Postcolonial Theologies

Postcolonial Theologies

An Introduction

Stefan Silber

CASCADE *Books* · Eugene, Oregon

POSTCOLONIAL THEOLOGIES
An Introduction

Cascade Books
An Imprint of Wipf and Stock Publishers
199 W. 8th Ave., Suite 3
Eugene, OR 97401

www.wipfandstock.com

PAPERBACK ISBN: 979-8-3852-0542-4
HARDCOVER ISBN: 979-8-3852-0543-1
EBOOK ISBN: 979-8-3852-0544-8

Cataloguing-in-Publication data:

Names: Silber, Stefan, author.

Title: Postcolonial theologies : an introduction / by Stefan Silber.

Description: Eugene, OR : Cascade Books, 2024 | Includes bibliographical references and index.

Identifiers: ISBN 979-8-3852-0542-4 (paperback) | ISBN 979-8-3852-0543-1 (hardcover) | ISBN 979-8-3852-0544-8 (ebook)

Subjects: LCSH: Postcolonial theology. | Globalization—Religious aspects—Christianity. | Liberation theology.

Classification: BR118 .S50 2024 (paperback) | BR118 .S50 (ebook)

VERSION NUMBER 08/14/24

Contents

Foreword

WITHOUT REALIZING IT, I had been dealing with postcolonial issues for a long time when, around 2010, I first came into intensive contact with this term and with the theories and studies associated with it. Latin American liberation theology and other theologies of the Global South had accompanied me since before I started my theological studies. Later, the diversity of intercultural and indigenous theologies also exercised a great fascination for me, especially while I lived and worked in Bolivia, from 1997 until 2002. All these theologies emerged in confrontation with contexts that today would be described as postcolonial. Postcolonial and decolonial[1] theories, which developed at about the same time have, however, only been engaged as important interlocutors for the further development of these theologies in the last fifteen years, more or less, at least in my perception.

It seemed, therefore, quite reasonable to me to deal with postcolonial theologies. At the same time, this confrontation resulted in a fundamental theological uncertainty for me. The vantage point from which I experienced this encounter was (and still is) that of a white male First World theologian living and working in Europe. It is precisely this location that is being questioned by postcolonialism because of its multiple hegemonic privileges. So what can it mean to research and write about postcolonial theologies from this perspective? This is an ongoing self-critical challenge.

1. For Decolonial Studies and the differences and relations between them and post-colonialism, see below, 1.2.

Visiting professorships in El Salvador (2017) and Bolivia (2018) on the topic of postcolonialism enabled me to self-critically sharpen my personal point of view in dealing with less privileged perspectives. These experiences have encouraged me to make the challenges of postcolonial theologies more accessible to German-speaking contexts. One reason for this is that our whole world is postcolonial and not just the states that emerged from the independence of the colonies. In this way, also the entire church and theology as a whole are being challenged by postcolonialism, especially, but not exclusively, in Europe. Our colonial past keeps intriguing us to face the postcolonial present and its problems.

This introduction to postcolonial theologies aims to provide a better understanding of the questions and challenges of postcolonial and decolonial studies to theology. It focuses on key questions of fundamental theology and method and works with numerous different examples from different theological disciplines. In each discipline, it will be possible (and necessary) to expand further considerations, for example, in exegesis, dogmatics, church history, practical theology, social ethics, and of course also in fundamental theology.

I would like to thank numerous interlocutors in Bolivia, Brazil, El Salvador, and from other Latin American countries, but also from other parts of the world, and last but not least, also from and in Europe for a variety of helpful suggestions and constructive criticism. I would also like to thank all the postcolonial theologians whose literature I have had the privilege of reading while dealing with these questions. Some of them are presented briefly and their theology is discussed in this book. I hope to have made good use of what I have learned. All errors and misjudgments are my own; I owe all the achievements and insights of postcolonial theologies to others.

Sailauf, February 1, 2021
Stefan Silber

Preface to the English Translation

IT IS WITH GREAT pleasure that I present this translation of my introduction to postcolonial theologies to the English-speaking public. It is
a book written in Germany and for Central European readers, and I
didn't change this transversal perspective for the English translation,
because location and perspective are something very important in
postcolonial studies. The topics and examples studied and analyzed
throughout these pages, however, have been elaborated and presented
by quite a number of authors living in and representing very different
cultural and social contexts of many parts of the globe. They are not
exclusively meant to be read and studied only in Europe; in most of the
cases, European theology is not even part of the primary audience. I
hope (and expect) that these multifaceted experiences will have something to tell to readers in English-speaking academia, as they did to me,
and it is with this expectation that I offer this introduction to theological studies and debates in this language.

On this occasion, I sincerely want to thank all the people at the Narr
Francke Attempto Verlag in Tübingen (Germany) and at Wipf and Stock
and Cascade Books who have worked hard and helped a lot to make the
publication of this translation possible. Also, I want to express my gratitude
to Jeannie Cohen, who carefully read the manuscript of my translation,
corrected, and improved it substantially. Thank you all very much.

Sailauf, September 7, 2023
Stefan Silber

1.

What Does *Postcolonial* Mean?
Some Basics

POSTCOLONIAL STUDIES AND THEORIES are becoming increasingly popular. The concept of postcoloniality now appears in many areas of the humanities and social sciences. In the last two decades, a diverse reception of these critical ways of thinking has also developed in theology worldwide. In Germany, however, discussion on this is still only beginning.

The term *post-colonial* can easily lead to misunderstandings. In a chronological sense, it only refers to the fact that these studies were created *after* the end of colonial rule, particularly that of Great Britain and France, in many Asian and African countries, as a result of and *after* the Second World War. From a qualitative perspective, however, postcolonial critique is about revealing the extent to which colonial rule, its ways of thinking, its formative cultural force, and its political and economic power structures have survived beyond the official end of the colonial period and—possibly in changed forms—continue to be effective.

The second potential misunderstanding is that the adjective *colonial* in a narrow sense only refers to facts and circumstances that are openly and directly related to colonialism. Postcolonial Studies, on the other hand, draw attention to the fact—and this will also be an essential topic of this book—that the colonial period and colonial relations had a much broader and deeper impact and history than is commonly assumed. Postcolonialism, therefore, also includes social and cultural phenomena in its analyses, while their connection with colonialism may not be apparent at first glance. Postcolonial Studies are not simply limited to a critique of historical colonialism, but rather analyze current cultural, economic, and political constellations to determine the extent to which they have been shaped by historical experiences from the colonial period up to the present.

Now, before this book will present an introduction to the developing postcolonial theologies, some basics about postcolonial theory need to be worked out as a first step: first, a very brief overview of the history and the concerns of Postcolonial Studies (with references to some very good introductory texts into these theories) will follow in 1.2. Then, the questions will arise as to why these studies are also important for theology (1.5) and why they should also be addressed today (1.4) and (interesting for my own context) particularly in Germany (1.3). Three short narrative approaches stand at the beginning, because they introduce the topic very well (1.1).

1.1. Narrative Approaches

The Tunisian historian and journalist Sophie Bessis recalls her childhood at the Jules Ferry Lyceum during Tunisia's colonial era:

> During the school break, national differences did not disappear in the face of the seeming ecumenism of children's fellowship. There were the Tunisians, Arabs or Jews, as opposed to the "French," a global entity whose homogeneity transcended the particular friendship that could be forged with each of them. Because the French girls crushed us with their contempt. Even if we didn't accept their arrogance, we didn't doubt their superiority.

> Because, firstly, they were blonde, with long, straight hair that could be thrown back with an elegant movement of the head. Faced with this almost angelic nature, the masochistic contemplation of the black and curly hair that adorned our heads caused us immense pain.

> They also went to communion. With wedding dresses, with tulle and veils, with a missal in hand and a wealth of pious pictures. . . . Who among us, Muslims and Jews, who shared the same darkness, did not even once in childhood dream of being a Catholic in order to experience this fairy tale? . . .

Before sixth grade, we had to choose which second language we wanted to learn. For my parents, the question was simple: we were Jews, but first and foremost Tunisians: so it was Arabic. After reading my application, my teacher called me over: "What a pity you didn't choose English!" she exclaimed. I long remembered her sad voice bemoaning the cultural regression to which her good student was being sentenced.[1]

In her memory, Bessis describes several characteristic aspects of colonial culture: The Tunisian children in no way doubted the (alleged) superiority of the French. This superiority had physical, external reasons (the hair), cultural and religious aspects (first communion, the language), as well as economic and social characteristics: "The French girls went on vacation 'to France.'"[2] This mythical country, described as a paradise by the girls returning from vacation, was separated from the Tunisian girls by a deep abyss. "The mere fact of belonging to this world . . . gave [the French children] a legitimate primacy."[3] The identity of the Tunisian girls, on the other hand, was consistently devalued ("darkness," "regression"), in line with the pedagogical ideal of the colonial school system. Accordingly, she comments: "We learned that there was little glory in being what we were."[4]

Only much later, when the author was able to travel to France as an adult, did she finally realize that the perceived abyss, the difference, and the hierarchical structure between the French and the Tunisian schoolgirls were not truths of nature, but a product of their colonial context.

Frantz Fanon, one of the precursors of postcolonialism and decolonization, describes in a memoir his first experiences in France. In his native Martinique, he had been aware of his skin color, but he was unprepared for how that skin color would appear in the eyes of white people:

> "Look, a Negro!" It was an external stimulus that flicked over me as I passed by. I made a tight smile. "Look, a Negro!" It was true. It amused me. "Look, a Negro!" The circle was drawing a bit tighter. I made no secret of my amusement. "Mama, see the Negro, I'm frightened!" Frightened! Frightened! Now they

---

1. Bessis, *Occidente y los Otros*, 15–16. Unless noted otherwise, the translations of all foreign language quotations in this book are by the author.

2. Bessis, *Occidente y los Otros*, 16.

3. Bessis, *Occidente y los Otros*, 16.

4. Bessis, *Occidente y los Otros*, 16.

were beginning to be afraid of me. I made up my mind to laugh
myself to tears, but laughter had become impossible.[5]

Only in the eyes of the others, who see him as a "negro," does he recognize the racism to which he is subjected, the mental and emotional
associations that are apparently linked to the color of his skin, "a racial
epidermal schema":

> I was responsible at the same time for my body, for my race,
> for my ancestors. I subjected myself to an objective examina-
> tion, I discovered my blackness, my ethnic characteristics; and
> I was battered down by tom-toms, cannibalism, intellectual de-
> ficiency, fetishism, racial defects, slave-ships, and above all else,
> above all: "Sho' good eatin."[6]

In contrast to the casualness with which he viewed his skin color
in the Caribbean, he interprets the racism experienced in Europe as a
seemingly "objective examination," as a supposed "ethnic characteristic."
Differences between light and dark skin color are not a reason for amuse-
ment, but a cause for fear. They mentally connect to cannibalism, superstition, and subjugation. These connections do not exist per se; they are
created by racism and sustained by colonialism. They have survived the
political independence of the former colonies from the European powers
and are also still alive in the former hegemonic countries.

My third example points to the diverse possibilities of resistance
against colonialism and its culture-shaping power. It is no coincidence
that it is taken from the field of Christian religion, because on the one
hand, this religion was an important element in stabilizing colonial rule,
but on the other hand, it always contained the potential for resistance and
the creative development of colonial and postcolonial contexts. This also
already gives expression to the main topic of this book.

The feminist and postcolonial theologian Kwok Pui-lan (Hong
Kong and USA) tells of a story that she found in an archive a long time
ago ("I have long since forgotten where I read this story").[7] A missionary in the early 1900s told of a Chinese woman "who could barely read"

5. Fanon, *Black Skin, White Masks*, 111–12.

6. Fanon, *Black Skin, White Masks*, 112. I only use the term *race* in literal quotations
in accordance with the original use. In line with the ongoing discussion in the German-
language discourse, I understand the term itself as racist and avoid it accordingly. The
same applies to the term *Negro* in the previous quote, in which it is already cynically
alienated by Fanon himself.

7. Kwok, "Verbindungen herstellen," 323.

but used a needle to poke out verses from the Bible to remove them. These were the verses in which the apostle Paul—according to the traditional interpretation—"advised women to be obedient and to keep silent in the church."[8]

Despite the colonial and missionary situation in which she found herself, this woman was neither subservient to nor passive in the face of religious instruction coming from Europe. "Instead of subscribing to Paul's sexist ideology, this woman exercised the freedom to choose and reject what she saw as harmful to women."[9] For Kwok, postcolonial theology consists not only in the memory of such women and their creative appropriation or rejection of European claims to power within the Christian religion, but also in a continuation of this practice by "postcolonial feminist critics . . . [who uncover] the myriad ways in which biblical scholars, including feminists, have either been involved in colonialism and neocolonialism or have been unaware of colonialism and neocolonialism."[10]

In addition, postcolonial theologies also reflect the spiritual potential that can be discovered or constructed in Christianity to resist the claims of domination, exploitation, and alienation that European-colonial Christianity presents.

People living in postcolonial societies today can often tell such stories of the persistence of colonialism and resistance to it themselves. They can identify immediately with it. Migrants in Germany, persons of color, and people who have gained intercultural experience during long stays abroad often relate more easily to these experiences than a large part of the German population, who do not attach the same importance to them. In the future, postcolonial theologies and theories will certainly gain in importance in the theological discussion in our part of the world and will be approved by some and rejected by others.

1.2. Postcolonial Studies: History and Concept

There are already some very good introductions into Postcolonial Studies, also in German language. The most important ones (in German) will be presented in the next section. The overview of the history and concept

8. Kwok, "Verbindungen herstellen," 323.
9. Kwok, "Verbindungen herstellen," 323.
10. Kwok, "Verbindungen herstellen," 323–24.

of postcolonialism intended here can therefore be relatively brief at this point. Moreover, in the central chapters of this book, I will present and discuss the key theoretical concepts and contents of Postcolonial Studies as based on their reception in theology. For an in-depth study of individual authors and concepts of Postcolonial Studies, it will be necessary to consult the relevant literature indicated here.

Postcolonial theories arise out of a multifaceted resistance to colonial rule during the colonial period. This resistance took place in everyday life, on a legal or philosophical level, in military, economic, and civil spheres. Numerous different forms of resistance are also attested in the area of religions. The theoretical work of postcolonialism builds on these practices and experiences. The strong focus of postcolonial and decolonial theories on discourses in the second half of the twentieth century should not obscure this long history of resistance and prophetic contradiction in all its complexity.

For Postcolonial Studies in the narrower sense of the word, as it is used today, the national independence of Asian and African colonies in the decades after the Second World War initially provided the impetus for critical studies in English-language history and literature that uncovered the influence of colonial power on the interpretation of history and literature. It was observed that the depiction and interpretation of historical events, on the one hand, and the content, narrative style, and construction of meaning of literary works on the other, obeyed the power interests of the colonial rulers in many respects, even after their political power had come to an end. Through critical analyses and alternative narratives, a different and liberating view of seemingly related facts could be developed. This critical perspective on the connection between colonial power and knowledge production was quickly taken up in other academic disciplines. The focus on texts, which is characteristic of literary and historical studies, has remained a central feature of Postcolonial Studies to this day as a sometimes critically questioned legacy.

A key event in the development of postcolonial theories is widely considered to be the publication of the 1978 study *Orientalism* by the Palestinian literary scholar Edward W. Said.[11] Said shows not only in literary and scientific works from the colonial period, but also in practical texts such as travel descriptions and bureaucratic documents, that in all of these areas knowledge about the spaces that are referred to as the

11. Said, *Orientalismus*.

Orient was (and is) constructed with the intention to better control the people who live there and to legitimize their exploitation.

At about the same time, the Subaltern Studies Group, an association of South Asian scholars led by the Indian historian Ranajit Guha, was criticizing European (primarily British) historiography on India and historically related states. With the concept of the *subaltern*, the group adopted a term of Antonio Gramsci, which became influential in postcolonial theories, to designate people who are subjected and exploited in different or even multiple ways.[12] An important member of this group was the Indian literary scholar Gayatri Chakravorty Spivak. She not only brought French poststructuralism into the debate, a field in which she was considered an expert, since she translated Jacques Derrida's *De la grammatologie* into English in 1976 and published it with a widely acclaimed introduction. She also represents a consistent feminist position in postcolonialism and integrates critical Marxist thinking in her work.[13]

Spivak also draws attention to the fact that the epistemological prerequisites of colonialism and the ideas and concepts with which it enforces its rule not only entail violence but already contain it as "epistemic violence."[14] The apparent knowledge that is generated in colonialism (and for its sake) exerts violence in itself, since it produces specific images of persons and people, through which people are valued and devalued and rule is established.

The Indian literary scholar Homi K. Bhabha links the areas of intercultural relations and psychoanalysis with the neo-Marxist and poststructuralist theories of postcolonialism. Bhabha also makes it possible to describe diverse, sometimes unconscious forms of resistance in colonial relationships. In a critical reception of Said's orientalism thesis, Bhabha draws attention to the fact that identities are never unambiguous and static; rather they are formed and changed in hybridization processes.[15]

An important precursor of the postcolonial movement was the psychiatrist and author Frantz Fanon, who was born in the French colony of Martinique in the Caribbean, lived in France and North Africa, and in this way became acquainted with the French colonial system from very

12. See Kerner, *Postkoloniale Theorien*, 103–6; see below, 4.4.

13. See Castro Varela and Dhawan, *Postkoloniale Theorie*, 161–228; Graneß et al., *Feministische Theorie*, 38–45.

14. Castro Varela and Dhawan, *Postkoloniale Theorie*, 193, and see 193–96; Brunner, *Epistemische Gewalt*.

15. See Castro Varela and Dhawan, *Postkoloniale Theorie*, 229–95.

different perspectives, not least in the Second World War and in the Algerian wars of liberation. His 1952 work *Black Skin, White Masks* (from which one of the above quoted narrative approaches is taken) is an influential reference point for the issue of racism within colonial relations.[16]

Dealing with racism is also one of the central concerns of Achille Mbembe's *Critique of Black Reason* published in 2013.[17] The Cameroonian political scientist Mbembe and Fanon show how racism pervades, shapes, and legitimizes all levels of European colonialism. Neither the emergence and historical development of colonialism nor its lasting consequences in the present are conceivable without this racism. Conversely, racist thinking and acting are experiencing a significant upswing as colonialism becomes established. The analysis of the construction of power relations between people of different skin colors is therefore also a core part of postcolonial thought.

Latin American theories that deal critically with colonial power relations are often grouped under the keyword *decolonial*. Latin American authors repeatedly distance themselves from Postcolonial Studies of Asian and North American influences. They criticize the fact that the economic and political aspects of analysis are weaker in postcolonialism and that Postcolonial Studies are strongly oriented toward European poststructuralist discourses. This criticism should be taken seriously, but not be generalized. It would be fatal to present post- and decolonial studies as two separate movements, homogeneous each of them but opposed to each other, as both share mutual relationships and also suffer internal differences and frictions. Above all, attention to these critical questions should not prevent a fruitful dialogue between the legitimate concerns of the various postcolonial and decolonial currents.[18] In this introduction, these critical aspects, justified as they may be in detail, are therefore not treated as a priority, nor are the various criticisms that exist within Latin American and Anglophone research respectively. Rather, the aim of this book is to present the range and effectiveness of post- and decolonial thinking and its effects on theology.

16. Fanon, *Black Skin, White Masks*.

17. Mbembe, *Kritik der schwarzen Vernunft*.

18. See Febel and de Medeiros, "Romanistik," 67–68, and my own argumentation in Silber, *Poscolonialismo*, 88–91. My decision to use the term *postcolonial* as an umbrella term for all these currents does not aim to monopolize other currents or make them invisible, but serves to simplify didactics. It also has biographical reasons, because it was through Postcolonial Studies that I explicitly came into contact with this diverse field of theory for the first time.

The Latin American decolonial theory tradition is fed by the works on dependency theory of the 1960s and 1970s, Immanuel Wallerstein's world system theory, and Enrique Dussel's intercultural philosophy of liberation. Dussel is also an important point of contact with Latin American liberation theology. Since many of the decolonial authors live and work in the USA, the discourse on these theoretical approaches is conducted in both Spanish and English.

The discussion received a severely anti-colonial accent with the introduction of the concept of *coloniality* by the Peruvian sociologist Aníbal Quijano,[19] who used it in an essay published in 1992 to describe the way in which formerly colonized states and cultures are entirely characterized by remnants of colonialism, even if national independence—as in the case of Latin America—occurred two centuries ago. For Quijano, this colonial way of thinking is fundamentally rooted in racism and has specific implications for economic exploitation and social exclusion. Later, the concept of coloniality was extended in many ways to include other postcolonial relationships.[20] A transdisciplinary working group of scholars in Latin America explored the interrelationships between European modernity, colonialism, and coloniality, as well as their diverse consequences in numerous social and political areas, under the keywords "Modernidad/Colonialidad" or "Modernity/Coloniality."[21]

One of the most prominent representatives of this group, the Argentinian literary scholar Walter D. Mignolo, refers in his work to the formative colonial legacy in European thought since the modern age and calls for "epistemic disobedience."[22] By this he means thinking beyond the limits set by colonial epistemology. Numerous decolonial theorists therefore fall back on indigenous and Afro-American thought and construct critiques of European and colonial thought systems from there.[23]

It is not only in Latin America that postcolonial thought is strongly influenced by feminism. Numerous authors worldwide analyze the reciprocal relationships between colonialism and sexism, in which

19. Quijano, *Kolonialität der Macht*; see below, 1.4 and 3.8.

20. See Lander, *Colonialidad del saber*; Maldonado-Torres, "Sobre la colonialidad"; Lugones, "Colonialidad y genero."

21. See Kerner, *Postkoloniale Theorien*, 90–94; Castro-Gómez and Grosfoguel, *Giro decolonial*, 10–13.

22. Mignolo, *Epistemischer Ungehorsam*.

23. On Mignolo and on decolonial thought, see Kerner, *Postkoloniale Theorien*, 90–97.

both mutually reinforce each other, and on the basis of which colonial thought until today has expressed itself clearly and in a special way in gender relations. Argentinian anthropologist Rita Segato, for example, examines the complex interdependence between colonialism, sexism, and racism in the lives of indigenous peoples.[24] The Bolivian sociologist Silvia Rivera Cusicanqui shows that a postcolonial feminist discourse must also include nonverbal elements.[25]

It is not only these last examples that make it clear that Postcolonial Studies are an extremely complex, heterogeneous, and differentiated field. It is still in the development phase and changes in a quite dynamic way. This lack of uniformity and sometimes even clarity is entirely understandable, since the postcolonial critique expressly refers to specific and concrete contexts that are shaped by their respective histories, cultures, and politics. It is to be expected that the outcomes will be very different. It is also not surprising that, at times, furious conflicts break out or continue between representatives of postcolonial theories. Moreover, none of these theories can do without a reference—of whatever kind—to European intellectual history, even while at the same time they criticize it in the strongest possible terms. Indian historian Dipesh Chakrabarty calls this a "postcolonial dilemma":

> The world of thought that arose during the era of European expansion and colonial rule seems as indispensable as it is insufficient for the description and analysis of one's own (non-Western) history and society.[26]

Despite the sometimes-conflicting disputes between different postcolonial currents and schools, what they have in common is that they not only regard colonialism as something that happened in the past, but criticize its current (cultural, epistemic, sociological, economic, political—and also religious) consequences as a fundamental cause of conflicts and problems of the present. This criticism is practiced today in numerous scientific disciplines, in interdisciplinary work, and in attempts to overcome the rigid division into scientific disciplines, which is also due to European intellectual history. Thence the call to "undiscipline" the sciences.[27]

---

24. Segato, *Crítica*.

25. Rivera Cusicanqui, *Sociología de la imagen*.

26. Quoted from Kerner, *Postkoloniale Theorien*, 76.

27. Walsh et al., *Indisciplinar las ciencias sociales*. See below, 4.7.

The focus on criticizing colonialism and coloniality means that there is a danger of reducing postcolonial contexts and cultures to their postcolonial condition, as if the centuries of European domination were all there is to these contexts. If this were the case, postcolonialism itself would remain trapped in Eurocentrism. However, the demand to think beyond borders made by Mignolo and others, and the change of perspective in the analysis of colonial and postcolonial relations made possible by Bhabha and Said, for example, open up a variety of ways out of the dilemma. The theological examples in this book will present some of these ways out and, at the same time, make visible the variety of content and methods involved in dealing with the legacy of colonialism.

Helpful Literature in German

There have been some very good introductions to postcolonial theories in the German language for a number of years. In particular, the already classic introduction by María do Mar Castro Varela and Nikita Dhawan must be mentioned here, now available in a third, expanded edition.[28] It is primarily oriented toward cultural studies and is mainly based on the presentation of Said, Spivak, and Bhabha and thus on the Anglophone, Asian variants of postcolonial theories.

Ina Kerner takes a different approach with her introduction, which has a stronger emphasis on political science and is structured thematically.[29] It also reaches beyond the Asian context and specifically addresses socioeconomic issues of postcolonialism. A good introduction to the basic concepts of Postcolonial Studies can also be found in the theological anthology by Andreas Nehring and Simon Wiesgickl (né Tielesch).[30] They relate the presentation of the central themes of Postcolonial Studies already with theology. After the German edition of the present book, Jens Kastner published an excellent introduction into Decolonial Studies that needs to be mentioned here.[31]

As early as 2002, Sebastian Conrad and Shalini Randeria published an anthology in which translations of important texts from Postcolonial

---

28. Castro Varela and Dhawan, *Postkoloniale Theorie.*
29. Kerner, *Postkoloniale Theorien.*
30. Nehring and Tielesch, *Postkoloniale Theologien,* 9–45.
31. Kastner, *Dekolonialistische Theorie aus Lateinamerika.*

Studies were made available to the German-speaking public.[32] They are suitable for a first contact with the global discussion; the editors' introduction connects them with German and Central European contexts.

In the anthology *Schlüsselwerke der Postcolonial Studies* by Julia Reuter and Alexandra Karentzos, German-speaking authors present some of the academics and their works already mentioned here (as well as a few others).[33] In addition, the reception of postcolonial theories in various academic disciplines (in Germany) is examined and discussed. The important question of how colonialism shapes German history, culture, and science is examined by numerous authors from different disciplines in the book *Deutschland postkolonial?* edited by Marianne Bechhaus-Gerst and Joachim Zeller.[34]

The *Handbuch Postkolonialismus und Literatur*, edited by Dirk Göttsche, Axel Dunker, and Gabriele Dürbeck, also presents Said, Spivak, and Bhabha as well as summaries of other Anglophone and Francophone authors, in just a few pages each.[35] As well as a look at various subjects of literary studies and different language areas, there is also a lexical overview of thirty key postcolonial terms that play an important role, but not exclusively in literary studies.

1.3. Postcolonial Germany?

Germany's[36] historical involvement in colonialism is not usually as present in our consciousness as the responsibilities of other European states such as the United Kingdom, France, and Spain. For this reason, postcolonial theories have so far received less attention in Germany than is the case, for example, in Anglophone countries.[37]

32. Conrad and Randeria, *Jenseits des Eurozentrismus.*

33. Reuter and Karentzos, *Schlüsselwerke der Postcolonial Studies.*

34. Bechhaus-Gerst and Zeller, *Deutschland postkolonial?*

35. Göttsche et al., *Handbuch Postkolonialismus und Literatur.*

36. In general terms, the name *Germany* refers not only to the expressly German states since the foundation of the *Deutsches Reich* in 1871, but also to the smaller predecessor states as well as for people and institutions in and from these territories. Due to my own history and contextualization, I shall only speak of Germany (in this sense), and not necessarily of the significance of Postcolonial Studies for other German-speaking contexts such as Switzerland and Austria, whose colonial history I have not sufficiently dealt with. See, for example, Purtschert et al., *Postkoloniale Schweiz*; Ruthner, *Habsburgs "Dark Continent."*

37. See Bechhaus-Gerst and Zeller, *Deutschland postkolonial*; Conrad and Randeria, "Einleitung," 39–42.

In fact, even Germany's explicit colonial history[38] continues to be ignored in many areas. Politicians in particular find it difficult to acknowledge the crimes committed by the German military and colonial officials, for example, in what is now Namibia. But even museums, art collections, and universities often do not face up to their historical responsibility in view of the art or ritual objects and other stolen property stored or exhibited in them. The arguments used sometimes seem to have come directly from the colonial era.[39] Even when it comes to the skulls, bones, and other body parts of people from colonial areas that are kept in anthropological or medical collections, German officials sometimes still resist proper repatriation and culturally appropriate burial. Church archives and museums for ethnology and/or mission history also have to face these challenges.[40]

In addition to the actual conquest of colonial areas for German rule, a broad current of colonial enthusiasm can be identified in the literature of the nineteenth and early twentieth centuries, in which wanderlust, fantasies of power, claims to superiority, curiosity, and tangible financial interests are combined. This colonialist enthusiasm can be traced until it merges into the ideology of National Socialism.[41]

In addition, numerous German settlers, researchers, military personnel, business people, missionaries, and adventurers who traveled to the colonies of other European states contributed to German colonialism without a German state or German institutions being directly involved. Through their contacts at home, these individuals also influenced colonial ideology in Germany. Last but not least, the importance of German banks for the European network of colonialism should not be underestimated.

In the present, the consequences of this history are subtler, but no less potent for that.[42] Sabine Jarosch speaks of "colonial wounds" in contemporary German society, in which colonial history is repeatedly and painfully felt. She gives examples of such wounds—among others:

> To this day, statues or pictures of black servants can be found in numerous German coffeeshops. Chocolate advertising uses the racist figure of the "Moor." Racist language practice in children's

38. See, for example, Gründer, *Geschichte der deutschen Kolonien*, with numerous historical documents.

39. See, for example, Nausner, "Langen Schatten," 200–201.

40. See Hölzl, "Wenn die Trommeln schweigen."

41. See also on the debate Geck and Rühling, "Vorläufer des Holocaust?"

42. See Nausner, "Langen Schatten," 203.

books is vehemently adhered to, even when those affected express how hurtful they find certain expressions. . . . There is massive political and social resistance to initiatives to rename streets currently named after colonial criminals. Black people and people of color . . . are subjected to more frequent police checks because they fit the "criminal profile" simply because of their skin color. People who do not have "white" pigmentation are repeatedly brought into the situation of feeling "othered," as not belonging to German society.[43]

Numerous initiatives in larger German cities have set themselves the task of making this presence of the colonial in everyday life visible by critically emphasizing it. With alternative city tours (some of which can also be experienced virtually), they draw attention to remembered protagonists of colonialism, former and current colonial institutions, monuments and street names, names and business signs of hotels and shops, etc., in order to point out the potency of colonial thought and attitudes up to the present day and to work toward a change in conception and behavior.[44]

Colonialism also continues to have an impact on experiences of everyday structural and subconscious racism reported by people of color and migrants in Germany. They are often associated with the cultural memories of the German colonial era, which, as described, are more comprehensive than the specific colonial rule of the German Empire. A problem that should not be underestimated and that is directly related to colonialism is the widespread and complex Islamophobia in Germany. With regard to such experiences with racism in Germany, Hito Steyerl and Encarnación Gutiérrez Rodríguez speak of the "colonial continuity of the Federal Republic"[45] and refer in particular to the work of feminists of color since the 1980s.

Michael Nausner, Austro-Swedish theologian, recalls that not only has Christianity in its history shown an "intimate complicity . . . with colonization," but that today's forms of migration are a "late consequence" of this colonial and missionary history.[46] In addition, he recognizes several connections between migration and church life in Central Europe: on the one hand, religions play an important role in the

43. Jarosch, "Koloniale Wunden," 47. For the concept of *othering*, see below, 2.1.

44. See Kerner, *Postkoloniale Theorien*, 61; http://www.freiburg-postkolonial.de and the detailed list of links on this website, which also refers to initiatives in other cities.

45. Steyerl and Gutiérrez Rodríguez, *Spricht die Subalterne Deutsch?*, 29.

46. Nausner, "Koloniales Erbe und Theologie," 75.

integration of migrants, but on the other hand, strong immigration also leads to the formation of diaspora religions and Christian groups with different cultural backgrounds. In this way, migrant Christian groups also carry postcolonial conflict constellations into churches and communities in Central Europe. In order to meet this challenge, Nausner advocates not leaving the theological examination of the phenomenon of migration to practical theology and missiology alone, but also asking systematic theology about the fundamental consequences of this complex challenge for theology and churches in this country.[47]

The German theologian Simon Wiesgickl, who also taught in Hong Kong, thoroughly worked out in his dissertation how the emergence and development of historical-critical exegesis in Germany would not have been conceivable without colonialism on the one hand and how, on the other hand, it also integrated numerous thought patterns and stereotypes of the colonial age. In exegetical texts, for example, Eurocentrism, the claim to superiority of German experts and even interactions with anti-Semitism can be detected, all of which also play an important role in German-style colonial ideology. Such critical investigations would also be extremely desirable in other areas of theology and the history of theology.[48]

Another postcolonial reality in the German church is the multilayered relationships between Germany and former colonial states of other countries through religious orders and aid organizations. Some of these relationships have existed for many decades and have often transformed their characters during this time. Nevertheless, they are originally based on colonial conditions, which are not always sufficiently recognized in the critical consciousness. However, postcolonial theories have already been discussed in some of these institutions.[49]

A fundamental aftereffect of colonialism in Germany, and one which has multiple consequences, can finally be made tangible on an epistemological level: European colonialism, particularly in the nineteenth century, would have been unthinkable without the ideological prerequisites of German idealism and the Enlightenment as a whole. Gayatri Spivak notes that Germany played a central philosophical and intellectual role in the elaboration and implementation of colonial ideology: "Cultural and intellectual 'Germany' . . . was the main source of the

---

47. See Nausner, "Koloniales Erbe und Theologie," 75–77.

48. Wiesgickl, *Alte Testament*. See also: Wiesgickl, "Gefangen in uralten Phantasmen."

49. See Pittl, "Anspruch und Wirklichkeit."

meticulous scholarship that established the vocabulary of proto-arche-typal . . . identity, or kinship" which served to name, evaluate, and contain colonial experiences.[50] With explicit reference to Kant, Hegel, and Marx, she writes: "Germany produced authoritative 'universal' narratives where the subject remained unmistakably European."[51]

These philosophies of the eighteenth and nineteenth centuries have shaped German ways of thinking up to the present day. The iden-titarian thought of the so-called Christian Occident is just one example of the exclusion of apparently foreign or "othered" cultures from the perspective of a supposedly dominant culture. The Eurocentric claim to superiority over dynamics of other parts of the world, which is still effective in many areas, can also be mentioned here. A Christianity that seems to have forgotten its Asian roots and sees itself as "European," especially in its Eurocentric Catholic variant, must face this critical question to a far greater extent.

1.4. Colonial Contexts Today

Even if most former colonies have now gained their national inde-pendence, colonialism is not a closed episode of the past. It shapes the present in many ways. Postcolonialism as a global scientific approach, therefore, also brings about a critical examination of the effects of the colonial era in the present. These are noticeable on very different levels: in economic dependency, in cultural hierarchies and exclusions, and on an epistemological level. At the same time, global movements acting against these continued effects of colonialism can also be perceived, on the same broad range of different levels.

Within international economic relationships, different conditions of exploitation are currently being discussed under the keyword of neo-colonialism. These differ from historical colonialism in that the exploited regions formally have attained national independence. However, through mining concessions, investments, and trade treaties, these neocolonies are being induced to produce what the international investor orders, rather than what is required by the local populace. This is particularly noticeable in the agricultural sector.

---

50. Spivak, *Critique*, 8.
51. Spivak, *Critique*, 8.

Another form of neocolonialism can be observed when jobs are created, for example in the clothing or information industries, in countries
that have significantly lower wage levels and poorer labor legislation than
industrialized countries. In many cases, poor countries themselves change
their legislation to investor-friendly conditions so that workers are forced
to work in extremely precarious conditions, sometimes resembling slavery. A third form of neocolonialism can be observed in outsourcing the
consequences of climate change to the countries and regions that have
least caused it. These three examples are intended to show the phenomena
of neocolonialism only as examples and not exhaustively.

As early as the 1960s, the Mexican sociologist Pablo González Casanova pointed out that despite national independence and numerous
other socioeconomic changes in the former colonies, economic structures persist that both continue to perpetuate global exploitation and the
development of what he calls *internal colonialism*, through which native
elites and certain regions of the country can perpetuate colonial power
relations over other parts of the country.[52] This is evident, for example,
in the systematic exploitation of rural and mining-affected regions, often
supported by a central government. Currently, such internal colonialism
is perceived in a particularly drastic way in the Amazon region.[53]

Further colonial and neocolonial contexts can be found in connection with the diverse migration movements of the present.[54] On the
one hand, neocolonial exploitation and the violent scenarios associated
with it are among the main push factors of migration, while on the other
hand, the pull factors that have to be identified include the widening
gap between the global winners and the losers of capitalist globalization. In addition, migrants who live in Europe—be it legally, tolerated,
or illegally—are often exploited under slave-like working conditions or
in other precarious employment relationships. As soon as they leave
their countries of origin and all the way through their migration to the
countries of destination, migrants are exposed everywhere to racism
and hierarchies of cultural superiority, which have their origins not
least in the centuries of European colonial practice.

Like the economic structures of colonialism, its cultural depths
have a longevity that cannot be easily overcome or broken through by
the end of the colonial era. Aníbal Quijano coined the term *coloniality*

52. González Casanova, *Sociología de la explotación*, 221–50.
53. See Porto-Gonçalves, *Amazonía*.
54. See Nehring, "Verwundbarkeit auf Abwegen."

to denominate the stubbornness of these cultural influences: "This relationship consists, in the first place, of a colonization of the imagination of the dominated; that is, it acts in the interior of that imagination, in a sense, it is a part of it."[55]

This means that people's imagination itself, their way of understanding everything, is colonized, with the effect that it is subject to the conditions of colonialism up to the present. At the same time, it is imagination itself that actively perpetuates these cultural conditions of colonialism by taking them for granted. This is the reason why the colonial devaluation of the native cultures and the subconscious appreciation of everything European have an equally lasting effect on the formerly dominated and the dominating, and have exerted a culture-shaping power up to the present day. According to Quijano, an important tool of coloniality is racism, since it uses superficial differences in people's appearance to assign cultural appreciation and devaluation to individuals.

Economic and cultural coloniality are mutually dependent and mutually supportive. Economic exploitation is legitimized and acceptable by degrading cultural (self-)assessment, and cultural devaluation is reinforced by growing poverty and precariousness. This mutual reinforcement of postcolonial experiences in different areas of society is an important topic of criticism in postcolonialism. It refers to the subconscious, stubborn power of colonial patterns of understanding that is taken for granted.

The effect of these legacies of colonialism can be described as epistemological: they change the way people perceive themselves and the world in which they live. Relationships between people of different origin, language, or skin color are subconsciously read according to a colonial interpretation and thus classified from the outset in this legacy of coloniality. The right of transnational corporations to exploit raw materials, energy production, and agricultural production is not questioned, because colonial memory does not doubt the supremacy and thus the privilege of the former colonial states. This happens both on the side of the previously colonized and on the side of the former colonizers.

This colonial memory also has an effect within the states of Europe and North America: colonial relations have changed and lastingly shaped the imagination not only of the dominated, but also that of the conquerors.

---

55. Quijano, "Colonialidad y modernidad/racionalidad," 12. Imagination, in the Spanish original, is *imaginario* and means the subject's way of imagining, interpreting, and understanding the world.

The superiority of those who are powerful today through capitalism is obviously also a cultural and political superiority. It seems legitimate as a result of factual circumstances and is academically backed up by a science that is just as prejudiced. Likewise, Eurocentrism and White supremacy often exert their cultural influence without being questioned.

Criticism of these apparently self-evident facts is an essential theme of Postcolonial Studies. They strive to uncover, criticize, and change the hidden structures of coloniality. The postcolonial theologies that are the focus of this book also aim to critique these deep-seated cultural beliefs, at the same time bringing the field of religions into focus. They ask, on the one hand, about the responsibility of religion for the development of this naturally hierarchical world of ideas of colonialism and, on the other hand, also about the consequences that colonialism in its turn had for the construction of theologies.

Postcolonial theologies and studies in general thus fit into a global network of resistance to coloniality and colonialism that already existed in colonial times. Such resistance has existed for about as long as colonialism itself, also within the churches and theology. However, theological resistance cannot claim to confront colonialism as one homogeneous bloc would another. It is indissolubly intertwined with colonialism through a variety of historical connections and is expressed in different strategies and practices.

Simultaneously with the neoliberal globalization, one can speak of a globalization of solidarity, of justice or of hope. In many places, people are trying to shake up the self-evidence of the diverse destructive structures of the present using very different methods. They themselves are also subject to the legacy of colonialism and therefore have to repeatedly question their own actions in a self-critical manner. An important element of this self-criticism is the diverse and developing field of Postcolonial Studies, which includes the self-critical view of one's own production as part of the postcolonial confrontation with one's own coloniality.

1.5. Significance of Postcolonial Studies for Theology

Christians are also part of these global processes—of colonialism, coloniality, and resistance. The links between the Christian mission and the violent acts of colonialism are widely known and have often been critically

analyzed. Already during the colonial period and afterward, Christians—
as individuals, but also as part of their church institutions—can be found
both on the side of the destruction and on the side of the resistance. Many
of them, like the Dominican Bartolomé de las Casas, were both colonizers
and critics of colonialism at the same time. A binary division into good
and evil, colonialism and resistance is out of the question from such a historical perspective. The critique of this kind of black-and-white thinking
is precisely an essential aspect of postcolonial theories.

The multifaceted interweaving of Christian and church actors in
colonial relations is an important reason why, for some years now, Postcolonial Studies have been actively appropriated in theology, at least in
a global perspective. The US theologian Joseph Duggan distinguishes
four phases in the development of postcolonial theologies:[56] He identifies a first stage—*avant la lettre*—already present in the liberation struggles against colonialism in the mid-twentieth century. Christians were
already actively involved in these liberation struggles and also produced
theological texts, often from the perspective of indigenous peoples.
However, in Duggan's view, the disregard of Christian and theological
literature from this period by mainstream postcolonial theologies un-
necessarily narrows the spectrum of these theologies.

A second movement developed from the application of postcolonial literary studies to the exegesis of the Bible. Since the turn of the
millennium, especially in India, Africa, and the USA, there have been
theologians who have begun to reread and interpret the Bible with the
help of postcolonial instruments. This second movement still has a great
influence on the development of postcolonial theologies. According to
Duggan, a third, more systematic and theologically oriented current
developed particularly in the USA, where theologians applied the instruments of Postcolonial Studies also to other theological disciplines and, in
particular, also sought dialogue with postcolonial feminism.

The fourth phase, which—as Duggan wrote in 2013—is "the most
complex and multifaceted one" and also "still developing,"[57] seeks an
explicit dialogue with postcolonial theorists, who are generally very
opposed to religion as they consider it a driving force of colonialism.
In this broad interdisciplinary dialogue, the self-critical question is
asked as to what role postcolonial subjects actually have in a theological

56. Duggan, "Erkenntnistheoretische Diskrepanz," 136–38.
57. Duggan, "Erkenntnistheoretische Diskrepanz," 137.

movement that is currently very active in the USA and in the English-speaking north of the planet. Indigenous and non-Christian authors are represented in this dialogue.

With Andreas Nehring and Simon Wiesgickl, the developments within the Ecumenical Association of Third World Theologians (EAT-WOT) can be added to this chronology. At the founding meeting of this association in 1976, the two authors locate an "epistemological rupture"[58] that in substance already approaches postcolonial concerns. In addition, other currents of theology from the Global South in the last few decades (such as Latin American liberation theology and the liberation theologies of other continents, feminist and eco-feminist theologies of the South, indigenous theologies from Latin America, North America, Africa, and Asia, etc.) can also be understood as a part of the diverse spectrum of postcolonial theologies. In the present, a complex dialogue is unfolding between these different currents.

The explicit recourse to Postcolonial Studies and the explicit addressing of colonial and postcolonial issues could justify speaking of postcolonial theologies as a current of their own. However, such a demarcation would imply a separation which does not exist from other comparable theologies and an inner homogeneity of this current. Rather, one has to imagine the postcolonial theologies as a diverse, critical, and dialogue-ready theological perspective that takes up the instruments of Postcolonial Studies in order to deal with challenges that arise from historical colonial contexts and is in lively exchange with other theologies of the Global South. This volume therefore also presents theological examples that are not described as postcolonial and do not refer explicitly to the methods of Postcolonial Studies.

It is currently hardly possible to give a complete overview of the panorama of postcolonial theologies. This is not only because of the described impossibility of distinguishing these theologies from related and neighboring currents and their inner diversity, but also because not all theological works that could be classified as postcolonial understand or label themselves as postcolonial or decolonial. Finally, one must also critically note that there are now works whose self-identification as postcolonial does not correspond to the methodology used.

As a theological perspective in motion and transformation, postcolonial theologies can currently be described as diverse and inconsistent.

---

58. Nehring and Tielesch, *Postkoloniale Theologien*, 44.

They do not have a geographic focus or center; on the contrary, they are scattered across all continents, often as a minority in their churches and academic relationships, which is why they sometimes characterize themselves as *diaspora*. The internet and social media are used happily and extensively, making global networking and communication possible. A lively ecumenical and sometimes interreligious cooperation is also developing.

Usually, no explicit distinction is made between the postcolonial theological works emerging from different Christian denominations. Rather, ideas from other churches are often gratefully taken up and received without further comment. The similarities in their (post)colonial issues are far often more important than their historically grown denominational differences. Indeed, historical confessionalism is even deconstructed as a colonial legacy. Like many border areas in postcolonialism, the borders between the denominations are problematized as (post)colonial instruments of power and need to be considered as open for dialogue.

Due to the attention paid to cultural as well as political and economic hierarchies and relationships of dependency in postcolonialism, postcolonial theologies also come into contact in many ways with both intercultural and liberation theologies. While intercultural theologies in the past often ignored questions of power relations and brought cultural encounters and learning processes to the fore, postcolonial theologies ask more about the possibilities of intercultural dialogue or negotiations between cultures under the influence of colonial power structures. In contrast to liberation theologies and various other political theologies worldwide, postcolonial theologies draw particular attention to (inter) cultural power relations, which in political theologies were often suppressed as secondary, or even as an obstacle, and draw attention to the fact that the analysis of cultural power relations is necessary to better understand social hierarchies and exploitative structures.

In both theological currents—political and intercultural theologies—there is now a growing interest in dealing with the questions and methods of postcolonialism. Postcolonial theologies therefore are also nourished by the dialogue with these two plural currents of theologies of the Global South.

The various forms of postcolonial theologies continue to show the importance that is attached to the specific local and historical contexts in each case. They do not try to give universal answers to supposed questions of humanity in general, but start from specific cultural and political power structures and other problems. As a result, they attain not only very specific contextual characteristics, but also, viewed globally, an extremely differentiated plurality: not only can they not be easily systematized, but in the comparative view they occasionally appear contradictory, inconsistent, and fragmentary. This inconsistency is a practical consequence of their fundamentally critical perspective on universalization, standardization, and reification in theology, which they criticize above all with regard to Eurocentric and colonial theology. One must therefore regard the contradictoriness and fragmentarity of postcolonial theologies as highly desirable indeed.

In this way, it is possible for postcolonial theologies to work in very specific ways on the diverse connections, for example, between colonialism and mission in history. Traces and remnants of colonial mentality appear in very different forms in the present, depending on their historical context and developments. They can be found in theology and church both in the (former) mission areas as well as in Europe and North America, up to the present. The complex relationships between cultures shaped by colonial and postcolonial power structures and the theologies that arose and are still emerging in them can be deciphered and changed with this postcolonial methodology.

In the Catholic Church in particular, which sees itself as a universal church and is organized centrally, global power relations and the cultures that are characterized by them are a major challenge for theology, and not just for the theologies of mission and religion, but also for ecclesiology, Christology, and other theological topics which are also subject to contextual influences.

The following chapters present some considerations in these contexts and show the far-reaching consequences of the reception of postcolonial thought in theology. Examples from all over the world and from different areas of theology will show that theology is being challenged fundamentally and must face up honestly to this demand.

The Filipino theologian Daniel Franklin Pilario names "three main objectives" of postcolonial theologies:

> (1) First is the deconstructive phase. Postcolonial theology seeks to investigate biblical documents, theological paradigms and doctrinal assertions to determine their complicity with the colonial enterprise. . . .

(2) Second is the project of reconstruction. Postcolonial theol-
ogizing attempts to do reconstructive readings of the so-called
classical texts from the perspective of subaltern voices or forward new texts and practices formerly suppressed by dominant
discourses. . . .

(3) Third, postcolonial theology opts for a hermeneutics [sic]
of resistance, that is, to read not only how the colonial powers
construct the colonized but also how the subaltern subverts the
same power used to dominate them.[59]

These objectives or phases of postcolonial theologies, which must not be
understood as a rigid sequence or structure, will also appear again and
again in the examples presented on the following pages. In this overview,
however, it becomes clear that the postcolonial criticism not only changes individual elements of theological work, but also questions traditional
theology in a fundamental way. The Austrio-Belgian theologian Judith
Gruber refers to this fundamental nature of theological reorientation: "A
German-speaking postcolonial theology is therefore not a new discipline
that may be marginalized. It gives a new direction to the epistemological
processes of theological discourse."[60] Postcolonial theologians in Europe
choose "an alternative method to the strategies of the established discourse; we are literally taking a different 'path' of doing theology, which
challenges us to also re-measure the 'map' of theology."[61]

Postcolonialism is—in this fundamental sense—of key importance
for theology in Europe and the West. On the one hand, it inquires into
colonialism, mission, Eurocentrism, etc. from a historical perspective.
On the other hand, this importance also presents itself from an epistemological point of view, since European theologies and their epistemes
are largely responsible for colonial and postcolonial distortions. Finally,
these questions also have consequences on a practical level in areas such
as parish community, school, and university, as will become clear in the
following chapters.

59. Pilario, "Mapping Postcolonial Theory," 47–49. See below, 1.6, for the similarities and differences between these "main objectives" in Pilario and the structure of this
book.
60. Gruber, "Wider die Entinnerung," 36.
61. Gruber, "Wider die Entinnerung," 36.

German Literature on Postcolonial Theologies

The publications in German on postcolonial theologies can still fit on one bookshelf.[62] The comprehensive anthology, *Postkoloniale Theologien. Bibelhermeneutische und kulturwissenschaftliche Beiträge*, published by Andreas Nehring and Simon Wiesgickl (né Tielesch) in 2013 offers not only an informative introduction to Postcolonial Studies right at the beginning, but above all a compilation of relevant contributions from Asia and North America.[63] This volume provides a good overview of the authors, topics, and methods but does not constitute a systematic introduction to postcolonial theologies. This limitation also applies to the follow-up volume *Postkoloniale Theologien II: Perspektiven aus dem deutschsprachigen Raum*, which the two editors published in 2018, and in which contributions originally written in German are presented.[64] These are rather disparate in terms of content. What they have in common is that they apply postcolonial methods to various thematic areas that the different authors consider important. At the same time, the volume makes visible and tangible the fact that postcolonial theologies are already being discussed in German-speaking countries.

The anthology on *Theologie und Postkolonialismus* edited by Sebastian Pittl documents the contributions to a conference on this topic that took place in 2017 at the Institute for World Church and Mission (Frankfurt/Main).[65] The bilingual conference volume (German and English) brings together above all reflections on missiology by scholars from all over the world and refers both to the diversity and the global significance of postcolonial theologies. The conference documentation, *Postcolonialism, Theology and the Construction of the Other: Exploring Borderlands*, also bilingual, discusses topics in church history, biblical studies, and systematic theology, and also considers the consequences for European theology.[66]

As early as 2013, an issue of the international journal *Concilium* (no. 2, 2013) on *Postcolonial Theology* was published, presenting translated articles from all over the world. Some of these contributions introduce the topic very well, while others can serve more as specific individual

---

62. See also the detailed and well-prepared overview by Nausner, "Zur Rezeption."
63. Nehring and Tielesch, *Postkoloniale Theologien*.
64. Nehring and Wiesgickl, *Postkoloniale Theologien II*.
65. Pittl, *Theologie und Postkolonialismus*.
66. Konz et al., *Postkolonialismus*.

examples for postcolonial theologies or related theological debates. The 2020 issue of the same journal on *Decolonial Theologies*, which unfortunately appeared in the German edition only under the title of "Gewalt, Widerstand und Spiritualität" ("Violence, Resistance, and Spirituality"; no. 1, 2020), presents this theological trend from a Latin American perspective. In this issue, younger authors in particular give an insight into diversity and methods. Unfortunately, the issue does not contain a systematic introduction to the decolonial variant of postcolonial theologies. The *Jahrbuch für Christliche Sozialwissenschaften* ("Yearbook for Christian Social Sciences") of 2020 (vol. 61) presents some articles, mainly from a social-ethical perspective, in which important traces are laid for the reception of Postcolonial Studies in the German-speaking discourse area of this theological discipline.[67]

The no. 1–2, 2012 issue of *Interkulturelle Theologie. Zeitschrift für Missionswissenschaft* ("Intercultural Theology: Journal for Missiology") mainly documents some of the essays that also appeared in the first volume by Nehring and Tielesch. Issue 2-3, 2019, under the heading "Postcolonialism—and what then?" contains some interesting articles on the history of religion, missionary history, and missionary studies that are written from a postcolonial perspective.

With *Theologien des Südens*, the Spanish theologian Juan José Tamayo introduces numerous newer theological methods of the Global South.[68] Postcolonial theologies are also presented, but unfortunately not systematically processed or fundamentally analyzed. The study "Südwind" by the Swiss theologian and philosopher Josef Estermann on contextual non-occidental theologies in the global South also documents and analyzes theologies from all over the world that are very closely related to the postcolonial ones.[69] Estermann only begins, however, to delve into the process of theological decolonization.[70]

In addition to other individual contributions and essays on postcolonial topics,[71] there are also two doctoral theses on theological questions in the German-speaking area: Sigrid Rettenbacher's postcolonial research into the theology of religion[72] and Simon Wiesgickl's critical reappraisal of

67. See Heimbach-Steins et al., "Vorwort."

68. Tamayo, *Theologien des Südens*.

69. Estermann, *Südwind*.

70. See Estermann, *Südwind*, 160–67.

71. Including already some critical discussions, e.g., Ackermann, "Identität."

72. Rettenbacher, *Außerhalb der Ekklesiologie*.

the history of historical-critical exegesis from a postcolonial perspective.[73] Both reach far beyond their specific questions and offer helpful material for deepening postcolonial theological concerns in German and for German-speaking contexts. The German translation of Joerg Rieger's christological study *Christ and the Empire*, which takes up postcolonial methodology, is also worth mentioning here.[74] Other important and interesting publications can be found in related disciplines such as the sociology of religion and intercultural and feminist theology.

1.6. Knowledge and Power in Theology: The Structure of This Book

The biblical scholar Rasiah S. Sugirtharajah from Sri Lanka describes the intention to "examine and uncover the connection between knowledge and power in the textual production of the West" as the "unifying force" of the diverse elaborations of authors of Postcolonial Studies.[75]

This intention can also be discovered in postcolonial theologies. It serves, therefore, as an important thread running through the following chapters, which will deal fundamentally with the connection between power and knowledge in theology. Every kind of knowledge is connected to a specific culture, although someone might want to understand it as a universal, ahistorical, and supracultural abstraction. Theological knowledge is also always culturally determined and therefore subject to specific power constellations that form at certain historical points in time in the cultures that shape theology.

While intercultural theology has made a valuable contribution to working out the connections between theology and culture, and liberation theology analyzed in particular the mutual relationships between power and theology, the complex triangular relationship between rule, culture, and theological production can be examined, analyzed, and criticized in the perspective of postcolonial theologies.

In recent decades, both in intercultural and in liberation theology, attention to this complex interrelationship has grown. It is not an exclusive achievement of postcolonial theologies to theorize it. This is not the point here. Rather, postcolonial theologies draw on support for

---

73. Wiesgickl, *Alte Testament.*
74. Rieger, *Christus und das Imperium.*
75. Sugirtharajah, "Postkoloniale Untersuchung," 125.

a more comprehensive and profound analysis from both liberation theology and intercultural theology, and at the same time can offer them a fruitful dialogue.

Culture must be viewed as a comprehensive, complex dynamic of various symbolic systems that include religion, society, economics, and politics.[76] It refers not only to art, language, and science, but to all areas of life, including the organization of everyday life, power relations, and the conceptual understanding of the world. A reduced concept of culture does not do justice to people's cultural self-experience and the intercultural experience of other people, especially not in colonial and postcolonial contexts. Likewise, power and rule must also be viewed as cultural factors that not only address legal, factual, or violently enforced dependencies, but also include psychological, cultural, and religious subordination as well as countervailing power and resistance. With Homi Bhabha and Gayatri Spivak in particular, it is important to relate, as is done in Postcolonial Studies, to the conceptions of power, domination, and hegemony as developed by Michel Foucault and Antonio Gramsci.[77]

The following five chapters represent a possible approach to the presentation of postcolonial theologies; they do not claim to be the only possible or best form of presentation. This structure was chosen because in this way four important, different aspects of postcolonial theologies can be presented transparently, and possible learning outcomes for us in Europe can then be shown. These aspects are related to each other in many ways. The individual chapters therefore refer closely to each other.[78]

Chapter 2 focuses on cultural and linguistic factors in postcolonialism. These questions are the focus of many theoreticians, many of whom come from literary studies. Postcolonial theories are therefore often identified with these factors or reduced to them. Equally important for an understanding of postcolonial theologies, however, is the aspect of power relations, which is the main objective of the third chapter.

---

76. For more details on my concept of culture, see Silber, *Befreiung der Kulturen*, 23–76.

77. See Castro Varela and Dhawan, *Postkoloniale Theorie*, 196–211; 231–32; 249–52.

78. The "three main objectives" of Daniel Pilario's postcolonial theologies quoted above (see 1.5) provided inspiration for the design of this chapter structure, with chapters 2 and 3 in this book corresponding to Pilario's "deconstructive phase," the fourth chapter to his "hermeneutics of resistance," and in the sixth chapter, "the project of reconstruction" of theology will be in the foreground. However, I did not keep Pilario's order of the three objectives or phases. See Pilario, "Mapping Postcolonial Theory," 47–49.

Colonialism is a power relationship, and it still has an impact on the many different configurations of power today.

The resistance that is offered to these power relations, also in theology, is the focus of the fourth chapter. This resistance and the countervailing power it represents also includes a number of specific methodologies used to criticize traditional theological forms. Nor does resistance end with criticism. Postcolonial theologies also develop theological alternatives in which they unfold theological implications of the counter-power that deals critically with colonialism. These are the subject of the fifth chapter. In some cases, these alternative theological constructions can arrive at completely new understandings of the Christian faith. The final, sixth chapter asks about the possibilities, conditions, and opportunities for learning from postcolonial theologies that arise for us in Central Europe.

This book is intended as an introduction to postcolonial theologies and their methodology, not as a systematic treatise. Postcolonial theologies should be *presented here* and not *represented*. This introduction aims to encourage further study. The literature used and presented is suitable for this, and may be used for further reference. Likewise, individual theological topics or objects of postcolonial theology cannot be fully and systematically worked out here: as Sigrid Rettenbacher and Simon Wiesgickl have shown, an entire doctoral thesis can easily be filled with specific postcolonial theological discussions.[79]

In addition, postcolonial theories have always been resistant to any systematization, as this is often accompanied by essentialization and hierarchization. Especially in theology, postcolonialism must also still be viewed as very young, dynamic, and in the process of change. For these reasons, instead of a systematic presentation, a benevolent approximation to postcolonial theologies seems more advisable.

For the same reason, this book is also not a "critical" introduction. While María do Mar Castro Varela and Nikita Dhawan describe their introduction to the postcolonial theories already in the first edition in 2005 as a "critical"[80] one in order to stimulate discussion of them, I think it is currently more necessary in theology to start with interest and to approach experiences of postcolonial theologies with curious attention. Of course, this does not rule out a critical examination, and this is also occasionally undertaken in this book.

79. See Rettenbacher, *Außerhalb der Ekklesiologie*; Wiesgickl, *Alte Testament*.
80. Castro Varela and Dhawan, *Postkoloniale Theorie*, 20–21.

The following chapters will introduce the terms, methods, and basic concepts of postcolonial theories with examples from the practice of postcolonial theologians. In this way, it will become clear how different strategies of postcolonial criticism are fundamentally changing theology. It should also be made clear that postcolonial theologies do not claim to be a new theological discipline or specific contextual theology, but aim at a reversal in theological methodology overall. Therefore, they do not assert that they are expanding the theological canon, but that they are changing it.[81]

My selection of postcolonial theological examples will always be meant as casual, illustrative, narrative, fragmentary, and non-exhaustive. I proceed likewise in the conviction that such an approach is more in line with the basic assumptions of postcolonialism than a well-ordered system that tends to classify and thus to order and subordinate. This may lead to simplifications, one-sidedness, and omissions. More experienced readers would certainly change the type of presentation at one point or another, choose different examples, or evaluate things differently. However, the aim of this introduction is to present postcolonial theologies in their basic features and to motivate readers to study them in depth. It is not intended to replace this extended study.

However, even a fragmentary theology is not unsystematic. Rather, it challenges the claim of a systematic theology that aims at a complete, conclusive, and verifiable presentation of a theological object. No such claim to power is made here. Instead, this introduction tries to throw different spotlights on a growing and transforming theological current through repetition, changing perspectives, and complementarity in apparently contradictory statements, which in their plurality should help to do justice to the basic concerns of this current to some extent. I am convinced that a closer look will reveal something like a mosaic-style pattern even if it consists of fragments.[82]

81. See below, chapter 6, for more detail.

82. For more detail on the theological presuppositions of fragmentarity in systematic theology, see Silber, *Pluralität*, 36–39.

2.

Praxes of Discourse

IN THE PRESENT, KNOWLEDGE can no longer simply be regarded as something that is objectively available or can be acquired reliably. Rather, it is generated, changed, passed on, and further developed in diverse discourses. In connection with power constellations, such as those found in colonial and postcolonial contexts, it is to be expected that the discourses that produce knowledge will also be permeated by these power relations and operate within them.

Postcolonial critique—and postcolonial theologies with it—therefore pays a great deal of attention to the various strategies and practices of discourse. Theology is itself a relational system of multiple discourses in which knowledge is produced. And theological discourses are also woven into diverse power relations. The production of theological knowledge in discourse practices must therefore be critically examined—especially from a postcolonial perspective—with regard to how it is influenced by power relations.

In this chapter, some important terms of postcolonial discourse criticism are presented, in particular based on their use in postcolonial theological texts. Two very important concepts stand at the beginning: othering or the invention of the other (2.1), and the essentialization or petrification of identities and concepts (2.2). They are strongly related to each other and in practice often appear in connection with each other. Cultural areas in which these practices of othering and essentialization are particularly evident are racism (2.3) and gender relations (2.6). The discourse on religion and religions is also shaped by external attributions that can have a petrifying effect (2.5). In colonialism, a more or less overt conviction of European superiority (2.4), which is also found, for example, in historiography (2.7), has a particularly strong effect.

Due to the diversity of these perspectives and their complex mutual influence, the concept of intersectionality or the overlapping of such perspectives is now increasingly being taken up in postcolonial debates (2.8).

What all of these more culturally or discursively oriented perspectives have in common is the common characteristic property of all cultural phenomena, that they have a formative effect on people's consciousness without always appearing openly. Certain cultural beliefs are taken for granted without being questioned. Rather, they are apparently known with an ostensible certainty because they already shape perception. Just as Sophie Bessis did not doubt in her childhood memories that the French girls in her school were superior to her,[1] so people today in very different postcolonial constellations know with deep conviction that some identities are like this and not different, certain people are less valuable or less advanced than others, and that historical processes happened as those in power had recorded them.

Postcolonial Studies question and criticize these deep, unconscious convictions and provide analytical means to break through the apparent certainty of cultural knowledge. They also reveal discourse practices in theology in which such stereotypes are used as a basis or justified as a result. In this way, they make an important contribution to the self-critical examination of theological discourses.

2.1. The Invention of the Other

The invention of the other is an important discourse strategy critiqued by Postcolonial Studies. It is about attributing certain qualities to other people, often within an assumed collective, through which these people are to be characterized and evaluated at the same time. By determining these properties as *different* from the asserted properties of the defining group (or subject), this strategy emphasizes the (putative) differences rather than the similarities common to individuals of both groups. The

---

1. See above, chapter 1.

people of the group thus defined appear to be fundamentally different: they are made into *others*. Postcolonialism calls this strategy "othering,"[2] which could be understood as "making into otherness"[3] or "turning someone into a stranger."

Gayatri Spivak has extensively analyzed and described the phenomenon of othering.[4] According to her, othering is not only about description, differentiation, or demarcation, but always also about devaluing and dominating those who are made different: it implies the confirmation of a power relationship through moral opposites such as wild/civilized, treacherous/reliable, etc., which are translated into apparent knowledge about the other. This knowledge and its production are in turn only accessible to the ruler in this power relationship. In this way, rule is seemingly legitimized.

Homi Bhabha also draws attention to the fact that these processes of othering do not take place according to a fixed pattern, but rather include ambivalences and transformations.[5] The imputed value of the other can oscillate between mockery and longing, nourished by subconscious fantasies and obsessions, so that the othered person can be a projection screen for one's own wishes, fears, and contempt at the same time.

The US biblical scholar Uriah Y. Kim shows how othering processes can also be found in the Bible. To this end, he first describes how the alienation of people has been legitimized in North American history up to the present day. He asks: "How can it be that the descendants of Europeans, who . . . never left Europe until 1492, are today considered 'natives' in these countries and also consider themselves so," while "the indigenous populations . . . live and count as others?"[6]

Kim combines this apparent legitimization with the need to stabilize the colonial power structure: in order for the powerful in the colonial system to be able to maintain their rule, even if they are in a numerical minority, the ruled are qualified as humanely, intellectually, and/or morally inferior. The actual superiority of the rulers thus becomes a seemingly natural and unquestionable reality. It can even become a fact of an ethnological or "racial" science.

2. See Babka, "Gayatri C. Spivak," 22–23.

3. Julia Reuter, *Ordnungen des Anderen*, 143, translates the term into German as "VerAnderung"—making someone different.

4. See Jensen, "Othering," 64–65, also below.

5. See Castro Varela and Dhawan, *Postkoloniale Theorie*, 232–33.

6. Kim, "Politik," 153.

In the case of the United States, Kim describes a further complexity of this process of change: While "national ethnic minorities (Irish, Italian, Poles, Greeks and other white Europeans) gradually became part of the majority group," neither the aborigines nor other immigrants succeeded: "Non-European ethnic groups (Black, Native American Indians, Asians, Latinos)"[7] were devalued compared to the other groups, isolated, labeled as minorities, and played off against one another.

While Kim neglects the inner differentiation and hierarchization of the population group considered as white, he nevertheless clearly shows how people are culturally (and thus unconsciously) classified into hierarchical groups of people solely on the basis of external characteristics and geographical origin.

Kim covers comparable processes of othering in the biblical book of Judges. This is not least due to the fact that the conquest of indigenous territories in North America by European immigrants in the eighteenth century was legitimized and glorified, among other things, with reference to the biblical narratives of land acquisition.

In Judges, the peoples of the land of Canaan are given individual tribal names, but they do not appear as differentiated peoples: they are constructed as a unit, as a hostile unit that threatens the identity and existence of the conquering people.[8] Likewise, the people of Israel are constructed as a unit whose internal differentiations are largely minimized. The differences between one's own unit and the foreign, enemy unit, on the other hand, are exaggerated in a binary, contrasting way.

On a superficial level, the text seems to use the strategy of othering to legitimize the devaluation and eventual elimination of one narrated group of people by another. At least that is exactly how the text was interpreted by the colonizers in the history of the North American conquest.

However, Kim's analysis also shows that, interestingly enough, the biblical text does not maintain this strict binary distinction on many individual points: in some episodes it is told how the Israelites behaved worse than the Canaanites (as in Judg 19:25). Then there are some Canaanites who show solidarity with some of the Israelites (Judg 1:24–26) and persons who cannot be clearly assigned to either group (Judg 3:31). What is more, one of the themes running through Judges is precisely

---

7. Kim, "Politik," 155.

8. See Kim, "Politik," 158.

the reiterated fact that "Israel has failed to maintain the essential difference between itself and the others."[9] The biblical text resists, at a subterranean narrative level, the narrative of othering that is maintained on the narrated surface. Processes of othering are thus subtly interrupted by the text itself.

The women appearing in the stories play a not insignificant role in the construction of the binary distinction between Israel and Canaan—as well as in breaking it.[10] On the one hand women are described in a patriarchal way as subordinate to men (also in a violent sense); on the other hand it is shown, for example in the narrative circle around Samson, that the Canaanite women who are doubly subordinated and devalued by the narrative have the threatening power to defeat even the strongest Israelite man: "Any woman can rob Israel of his manhood."[11] Here, too, the superficial duality of the text's praxis of othering is broken ironically.

Kim contextualizes the editing process of the book of Judges in a much later epoch than the narrated one. At the time of the redaction of the book, there was no longer any talk of a military conquest of the country. Kim puts the function of othering in the text in relation to the desire to strengthen one's own group identity and condemn possible deviations from this identity.[12] In his interpretation, the acts of violence related to othering that are narrated in Judges can therefore precisely *not* legitimize discourses of othering in the present and the violence that accompanies them. A contemporary interpretation of the book of Judges must consider this contextualization as well as the ongoing reality of othering in postcolonial societies. Otherwise, in colonial or postcolonial contexts, the text can acquire a meaning that does not correspond to the original intention of the biblical text. At the same time, Kim unmasks the superficial claiming of the land-acquisition narratives by the North American conquerors and the effects of this appropriation up to the present.

Uriah Kim's postcolonial interpretation of the book of Judges is a good example of how the theories and tools of Postcolonial Studies can be used to challenge biblical texts and theology in general. In this way, discourse practices can be uncovered that already shine through in the biblical and theological texts and serve to legitimize othering and other forms of securing claims to power in the present. But it can also be shown

9. Kim, "Politik," 158–59.
10. See Kim, "Politik," 159.
11. Kim, "Politik," 159.
12. See Kim, "Politik," 160.

to what extent a certain use of biblical texts is abusive and is primarily intended to support colonial interests. Finally, the way that a postcolonial interpretation of biblical texts can help to recreate and strengthen the liberating message of the Bible becomes visible.

Moreover, othering does not only occur in colonial contexts, but is used in many other processes of exercising and legitimizing power, including racist, sexist, and clerical settings. In this respect, postcolonial methods can also have an enlightening and liberating effect in other contexts in which an explicitly colonial background is not immediately apparent.

2.2. Petrification of Identities

The invention of the other is exacerbated when clearly defined, static, and apparently unchanging identities are ascribed to the other—and thus to a certain extent also to the subject itself. The negative evaluation and subordination of the (fictitious) others cause, in this way, the consolidation and petrification of one's own claim to dominance. The other appears inferior simply because he/she appears to belong to a group of people that has been constructed as inferior, so that the claim to power made over that group (and the one person defined as other) appears legitimate. This process is called essentialization or naturalization in postcolonial theory.[13] The culturally ascribed identity is understood as if it were *naturally* or *essentially* connected to a specific group of people and the associated individuals.

In particular, racism and sexism in their various forms work with these essentializations. People with certain phenotypic characteristics, such as skin or hair color, or people who are read as belonging to a specific gender, are assigned a culturally determined identity formation that appears to be common to all individuals in this group. In racist and sexist discourses, seemingly scientific analyses, systematizations, and justifications are often part of the essentialist presentation, so that these petrified attributions of identity are also taught, learned, and used with academic underpinning.

Racism and sexism were used as important instruments of colonial rule and still represent central elements of postcolonial cultural contexts (see 2.3 and 2.6 below). In addition, cultural, ethnic, or national identities

13. See Kerner, *Postkoloniale Theorien*, 67.

have served as material for petrification. The theologian Namsoon Kang from Korea, who teaches in the USA, shows, for example, that an essentialist image of Asia and Asian theologies was constructed in theology. With explicit reference to Edward Said, she writes: "The image of the Orient tends to be immobile, frozen, and fixed forever; therefore, the possibility of the transformation and development of the Orient is denied."[14]

The colonialist devaluation of Asia and everything Asian (in an essentialized sense) corresponds to an essentialist counter-strategy, which Kang also criticizes, in which Asian theology "is glorified, mystified and idealized as the wisdom of the East."[15] In this counter-strategy, Asian theology also appears to be fixed and unified: certain mystical or wise examples of Asian theologies are constructed as paradigms or essences of Asian theology and defined as the *other* of rational and discursive Europe. According to Kang, this is practiced "both by the people of the Western hemisphere and by Asians themselves."[16]

Asian theologians who do not conform to this Western mystical cliché but use theological methods identified as Western ones can then quickly be denounced as alienated or colonized. Feminism in particular can thus be excluded as something apparently non-Asian, both from the Asian and from the Western side.[17] Here Kang expressly refers to the feminist-postcolonial theorist Chandra Talpade Mohanty, who had already in 1984 pointed out that it is difficult for people from Asia, especially in the academic context, to assume an identity in the West or toward the West that does not correspond to the clichéd idea of the Asian.[18]

But Kang also uncovers essentialist approaches in Western feminist theology: Taking her cue from a work by Rosemary Radford Ruether from 1998, Kang shows how Ruether "by mentioning various individual feminist theologians in the West" "seeks to avoid the trap of generalization,"[19]

---

14. Kang, "Wer oder was ist asiatisch," 205. For Africa, the Congolese theologian Boniface Mabanza writes in a similarly pointed manner: "There is no such thing as Africa. Africa exists only in the plural." Mabanza, *Leben bejahen*, 138.

15. Kang, "Wer oder was ist asiatisch," 205.

16. Kang, "Wer oder was ist asiatisch," 205.

17. See Kang, "Wer oder was ist asiatisch," 208.

18. See Kang, "Wer oder was ist asiatisch," 211–12; and Mohanty, "Under Western Eyes."

19. Kang, "Wer oder was ist asiatisch," 213. She refers to Ruether's book *Women and Redemption*. In the more than twenty years since this book was published, the way non-Western feminist theologies are presented in the West has also changed. The basic problem of essentialism nevertheless remains virulent in other forms.

but then falls into exactly this trap when presenting the feminist theology of the Global South by letting the individual theologians disappear namelessly into the categories of Latin America, Africa, and Asia.

Within theology in Asia itself, women and their role in society can also appear essentialized:

> In Asian theological discourse on women, for example, women are portrayed as mere victims or liberating personalities, rising above all pain and suffering with an amazing, redemptive power.[20]

On the other hand, women as perpetrators, women as members of the power elite or in other social roles are not considered. Their cultural, ethnic, national, and class-related differences and personal, individual characteristics are also not taken into account: "Asian women are viewed one-sidedly as victims and any historical-cultural peculiarities are denied to them."[21] Furthermore, both the internal diversity of the group labeled as Asian women, as well as the diverse relationships of similarities and differences between Asian women on the one hand and non-Asian women or Asian and non-Asian men on the other hand, need to be considered.

For example, Kang also criticizes the theologian Aloysius Pieris from Sri Lanka, who identifies the experience of poverty and the diversity of religions as two common denominators of Asian theology.[22] Other challenges in Asian contexts that cannot be linked to these two broad categories could not be the subject of an Asian theology in the sense of this definition.

Kang expressly does not reject the use of an essentialist notion of Asian theology by theologians from Asia, since she sees it as an understandable counter-reaction and legitimate practice of resistance against Western devaluation. This relates to Gayatri Spivak's controversial concept "strategic essentialism":[23] under certain conditions, essentialization can be used as a means of resistance, to mobilize people, or to mark a counter-position as a strategic instrument if the danger of petrification is counteracted.

20. Kang, "Wer oder was ist asiatisch," 209.

21. Kang, "Wer oder was ist asiatisch," 211.

22. See Kang, "Wer oder was ist asiatisch," 208, with reference to an article by Pieris from 1980.

23. Babka, "Gayatri C. Spivak," 24; see Kang, "Wer oder was ist asiatisch," 207.

However, the negative effects of these essentializations must always be viewed critically and self-critically. In particular, both internal differences between the people who fall under a strategic essentialism and the relationships that prevail between the positions marked as different must be identified and analyzed. Otherwise there is a danger of isolation of the various identities that see themselves as pure and unchangeable. Kang therefore expressly warns: "Nowadays it is perfectly clear that whatever isolates itself, be it Western or Asian theology, petrifies. And everything that petrifies dies."[24]

In addition to such petrified attributions of identity, which can be aimed at people from other regions, cultures, and ethnic groups, essentializations can also be found in other discursive areas. Terms and concepts can also be used in essentialist ways, as if their meaning were fixed and immutable.

In theology such generalizing terms also are often used uncritically and can lead to essentialization and political, but also theological, petrification and thus be used for the conscious or unconscious exercise of power. The Argentinian-Scottish feminist theologian Marcella Althaus-Reid uses the example of grace to analyze how theological doctrines, when applied in a petrified way, can be used to justify violence, exploitation, and murder. During the conquest of Latin America, she writes, the concept of grace was misused to devalue the natives of the continent as pagans, as "inferiors."[25] All kinds of "sins" were constructed for this purpose: "Cannibalism, deviant sexual behavior, laziness and lack of spiritual seriousness" could serve "as vehicles for mercy," even if they were "(as in the case of cannibalism) pure fantasies in view of the actual identity of the natives."[26] The indigenous people had to pay for the grace of evangelization with their land, their labor, and often enough with their lives.

Althaus-Reid notes a similar misuse of a petrified doctrinal concept when speaking of mercy during the Argentine military dictatorship (1976–83), which led to the death or disappearance of tens of thousands of Argentine nationals. The claims of petrified doctrines, which had moved away from their original biblical and theological meaning and only clung to Christianity in terms of terminology, could underpin the legitimacy of the dictatorship and its crimes:

24. Kang, "Wer oder was ist asiatisch," 219.
25. Althaus-Reid, "Gnade und Anderssein," 430.
26. Althaus-Reid, "Gnade und Anderssein," 432.

Certain sermons at the time spoke of a country that needed redemption from communism, following the example of Jesus on the cross, and said that redemption was to be accomplished "through the blood" of fellow citizens.[27]

Such practices, which should be evaluated critically, can also be found in political and liberating theologies. R. S. Sugirtharajah, for example, criticizes Latin American liberation theology for tending to "reify the poor" and then "romanticize" them.[28] Reification can be compared to what is referred to here as essentialization or petrification. The poor, the women, the workers, the laity, the excluded (etc.) are classical "*masterwords*"[29] in Gayatri Spivak's terminology. By *masterwords* she understands words that, as powerful generic terms, designate a heterogeneous group of people in a way as if they were homogeneous. At the same time, through the power of generalization, these terms exercise dominion (in the sense of the *master*) over these people, homogenizing them and making their individual differences disappear. Of course, this dominance is not exercised by the concepts themselves, but by those who use them. By pointing them out as *masterwords*, this exercise of power can be made visible.

2.3. "Black I Am and Beautiful" (Song 1:5): Racist Traditions

As for the Bible verse quoted in the title (in my own translation), the devil is in the detail: Maricel Mena López, Claudia Pilar de la Calle, and Loida Sardiñas Iglesias point out the difficulty involved in translating one little word: what exactly does "and" mean?[30] In the past, this word was often translated adversatively. Even today, the 2016 German (Catholic) standard translation also writes here "I am black, but beautiful," i.e., understands the adjectives in contrast to each other, while the 2017 German Luther translation formulates in the same place: "I am black and very lovely." In the Hebrew text there is a *waf*, meaning "and."

27. Althaus-Reid, "Gnade und Anderssein," 431.

28. Sugirtharajah, "Postkoloniale Untersuchung," 62.

29. Spivak, *Post-Colonial Critic*, 104, see Castro Varela and Dhawan, *Postkoloniale Theorie*, 67–68.

30. Mena López et al., "Bíblia e descolonização," 133–35. See the detailed analysis in Caldeira, "Hermenêutica Negra Feminista."

The three authors refer to the Jerusalem Bible Commentary (1998 Brazilian edition) according to which "a sunburned woman tending vineyards can be but a slave, unlike fair-skinned women"[31] and they quote from the commentary: "The ancient Arab poets contrasted the fair skin of the girls of good birth (here the daughters of Jerusalem) with the male and female slaves who worked in the open air."[32]

Here the Brazilian-colonial relationship between white slave owners and black slaves is projected back into the time of the Song of Songs. The Bible text does not say that the daughters of Jerusalem and the speaker belong to different social classes or that the former are lighter in color. However, this racist interpretation of the beginning of the Song of Songs has a long tradition. The three theologians therefore also quote the church father Origen, who takes up this passage:

> Black by the shame of race, but beautiful by repentance and faith; black by sin, but beautiful by penance and the fruits of penance
> . . . . She, who is black, is neither created so by nature nor by the Creator, but has inadvertently suffered this situation.[33]

Origen compares the beautiful black woman to the soul that has become black through sin but can rise to the light by rejecting blackness. "Black" means therefore negative and removed from God, while "white" points to being redeemed and freed from sin. It doesn't seem to have crossed the mind of Origen, who had been born in North Africa, that there are actually people whose dark skin color is indeed "created by the Creator."

There is a deep racism in this imagery, which is evident in the stubbornness of the adversative translation of the verse until the present, and has deprived Black girls and women of a positive opportunity to identify with themselves, their skin color, "their eroticism, sensuality and beauty."[34] The translation and impact history of Song 1:5 is just one example of the racism that has shaped Christian theologies since it gained a foothold in Europe and developed in a European way.

---

31. Mena López et al., "Bíblia e descolonização," 134.

32. Mena López et al., "Bíblia e descolonização," 134; quote from the Jerusalem Bible without further information.

33. Mena López et al., "Bíblia e descolonização," 134; ellipsis original, quote by Origen from *Patrologia Graeca* 13, 103–12.

34. Mena López et al., "Bíblia e descolonização," 134.

In Postcolonial Studies, European racism is seen as one of the most influential basic structures of colonialism and postcolonial conditions. For Aníbal Quijano, today's globalized world represents "the culmination of a process that began with the constitution of America and the constitution of colonial/modern and Eurocentric capitalism as a new pattern of world power,"[35] using "America" here to describe the invention of a world to the west of Europe and new for Europeans. Racism is "one of the fundamental axes"[36] in this process, based on a division of humanity according to "phenotypic differences between victors and vanquished."[37] According to Quijano, racism is

> the social classification of the world's population according to the idea of "race," a mental construction that expresses the basic experience of colonial domination, and which has permeated the most important dimensions of world power ever since, including its specific rationality, Eurocentrism.[38]

This social classification continues to the present day, since "a systematic racist division of labor" also prevails in globalized capitalism, in which "every type of labor control is linked to a specific 'race.'"[39]

Achille Mbembe also combines the conquest of America, the slave trade, European racism, and the emergence of modernity into a unit that has consequences up to the present day:

> In many ways, our world has remained a "world of races" to this day, even if it doesn't want to admit it. The racial signifier is still the essential, if occasionally disputed, language of representation of self and world, relation to the other, memory and power. The critique of modernity will remain unfinished until we understand that its emergence coincides with the emergence of the racial principle and the slow transformation of that principle into the privileged matrix of domination techniques.[40]

This racist interpretation of the world was taken up in the history of colonial missions and pervaded missionary practice. In an investigation

35. Quijano, "Colonialidad del poder, eurocentrismo," 201.

36. Quijano, "Colonialidad del poder, eurocentrismo," 201.

37. Quijano, "Colonialidad del poder, eurocentrismo," 119.

38. Quijano, "Colonialidad del poder, eurocentrismo," 201. "Race" (*raza*) in the original without quotation marks.

39. Quijano, "Colonialidad del poder, eurocentrismo," 201.

40. Mbembe, *Kritik der schwarzen Vernunft*, 111.

into the history of missions, German historian Richard Hölzl shows how German missionaries in Africa during different eras of colonialism made different use of racist prejudices, but were never free from racism.[41]

A racist interpretation of the Noah story played a key role over the centuries: because Noah cursed his grandson Canaan (and with him his son Ham), according to Gen 9:20–27, and Ham is considered the progenitor of some African peoples in Gen 10:6, many theologians since the sixteenth century have argued that the curse of Noah affected the people of Africa as a whole.[42]

Hölzl quotes a travelogue by the Spiritanian superior Anton Horner (1827–80), which—from today's perspective—contains intense racism:

> Of the five continents, Africa is undoubtedly the most unfortunate and desolate. . . . Populated by Cham, Noe's second son, that continent is still under the heavy pressure of the father's curse.[43] . . . The black color of the descendants of Chanaan still testifies to the fact that their race has suffered Heaven's wrath in the beginning.[44]

In the opinion of these missionaries, the fatal consequences of the biblical curse can be redeemed through the mission and the hoped-for baptism, but the assumed and claimed inferiority of people with black skin cannot be eliminated.

Hölzl concedes that later actors presented a less prejudiced approach through the help of ethnographic studies. However, racism then took on other forms, for example in that individual observations among certain African peoples were generalized, essentialized, and "detached from the social interaction of observer and observed and constructed as timeless otherness."[45]

Even apparently positive and benevolent descriptions can contain a racist imbalance. Hölzl quotes the travelogue of the Benedictine missionary Alfons Adams from 1899:

> Whenever I saw Wahehe with her bold facial expression and strong figures, crouching on the ground by the fire or lying on the cowhide, happily conversing, consuming one mug of beer

41. See Hölzl, "Rassismus, Ethnogenese und Kultur."
42. See Hölzl, "Rassismus, Ethnogenese und Kultur," 11.
43. Hölzl, "Rassismus, Ethnogenese und Kultur," 12.
44. Hölzl, "Rassismus, Ethnogenese und Kultur," 13.
45. Hölzl, "Rassismus, Ethnogenese und Kultur," 16.

after the other, I couldn't help but think of our heroic ancestors, the Germans, who impressed the civilized Romans simply
by their tremendous thirst.[46]

The comparison with the Germans is meant flatteringly here, but it
not only reproduces a classic othering, but also denies contemporaneity
through the parallelism with "our ancestors," and thus negates cultural
equivalence. This practice is characterized in critical ethnography as a
"denial of coevalness,"[47] i.e., a negation of contemporaneity.

In a later epoch, Hölzl identifies a more self-critical and covert "racism behind closed doors"[48] among the missionaries, based on a concept
by Homi Bhabha, in which the devaluation of African people was no
longer openly expressed or even theologically justified, but "using the
means of the unspoken, of irony and casualness"[49] was brought into the
discourse in such a way that prejudices and stereotypes no longer had to
be explicitly named, but were assumed to be known and could thus be
called up indirectly. The analyses of some photographs from missionary-
colonial contexts of the twentieth century, with which Hölzl uncovers the
racist relationships and ideas recognizable in the pictorial compositions,
are extremely revealing in this respect.[50]

The concept of racism is currently subject to some expansions
and clarifications. In a critical analysis, Fabian Lehr, German-Austrian
Marxist, points out that racism is not only expressed in behavior toward
Black people, especially in Europe.[51]

This is an important addition to the anti-racist considerations in
postcolonialism, since these are often based on the relationships between
people from Europe and Africa and the other colonial states, as well as
with people who have been kidnapped to other regions and cultures
through the international slave trade. Lehr, on the other hand, shows that
there is also a racism with deep cultural roots in the Western European
states, which is directed against people from Eastern Europe and which
has its origins at least as far back as the Middle Ages. He demonstrates

46. Hölzl, "Rassismus, Ethnogenese und Kultur," 18.

47. Hölzl, "Rassismus, Ethnogenese und Kultur," 19, following Johannes Fabian,
Time and the Other: How Anthropology Makes its Object.

48. Hölzl, "Rassismus, Ethnogenese und Kultur," 24.

49. Hölzl, "Rassismus, Ethnogenese und Kultur," 25.

50. See Hölzl, "Rassismus, Ethnogenese und Kultur," 27–33.

51. See Lehr, "Zum europäischen Rassismus."

racist prejudices against people from the former so-called Eastern bloc (this term also contains an essentialist charge) to the present day.

Irrespective of whether one wants to expand the concept of racism with Lehr, this example nevertheless points out that a one-sided determination of the concept of racism to include relationships between people of a certain skin color also assumes essentializing traits and is in danger of occupying racist positions itself. Anti-racist analyses from Postcolonial Studies and theologies can also shed light on the relationships between other people who have been essentially assigned to different social groups. At their root, they often draw attention to the problem of constructions of European superiority.

2.4. Constructions of European Superiority

The invention of *others* and the essentialization of their identities often served to construct European claims to superiority in numerous cultural areas during the age of colonialism. European science and rationality in particular were considered superior to those of non-European cultures.[52]

Such a claim to superiority can still be identified today. It is now rarely imputed to Europe in a geographic sense. However, in a cultural and historical sense, European traditions of thought, from antiquity through the Renaissance and the Enlightenment to postmodernism, are still considered to be of universal significance. European way of thinking is still often maintained to be more advanced, more rational, more critical, and more efficient than the thought traditions of other geographical and cultural areas.

It is also associated with the claim of universality. European traditions of thought are no longer classified as European in the sense of a regional cultural imprint, but as universal, belonging to humanity and appropriate to reality.[53] Their European origin is often not denied—in a historical sense—but is not used to contextualize it culturally, but in a circular argument as proof of European superiority, since this apparently universal rationality has its historical roots in Europe.

As an example of such a circular argument, the German theologian Joerg Rieger, who teaches in the USA, cites an argument of Friedrich Schleiermacher, who regarded the political superiority of Europeans

52. See Contreras Colín, "Kritik," 159–60.
53. See Chakrabarty, *Provincializing Europe*, 29–30.

in the colonies as proof of the better development of their culture and the correctness of their religion: in Schleiermacher's opinion, given the enormous superiority of the Christian nations in terms of civilization and power, contemporary missionaries did not need any further legitimation through miraculous signs.[54]

This European claim of superiority is also evident in other realms of theology.[55] The cultural contextualization of Christianity in Greco-Roman thought, which had already begun at the time the New Testament was written, is declared to be the basis of a universal theology from which the theologies of other cultures should be nourished and cannot depart. The origin of Christianity in a non-European culture is deliberately suppressed; its Jewish roots are declared to be an ultimately dispensable "particularism."[56] In this way, European theologies become the benchmark for theology in general. Edward Schillebeeckx therefore also notes critically: "Previously it was assumed that the theology of the churches in the West was of course supra-regional, universally valid and immediately accessible to every human being—regardless of what culture he or she came from."[57]

In this way, theological awakenings on other continents can always be warded off by referring to the universal claim of European theology. This tendency can even be found in the early reception of liberation theology by the New Political Theology, when authors like Johann B. Metz maintained that the former depended theologically from the latter.[58]

Paulo Suess criticizes European theology's claim to universalism as a falsification of Christianity.[59] For Suess, this universalism is closely related to the claim of European thought to represent science in the singular, thereby devaluing or excluding alternative or competing forms of knowledge:

> Universalism leaves the first and last word to science, which it sees as universal because it is not subject to contextual influence. Therefore, the locally-anchored knowledge is to be regarded as

54. See Rieger, "Theology and Mission," 204.

55. See also my discussion in Silber, "Eurocentrismo."

56. For example, Pannenberg, "Notwendigkeit," 147. See, on the other hand, Estermann, *Südwind*, 163–64.

57. Schillebeeckx, "Vorwort," 8. However, I cannot agree with his optimism that this has changed "at the latest since the emergence of liberation theology" ("Vorwort," 8).

58. See, for example, Metz, *Zum Begriff*, 164.

59. Suess, "Prolegomena," 193.

on a lower level due to its regional reach and excluded from a dialogue with science. Scientific universalism became an instrument of domination like racism and patriarchy. In the field of theology, this question appears in the form of the dispute between universal theology and local theologies.[60]

However, European theology cannot claim to be a universal theology, but is itself a local, contextual theology that is in direct exchange with its local contexts and their epistemic horizon. The deconstruction of this European universal claim is an important theme of the Indian historian Dipesh Chakrabarty, who speaks of the need to *provincialize Europe*,[61] i.e., to restore to the continent the regional (and internally plural) character that is actually its own, and thus deconstruct the claim to a universal character as an attempt to hegemonize global thinking.

The German theologian Elmar Klinger takes up this challenge of provincialization when he writes:

> European theology is not used to giving European theology the title European. . . . The title "European" to refer to it must sound like a challenge to the ear of a European theologian, and it is. Because, in the opinion of those theologians who use it, it is a title that describes European theology as belonging to a certain cultural group and narrowing its perspective.[62]

Constructions of European superiority and the claim to the universal significance of one's own can also be found concealed in the history of European theology. Thus, they often continue to exercise their influence today without this being immediately apparent. Simon Wiesgickl uses the example of the development of the historical-critical method in German-language biblical studies to show the diverse interactions between European superiority, colonialism of the eighteenth and nineteenth century, and the emergence of an extremely influential exegetical method to the present day.[63] The critical analysis of the contexts in which biblical narratives were situated or edited often made use of the orientalist constructions of colonial travelogues of the time.

Wiesgickl adopts Edward Said's critique of European ideas about the Orient. He demonstrates that biblical scholars, who are among the

60. Suess, "Prolegomena," 192.
61. Chakrabarty, *Provincializing Europe*; see Kerner, *Postkoloniale Theorien*, 76–80.
62. Klinger, "Theologie im Horizont," 47.
63. See Wiesgickl, *Alte Testament*, 121–231.

founders of historical criticism, envision religious, political, and economic contexts for biblical texts that relate more or less to the same geographic area but to completely different historical and cultural epochs.
In addition, Wiesgickl describes the notion of a gradual development of
mankind that is developed in the nineteenth century, and according to
which both the biblical contexts and the subjects of the colonies of their
time were in a kind of "childhood age of mankind,"[64] while Europe had
already reached adulthood.

This claim of European superiority has a particularly dramatic effect
in the idea documented by Wiesgickl of historical-critical Bible scholars
who actually thought they were helping to improve the Bible text by con-
verting, shortening, or correcting biblical traditions:

> The biblical books were seen by scholars as an unsorted hoard
> of miscellaneous texts, not differentiated according to genre, au-
> thenticity and character, which German Old Testament scholars
> would now have to put in order.[65]

This seemed possible, because "German scholarship," as Wiesgickl
proves with documents from the time, "understands its counterpart
better than this counterpart is able to visualize itself."[66] The idea that
German literary studies and theology should be able to do this better
than other European disciplines is no coincidence and was underpinned
with nationalistic and chauvinistic arguments during the period under
study. Wiesgickl also uncovers interactions between anti-Judaism and
biblical studies, insofar as a high and at the same time chauvinistic appreciation of the Old Testament texts could go hand in hand with a
radical devaluation and rejection of contemporary Jewish authority in
the interpretation of their own holy texts.[67]

The European idea of human development criticized by Wiesgickl
is linked by the Brazilian theologian Alfredo J. Gonçalves with Hegel's
doctrine of the *Weltgeist* (world spirit): according to this idea, mankind
would "become more and more civilized, that is, progressive and modern
at every stage of its history."[68] This would, of course, be done under the
leadership of Europe, so that the other parts of the world would always be

---

64. Wiesgickl, *Alte Testament*, 176.

65. Wiesgickl, "Gefangen in uralten Phantasmen," 182.

66. Wiesgickl, "Gefangen in uralten Phantasmen," 182–83.

67. See Wiesgickl, *Alte Testament*, 173.

68. Gonçalves, "Crisis," 86.

in a stage of development corresponding to an earlier epoch of Europe's history. In other words, they are always lagging behind European developments without any possibility to ever reach them.

Kwok Pui-lan shows that this ideology of development also had consequences for European religious studies. Non-Christian religions were regarded as forms of religion that were not yet so highly developed, like precursors to Christianity, so to speak. Colonization and mission would then serve to further develop and modernize these religions. In this way they could reach a stage of development similar to that of Christianity. In Protestant religious studies, Christianity was still considered the fulfillment of all religions[69] at the time of the Edinburgh Missionary Conference in 1910.

But even in the present, similar ideas of a Christianity that is simply more advanced than other religions or of a European Christianity in comparison to which the churches of other continents are less developed can be demonstrated. For the Protestant theological tradition, Kwok mentions the influence of Karl Barth, whose differentiation of faith and religion has in turn led to a devaluation of non-Christian religions.[70]

Colombian biblical scholar Maricel Mena López deftly deconstructs the hegemony of white, European stereotypes in biblical scholarship: she examines the African and Asian roots of biblical texts.[71] She maintains that the Bible is not a European book, even if it made this claim in Latin America. Nor is it "100 percent Semitic,"[72] as Mena López points out, but it arose out of a centuries-long dialogue with peoples, religions, and cultures of a broad geographical region that stretches across Asia, Europe, and Africa. The Bible is therefore connected to Africa by way of Egypt, Kush, and beyond, in a variety of direct ways and can thus also be related to today's Afro-American cultures in Latin America without having to take the detour via the European conquerors.

2.5. Do Religions Actually Exist?

The question in the heading may appear unexpected at first. However, postcolonial criticism of the epistemological category of the concept

---

69. See Kwok, *Postcolonial Imagination*, 189–97.

70. See Kwok, *Postcolonial Imagination*, 196.

71. See Mena López, "Raíces afro-asiaticas y la descolonización."

72. Mena López, "Raíces afro-asiaticas y la descolonización," 77.

religion can lead to the question of what is actually meant by this term: To which cultural and historical phenomena does the term apply and in what way? Is there a power interest associated with its use as an attribution to certain phenomena? What function did it perform, for example, in the legitimization and practice of colonization?[73]

Current religious studies also discuss justified doubts about the consistency of the concept of religion, especially in its application. If Religious Studies want to remain neutral toward the self-definitions of religious communities, especially confessionalism, they are faced with the problem of deciding how exactly a religion can be recognized, defined, and described. As Ulrich Berner writes:

> The problem with all these attempts at order and classification . . . lies . . . in the tendency towards essentialization, i.e., the tendency to define the "essence" or the "central meaning" of individual religions or of religion in general.[74]

For example, how important is the Bible or the Eucharist for Christianity? The answer will be different depending on the Christian denomination one is studying. The same applies to the importance of the observation of the Sabbath in Judaism or the understanding of the Qur'an in Islam. Berner takes up the problem again, quoting Pierre Bourdieu with the statement that many "contents of faith and practices commonly referred to as Christian" often "have little more in common than the name."[75]

Religions should not be conceptualized as homogeneous institutions or communities, but were often treated as such in colonial practice. For colonialism, it was necessary to homogenize religions conceptually in order to be able to master and manipulate them more easily through essentialization and to stabilize colonial rule over and through them. Colonial religious studies supported this practice by declaring various forms of a religion to be "deviant" or "heterodox" currents, often in agreement with native elites with whom colonial officials worked.

---

73. See also for what follows: Daniel, *Grenzen des Religionsbegriffs*; Rettenbacher, *Außerhalb der Ekklesiologie*, 299–324; de Jong-Kumru, *Postcolonial Feminist Theology*, 92–98; and Silber, *Pluralität*, 167–83.

74. Berner, *Religionswissenschaft*, 13.

75. Berner, *Religionswissenschaft*, 31.

Kwok Pui-lan criticizes this Western practice of religious studies as a "reification of religions,"[76] i.e., their petrification or essentialization. What is dynamic, flexible, and geared toward exchange in a religion is pushed back in favor of a rigid, apparently scientific concept of distinguishable religious communities.

As the Chinese theologian Lai Pan-chiu explains, this exclusion can even affect Christian traditions in a colonial setting: in the time of colonial mission, traces of Christianity in Asia originating from Nestorian, Arian, and Monophysite Christians at the time of their persecution in the Roman Empire were found, yet not taken up as something peculiar to Christianity, but rejected as heterodox. Today, however, they can contribute to the development of a separate, inculturated Chinese Christian identity.[77]

The reification or petrification of religions leads to a separating or distinguishing demarcation of one religion from the other. The various relationships that members of the religions develop with one another are marginalized or declared to be deviant. For example, the possibilities of the worship of Virgin Mary in Hinduism[78] or the observance of the Sabbath in Christianity on Saturday instead of Sunday seem to be atypical for the respective religion. However, they represent examples of practices that are used in a self-evident way by members of many religions when they come into contact with the rites and beliefs of members of other religions in their own contexts. Such phenomena indicate that an essentialist description of religions is not at all appropriate to their lively cultural and intercultural dynamics.

Rather, any study of religions must consider the fact that there are multiple relationships between religions, not just similarities but also interdependencies, shared and interwoven histories. The concept of "entangled histories" advocated by the postcolonial ethnologist Shalini Randeria to label the fact that seemingly separate histories are always intertwined has particular justification here.[79]

Sigrid Rettenbacher, for example, shows in her dissertation how various religious communities have repeatedly developed their relationships, differences, and demarcations through negotiations in discourse

76. Kwok, *Postcolonial Imagination*, 205.
77. See Lai, "Teaching Global Theology."
78. See Baumann, "Götter, Gurus," 234.
79. Conrad and Randeria, "Einleitung," 17.

over the course of history.[80] According to this reading, Christianity and Judaism were connected to each other for much longer and only separated into two distinct religious communities when Christianity had gained a position of power in the Roman Empire. The external demarcation between the religions that will be perceived as separate in the future corresponds exactly to an internal essentialization:

> With the separation or creation of Judaism and Christianity in the fourth century, the difference between orthodoxy and heresy was also established at the same time, so that from then on it could be clearly defined who was inside and who was outside.[81]

R. S. Sugirtharajah draws attention to the interdependence of Christianity with Asian religions: Through "merchants, craftsmen, migrants and those fleeing religious persecution,"[82] Christianity spread in the first centuries to all parts of the world accessible at the time, including what today is Japan, without specifically pursuing mission in the contemporary (or colonial) sense of the term. Conversely, traces of Eastern wisdom and cultures can also be found in Christian traditions. Thus, Sugirtharajah correlates the historically attested "religious act of voluntary self-sacrifice" performed by the Indian (Buddhist?) emissary Zarmanochegas in 37 BCE in Athens, with the self-immolation alluded to by Paul in 1 Cor 13:3.[83] In this respect, religious traditions must always be read as hybrids and refer to interreligious relationships.

In postcolonial criticism, the very concept of religion is called into question. The British religious scholar Richard King judges that the term religion itself is "a Christian theological category," "the product of the culturally specific discursive processes of Christian theology in the West and has been forged in the crucible of interreligious conflict and interaction."[84] By including this Christian theological term in Western religious studies, Kwok Pui-lan argues, it acquires an interpretative power over all phenomena worldwide that are designated by it, regardless of their cultural peculiarities, even in secular academic and non-academic contexts. "In this way, Christianity continues to serve as the

---

80. See Rettenbacher, *Außerhalb der Ekklesiologie*, 88–89.

81. Rettenbacher, *Außerhalb der Ekklesiologie*, 96–97.

82. Sugirtharajah, "Postkoloniale Untersuchung," 136.

83. Sugirtharajah, "Postkoloniale Untersuchung," 141.

84. King, *Orientalism and Religion*, 40; see King, "Philosophy of Religion," 44–48.

prototype of a religion, and the standard for evaluating other wisdom traditions," Kwok concludes.[85]

Sigrid Rettenbacher also argues (with Daniel Boyarin) that the concept of religion does not exist as an "epistemological category"[86] before the fourth century CE. This category and with it the religions of Christianity and Judaism were "invented"[87] in order to be able to describe what began to be differentiated through the separation of Jewish and Christian communities. This concept, coined for a specific case, should therefore not be applied to completely different cultural phenomena in distant contexts.

Rettenbacher adduces numerous examples to show the consequences of this for colonial religious studies. She demonstrates how the colonial depiction of Hinduism specifically looked out for phenomena that were known from Christianity, namely sacred scriptures and spiritual elites, without asking whether such institutions actually had an important meaning in the "religion" under investigation—or which could have been that meaning.[88] One can speak of a Western invention of Hinduism in the interests of the colonial power and the local elites working with it.

It is no longer surprising that, if Religious Studies are shaped by such basic assumptions, the direct comparison between Christianity and the religions of the colonized peoples generally should end in favor of the religion of the colonial masters. Kwok Pui-lan also detects this self-understanding of one's own superiority in secularized Religious Studies and in liberal Theology of Religions, for instance in John Hick. His assumption that all religions are responses to the same transcendent reality, according to her critique, blurs the actual differences between religions and again views them from an apparently superior Western perspective—now that of pluralism.[89]

Such a leveling pluralism does not do justice to the real and very complex plurality in the world of religious phenomena: "Instead of grounding our thinking in the liberal paradigm of religious pluralism, we must begin to envision a postcolonial theology of religious difference," Kwok writes.[90] This theology will no longer focus on religions as essen-

85. Kwok, *Postcolonial Imagination*, 189.

86. Rettenbacher, *Außerhalb der Ekklesiologie*, 101.

87. Rettenbacher, *Außerhalb der Ekklesiologie*, 101.

88. Rettenbacher, *Außerhalb der Ekklesiologie*, 199–200.

89. See Kwok, *Postcolonial Imagination*, 199.

90. Kwok, *Postcolonial Imagination*, 203.

tialized and delimited entities, but rather on the relations and differences between the experiences of people from different cultural, philosophical, religious, and ordinary contexts.

At the same time, a postcolonial theology of religions will not look only at the differences between religious experiences, ideas, and practices, but also at their similarities, overlaps, and complementarities. This is how the Malaysian Jesuit Jojo Fung, who teaches in the Philippines, talks of the different experiences of the spirit in the indigenous world, in shamanism, in Chinese culture, in the Bible, and in secular modernity and relates the different ideas to one another.[91] In this way he can show that it is unfair and inaccurate to attribute primitiveness to shamanism and indigenous religions, and to view secular modernity (or Christianity) as progressive. Rather, for Fung, these different descriptions of the spirit show different expressions of the human search for a relationship with the Spirit of God described in the Bible. From a Christian point of view, and in Fung's analysis, representatives of shamanism must therefore be respected and valued as partners in dialogue.

2.6. (Post)colonial Gender Relations

The colonial discourse practices described so far also have an effect in the area of gender relations, and they are also critically analyzed by postcolonial feminist theology in particular. Othering and essentialization are classic methods of classifying women as the other or second gender from the perspective of male dominance. They also served to confirm European superiority in colonial contexts.

Binary gender constructions tend to be conceived in a dualistic and exclusive way. Gender identities that do not fit into this dualism are then classified as deviant or unnatural, exceptional or simply nonexistent. The examples in this section mostly criticize a patriarchal-dualistic gender construction without explicitly drawing attention to the deeper problems of a two-gender image of humankind. However, this further criticism is also triggered by these feminist considerations and must always be kept in mind.[92]

Colonialism has also affected the relations between the sexes in the fields of churches and theology and often changed them radically for the

91. Fung, "Postcolonial-Mission-Territorial Hermeneutics."
92. See the section on queer theologies, 5.5.

worse. Musa Dube, theologian and biblical scholar from Botswana, shows how the way European missionaries dealt with precolonial concepts of God in Botswana was shaped by patriarchal and Eurocentric prejudices and led to intracultural disruptions in gender relations.[93]

Before the arrival of the missionaries, the local population knew a system of higher and lower deities, which they imagined to be gender-neutral. The ancestors who were part of this spiritual structure were also referred to with a gender-neutral plural form. The "priestly figures"[94] that existed in Setswana culture could be male or female; in the religious tradition of the Batswana ethnic group, women had the opportunity to bring their spiritual abilities into the community and to identify and relate to divine beings.

According to Dube, through the mission and the introduction of a translation of the Bible into Setswana, the formerly gender-neutral supreme deity, *Modimo*, was masculinized and identified with the biblical God Father. The lesser deities were declared to be demons, and the priestly roles and functions previously open to both sexes were interpreted as a witch cult. In this way, colonialism dramatically changed gender relations:

> The colonial process alienated the Batswana from their cultural symbols of power and particularly marginalized indigenous women; the men could at least identify with Modimo, God the Father, and with his Son who is the head of the church, just as men are the heads of the family (see Eph 5:22).[95]

This apparently theological-biblical stratification of (male) God and demons, men and women, husbands and wives was reinforced in colonial practice by educational and administrative institutions, economic structures, and trading systems that were patriarchally organized along the lines of the European model. In this way, the essentialist conception of God in Eurocentric theology coupled with a hierarchical gender dualism and the patriarchal organization of everyday life resulted in fatal epistemic violence, the victims of which were primarily women.

Kwok Pui-lan cites other examples from Asia and Africa of how social and cultural gender relations were worsened by colonialism.[96] The

93. See Dube, "Postkolonialität," 106–8.
94. Dube, "Postkolonialität," 106.
95. Dube, "Postkolonialität," 107.
96. See Kwok, *Postcolonial Imagination*, 153–55.

Filipino nun and theologian Mary John Mananzan, whom she quotes, describes the drastic effects of the Catholic Spanish mission in the Philippines on the role of women in society and their self-esteem:

> In the 16th century, Spain brought Christianity and Western civilization with its patriarchal character to the Philippines. The same misogynist sentiment that prevailed in the Western church was brought to the islands.[97]

While women in the Philippines largely enjoyed the same rights and social standing as men before the arrival of the missionaries, colonialism restricted their responsibilities to the family household and massively curtailed their participation in society. The justifications with biblical and theological arguments seemed obvious in the European culture of the time.

For the Bolivian theologian Cecilia Titizano, "Indigenous women have suffered and survived tremendous violence under the colonial civilizing mission"[98] as colonial exploitation and sexual violence went hand in hand with a demonization of indigenous cosmovision that devalued female deities as well as women's life experiences and wisdom. For Titizano, the commitment to the dignity and rights of women therefore requires challenging the patriarchal Christian image of God the Father.

Instead, she points to the precolonial female deity of *Mama Pacha* (or *Pachamama*) as a figure of identification for both female and indigenous worlds of experience. As "Earth Mother" (a possible translation of the Andean *Mama Pacha*), she also integrates experiences of the agrarian and the ecological world and—theologically—of creation. Titizano does not claim to replace the Christian Father-God with Pachamama, but draws attention to the possibility of a more holistic image of God and describes the destruction caused by colonial mission.

Another postcolonial strategy of reappropriating the feminine aspects of the deity is described by the Peruvian-Mexican theologian and anthropologist Héctor Laporta. His field research in various shrines of the Virgin Mary in Latin America showed that the figure of the Mother of God was enhanced by her worshipers in ritual and festival:

> My ethnography confirms that the worship of Our Lady of Guadalupe disrupts the colonial order and transgresses Catholic Church dogmas and policies. In so doing the devotion to

---

97. Mananzan, "Frauen und Religion," 120; see 119–21.
98. Titizano, "Mama Pacha," 132; see 129–35.

> Our Lady of Guadalupe breaks with the impositions of colo-
> nial values such as power, race, and language, subverts Catho-
> lic doctrine, and goes outside the control of the physical space
> of the church.[99]

While not overtly in the liturgical language but implicitly in the festival practice, the figure of the Virgin of Guadalupe is treated like a Goddess—in particular as the embodiment of the ancient Mexican deity *Tonantzin*.[100] In this practice, colonial patterns are broken. At the same time, other colonial social and cultural values are also violated by the festival. Laporta interprets the procession with the figure of the saint and the festival that follows, both of which take place outside the walled ecclesiastical space, as a departure from the colonial order and a break with it. Even the excessive consumption of alcohol and the sexual per-missiveness that can be experienced at these festivals are seen as signs of a rupture in the colonial social order, motivated and supported by the reappropriation of the Goddess: "Mary jumps off the official stage and participates actively in the *fiesta*, where music, drink, food, and romance are important part of the celebrations."[101]

However, it should be noted critically that violence against women in Latin America is often a direct result of the massive consumption of alcohol, not least at these festivals. An overly uncritical assessment of these celebrations as a break with the colonial order is therefore not appropriate. Nevertheless, the example shows how a postcolonial examination of religious institutions and processes can contribute to a decisive theological change of perspective.

These few examples of colonial and postcolonial gender relations and strategies to overcome them cannot suffice as an introduction into the complex field of postcolonial feminist theologies or studies.[102] For the time being, they only point to the fundamental importance of feminist critique in postcolonialism. In the following sections and chapters, even more examples from feminist perspectives are described, which will con-tribute further important aspects to this transversal theme.[103]

99. Laporta, "Decolonizing," 109; see 108–13.

100. Laporta, "Decolonizing," 110–11.

101. Laporta, "Decolonizing," 111. Translation corrected by the author.

102. See Kwok, *Postcolonial Imagination*; Dube, *Postcolonial Feminist Interpretation*; and de Jong-Kumru, *Postcolonial Feminist Theology*.

103. See especially 3.3, 3.6, 4.2, 4.3, 5.4, and others.

2.7. Who Writes (Church) History?

A powerful instrument of colonial discourse was, and is, the writing of history. Against the claim to neutrality made by some schools of historic science, Postcolonial Studies make the criticism that authors of historiography give preference to their own perspective and thus also pass it on to their future readers.

The American scholar of religions Randall Styers examines the importance of postcolonial theories for the study of church history. He quotes the Tunisian-French sociologist Albert Memmi, who says

> that "the most serious blow suffered by the colonized is being removed from history." Colonizers have indeed exercised extraordinary power in defining what counts as history, who counts as a subject, and what counts as knowledge.[104]

The South Asian Subaltern Studies Group, which is considered one of the founding initiatives of Postcolonial Studies, devoted itself particularly to this problem in historiography: Who are the authors, which actors are named and which are kept secret? How are they and their practices characterized? Above all, Dipesh Chakrabarty criticizes the practice in historiography of always examining the history of non-European parts of the world in relation to and in comparison with Europe; while European historiography apparently could be done without reference to the rest of the world.[105] At the same time, these critiques create a "history from below,"[106] in which subaltern actors can also have their say, for example by means of interviews.

US church historian Elizabeth A. Clark asks similar questions to those of the Subaltern Studies Group while opening a forum meant to address postcolonial inquiries to church history scholarship:

> Who is entitled to engage in this theorizing? Whose voices get recovered? Can Westerners "authentically" represent the views of those whom their own cultures have repressed? Does not the formation of Christian identity, like all identity-construction, depend upon setting up an "other" as a negative foil, in this case, the non-Christian, the heretic, the apostate? Have political and economic—"material"—forces become submerged in the

---

104. Styers, "Postcolonial Theory," 854. The quotation of Memmi is from his 1957 book *Colonizer and the Colonized*.

105. See Chakrabarty, *Provincializing Europe*, 27–46; 97–113.

106. Kerner, *Postkoloniale Theorien*, 151; see 150–52.

academic discussion of "representation," of literature and textuality? Has the history of the colonized been lost in the process?[107]

In addition, the indigenous scientist Linda Tuhiwai Smith from New Zealand questions the European concept of history itself from a feminist perspective: "history is the story of a specific form of domination, namely of patriarchy, literally 'his-story.'"[108] Therefore, it is not a given for the indigenous struggle for decolonization to advocate that indigenous authors should want to participate in the production of Western historiography. Rather, Smith questions essential foundations of the Western understanding of history. In order to be able to tell one's own story, indigenous practices of memory and storytelling, in particular narrativity, plurality, and alternative rationalities, must be allowed and valued. In this way, historiography also becomes an arena for debate about the past and the injustices inherited from it. With that in mind, as Smith writes, "the need to tell our stories remains the powerful imperative of a powerful form of resistance."[109]

Latin American theologians and historians also complain that the history of the missions and the colonies was and is usually written by Europeans and with European methodology. The history of the subjugated is made invisible in this way. Enrique Dussel criticizes European historiography of the conquest of America as an "aristocratic history":

> A certain Christianity was recorded and another one left on the margins. . . . Furthermore, history has almost always been written from the perspective of an elite culture that is itself culturally dependent. We were educated in universities, in seminars, in Europe or under European influence, and that gave us a certain perspective on reality. Even if we now provide a "scholarly" description (and that is assumed here), this is a highly erroneous interpretation.[110]

The Mexican theologian Alejandro Castillo Morga points out how, since the conquest of Latin America, indigenous knowledge, self-image, and historical awareness have been repeatedly delegitimized, reinterpreted, and destroyed.[111] This self-understanding of the history

107. Clark, "Postcolonial Theory," 848.
108. Smith, *Decolonizing Methodologies*, 29; see 28–41.
109. Smith, *Decolonizing Methodologies*, 35.
110. Dussel, *Desintegración*, 101.
111. See Castillo Morga, *Sabiduría*, 127, and 125–81.

of America's indigenous peoples "is expressed in their way of being, in their ways of life, their worldview, myths, customs and habits, and of course in their word."[112]

In the face of conquest, colonization, and mission, this self-image was partly destroyed and partly reinterpreted according to prevailing interests. But Castillo also shows how the indigenous wisdom developed strategies of resistance through which it was possible to preserve and pass on their own historical consciousness, at least in a transformed form. Using a Nahuatl term widely used in Mexican decolonial discourse, Castillo calls this strategy *nepantla*, which can be translated as "to step in between," opening a space in which hybridity and mesticity[113] become possible.

In this space it is possible to resist collectively within the colonial framework using the combined means of the colony and one's own tradition. The historical memory that is formed here draws on both traditions, but primarily uses the language and terminology of the conqueror to preserve and pass on the indigenous traditions in a way that does not seem suspicious to the powerful.

However, the aim of this analysis is not to distill a kind of pure indigenous historical memory in this way, but to describe the forms of resistance through which it was transformed and passed on. In this way it is possible to learn not only from the original indigenous wisdom but also from the experiences of resistance in past and present.

The history of the subjugated and their resistance is therefore not doomed to be lost. Rather, it is possible, with suitable methods, with consideration for the voices of the subalterns themselves and by correcting historical scholarship shaped by Western ideas and the idea of history itself, to construct alternatives, in which this subaltern history can be remembered and passed on. This is how Randall Styers sums it up (in a foreword to postcolonial church-historical contributions):

> Colonization has rarely succeeded in the effort to expunge the colonized from history. Just as postcolonial writing demonstrates the potential for fighting one's way into the revision of

112. Castillo Morga, *Sabiduría*, 125.

113. See Castillo Morga, *Sabiduría*, 129. Castillo translates *nepantla* in Spanish as "*situarse en medio*." *Mesticity* or *mestizaje* in Spanish refers to the specific (and internally diverse) cultural and ethnic development of Latin American peoples in the centuries of colonialism. It is also used to characterize cultural developments of Latino/a ethnic groups in the USA.

the historical narrative, so also the papers that follow offer new insights into how the historian can contribute to efforts to contest and amplify that narrative.[114]

2.8. Intersections of Different Axes of Coloniality

The feminist theoretical concept of intersectionality is used very frequently in Postcolonial Studies. Gabriele Winker and Nina Degele locate the origin of this concept in the "experiences of Black women who did not find themselves mirrored in the feminism of Western white middle-class women,"[115] especially in the USA of the 1970s. Accordingly, experiences of oppression due to racism and sexism cannot simply be added together, but rather overlap and influence one another. These overlaps or crossings have been called *intersections* since the 1990s, while *intersectionality* refers to the theoretical concept and systematic analysis of their mutual influence.

Over time, other axes of unequal treatment, exclusion, or exploitation were added to this increasingly complex method of analysis. The theologian Namsoon Kang mentions "gender, race, ethnicity, class, sexuality, (dis-)ability, nationality, citizenship, religion, etc."[116]—and the final "etc." particularly points to the fundamental incompleteness inherent in the concept. Age, education, and occupation also appear as other important categories that can be included in the analysis.

Winker and Degele make it clear that these different axes of social structure are not independent of each other and must therefore be analyzed in their relationship to one another, since these "categories appear in an interwoven way and may strengthen, weaken or even change each other."[117] The "goal is the comprehensive theoretical and, above all, empirical analysis of the importance of various categories of difference in phenomena and processes of all kinds."[118]

With regard to postcolonial theological scenarios, Namsoon Kang speaks of an "entanglement of colonialism, gender and religion."[119] Beyond the immediate historical effects of colonialism, it is necessary to

114. Styers, "Postcolonial Theory," 854.
115. See Winker and Degele, *Intersektionalität*, 11.
116. Kang, "Jenseits," 181.
117. Winker and Degele, *Intersektionalität*, 10.
118. Winker and Degele, *Intersektionalität*, 10.
119. Kang, "Jenseits," 181.

uncover how it is intertwined with other power structures and mechanisms of exclusion. To construct postcolonial theories implies therefore

> analyses of multiple complex relationships of domination and
> oppression and of power and knowledge that are inseparable
> from one another, but cannot be traced back to one another.[120]

Kang explains that each of these axes—she largely limits her analysis to colonialism, gender, and religion—tends to produce binary structures of "center and periphery, . . . inclusion and exclusion."[121] However,
the overlaps make it increasingly "difficult to define precisely who 'we'
and who 'they' are. The *we* as a singular-monolithic identity becomes
impossible, problematic and even dangerous."[122] Moreover, and especially in colonial-missionary constellations, "religion appears as a holy
sanction of such power asymmetry."[123]

The analysis of these complex and interwoven intersections is
further complicated by the fact that power relations are often not
clearly visible and recognizable, but distorted, obscured, and masked.
In particular, those who wield power in (post)colonial contexts often
remain unrecognized because their position "is often invisible and
camouflaged."[124] Last but not least, religion often plays a decisive role in
this intended invisibility, for historical reasons.

From her investigation, Kang concludes five consequences for
the production of theology in postcolonial spaces using the tools
of intersectionality: first, it is important to "deconstruct the Western
construction of a binary fixedness."[125] This means uncovering the processes of othering and essentialization, also described in this chapter,
and revealing their functioning and direction. A second consequence
is the dissolution of the hegemonies constructed along the various intersecting axes, such as Eurocentrism and sexism. She warns against
"postcolonial revenge,"[126] i.e., the desire to simply reverse the balance of
power between men and women, center and peripheries, colonized and

---

120. Kang, "Jenseits," 182.

121. Kang, "Jenseits," 181.

122. Kang, "Jenseits," 181.

123. Kang, "Jenseits," 182.

124. Kang, "Jenseits," 182.

125. Kang, "Jenseits," 185.

126. Kang, "Jenseits," 186, with a term used by Leela Gandhi, from her book *Post-colonial Theory*.

colonists. Rather, she says, this deconstruction of the hegemonies serves to "question theological norms and standards."[127]

As a third consequence for theology, Kang calls for "promoting hypersensitivity to the marginalized."[128] Within intersectional settings, these marginalized are harassed in multiple ways, namely on the various intersecting axes. Any partiality for them—which she considers a Christian obligation due to the discourse on the final judgment in Matt 25:31–46—falls under the suspicion of those in power. Therefore, Kang also draws the further conclusion of "radically" recognizing the legitimacy of the standpoints, perspectives, and experiences of the marginalized.[129] For Kang, the theological reason for this—as a fifth and final consequence—lies in the fact that the marginalized are made in the image of God. To demonstrate and rehabilitate this likeness is for Kang a decisive theological effect of intersectional analysis.

For Namsoon Kang, this critical theological analysis and reorientation takes place in the space of the church and the theological tradition, and transcends both at the same time. These advancements are necessary to restore to Christianity the liberating character it lost through imperial and colonial influence.

2.9. Hegemony: Conclusion

In colonial contexts, the various discourse practices presented in this chapter ensure that the military, political, and economic rule of colonialism is also culturally secured and can even be taken for granted. Deep-rooted and culturally anchored convictions are not easily challenged, and so the asserted superiority of the European, white, Christian, and male conquerors is secured by cultural domination.

This self-evident conviction can be described as *hegemony*, in the sense given to the term by the Marxist philosopher Antonio Gramsci, which has been widely adopted in Postcolonial Studies. According to Bill Ashcroft et al., the Gramscian concept can be resumed in this way: "Fundamentally, hegemony is the power of the ruling class to convince other classes that their interests are the interests of all."[130] Hegemony is primar-

---

127. Kang, "Jenseits," 186–87.

128. Kang, "Jenseits," 187.

129. Kang, "Jenseits," 188.

130. Ashcroft et al., *Post-Colonial Studies*, 106.

ily a cultural effect. Gramsci contrasts it with open and direct forms of exercising power that can be seen and felt. Rather, hegemony relies on the power of inner conviction:

> Domination is thus exerted not by force, nor even necessarily by active persuasion, but by a more subtle and inclusive power over the economy, and over state apparatuses such as education and the media, by which the ruling class's interest is presented as the common interest and thus comes to be taken for granted.[131]

In the context of colonialism, the concepts and practices described in the previous sections, such as othering, essentialization, Eurocentric superiority, patriarchy, etc., lead to a culturally perceptible hegemony in the sense of Gramsci, the implicitness of which one can hardly escape. Even after the end of political colonial rule, this hegemony remains in the cultural sense—it becomes Aníbal Quijano's *coloniality*.[132]

The concept of hegemony can also explain why colonial values and devaluations persist instead of being fought even after independence has been achieved. The deep cultural roots of colonial beliefs means that they remain hegemonic even in the postcolonial period.

> Consent is achieved by the interpellation of the colonized subject by imperial discourse so that Euro-centric values, assumptions, beliefs and attitudes are accepted as a matter of course as the most natural or valuable. The inevitable consequence of such interpellation is that the colonized subject understands itself as peripheral to those Euro-centric values, while at the same time accepting their centrality.[133]

Nehring and Wiesgickl explain that exactly the same problem can also be found in ecclesiastical and theological contexts:

> For theology, important starting points arise here for the question of how people of other religions and cultures could accept a missionary Christianity from Europeans, what they adopted

---

131. Ashcroft et al., *Post-Colonial Studies*, 106–7. The term *cultural hegemony* is currently also used by new-right and neo-fascist movements to draw attention to the fact that a desired takeover of power also requires the achievement of an interpretational sovereignty in civil society based on conviction and cultural self-evidence. See Pittl, "Schmittsche Gespenster," 176.

132. See also sections 1.2, 1.4, and 3.8.

133. Ashcroft et al., *Post-Colonial Studies*, 107.

from it and where they developed forms in which resistance to the Western missionaries was possible.[134]

In the vast majority of colonial systems of European provenance, church and missions were central actors who took advantage of colonial rule and at the same time often legitimized it. Contemporary theology usually underpinned the respective arguments, although of course at the same time there existed theological resistance to certain excesses of colonialism or even to the colonial project. In this sense, Musa Dube criticizes

> the colonial ideology of oppression that characterizes its victims as human beings who must be rescued from their own terrible inadequacy. This colonial construct continues to portray the West as the center of all cultural achievement, a center with a supposed redemptive impulse, while degrading all other cultures to a project of civilization, Christianization, assimilation and development.[135]

In addition, a specifically theological interest in a Eurocentric hegemony can also be recognized.[136] Catholic centralism in particular, which for several reasons was structurally expanded and organizationally secured at the same time as European colonialism was prospering, created its own particular systems of belief in the superiority of European (Roman) scholarship in general and theology in particular. This specific Catholic version of Eurocentrism survived periods of crisis in the humanities, such as humanism, the Reformation, the Enlightenment, and postmodernism, largely unscathed.

So critical analysis shows that theologians from postcolonial contexts who want to present an independent version of contextual theology have to deal with the corresponding discourses in European theology as a matter of course, while for theology in Europe—even in a globalized world church—it is apparently possible to have theological discourses that claim to be universal without any reference to or dialogue with the theologies of the Global South.

These implications based on Eurocentric colonial hegemony are dissolved and deconstructed in the postcolonial critique. The dialogue with other knowledge systems and traditions and the engagement of critical and resistant epistemologies also contribute to break the spell of

134. Nehring and Tielesch, *Postkoloniale Theologien*, 21.

135. Dube, *Postcolonialität*, 95.

136. See Silber, "Eurocentrismo."

this hegemony. While these forms of resistance and the construction of alternative forms of knowledge will be the subject of the fourth and fifth chapters, the next chapter focuses on the postcolonial critique of the more direct forms of oppression and exploitation. To take up Antonio Gramsci's well-known formula: "State = political society + civil society (in other words hegemony protected by the armor of coercion)."[137] If this chapter has dealt primarily with questions of hegemony, the next one is devoted more to coercion.

137. Gramsci, *Gefängnishefte*, 783.

3.

Power Relations

IF GRAMSCI REGARDS THE state as hegemonic rule secured by coercion, then colonialism and the postcolonial relations of power that followed can also be analyzed as power relations that are discursively or hegemonically justified and maintained by external coercion. The colonial power relations, which were mostly secured by the military and the police, were transformed over time, especially after the respective formal state independence of the colonial areas, into a variety of other power relations that were of a political and economic nature, racist, or gender-related. Church and missionary power asymmetries also continue colonial power structures to the present day.

It is not uncommon for these power relations to be veiled by discourse. In this respect, there are, of course, close connections between the themes and analyses of this chapter and those of the previous one. Therefore, overlaps cannot always be avoided. In this chapter, however, the focus lies in the external, structural, institutional, and legal aspects of the critique of postcolonial power relations. Contrary to a widespread criticism, postcolonial theories not only deal with cultural and discursive aspects of domination, but also aim at social and political conditions that work on a more structural level. However, the synergy of analyses at the structural and discursive levels gives Postcolonial Studies an advantage in uncovering the complex and varied forms of rule that colonialism created, bequeathed, and further developed.

After the end of colonialism, these structures did not simply survive but were transformed and deformed in many ways, not least under the influence of the resistance and independence movements. The purely historical memory of colonial power relations can therefore only serve as one element of their analysis. In addition, Postcolonial Studies also make use of other tools of power analysis in order to be able to deconstruct the complex and often veiled character of the postcolonial power structures.

Without claiming to be exhaustive, this chapter presents various aspects and perspectives of the structural exercise of power in postcolonial contexts. As in the last chapter, they are again illustrated with examples from postcolonial theological work in order to document the effects of these analyses on theological methods and content. At the same time, the contribution that critical, postcolonial theologies make to the analysis of power relations and, at the same time, to the resistance against them becomes visible.

In addition to open power relations, e.g., in the political sphere (3.1), structural dependencies can also be found in the economy (3.2), in religion (3.3), and in land ownership (3.4). Questions of belonging and exclusion have both discursive and structural aspects (3.5). Other elements of postcolonial-theological analysis presented here are violence against women (3.6) and invisibility in oppressive conditions as a power strategy (3.7). Finally, with the concept of the coloniality of power (3.8), an interim conclusion is drawn to sum up the two rather analytical and deconstructive chapters 2 and 3.

Similar to the cultural and discursive forms of hegemonic rule examined in the previous chapter, the power relations that are the focus of this chapter also present a certain self-evident or even apparently God-given character. Since Christian mission usually represents an important element of postcolonial cultures, the existing power relations are often seen as religiously legitimized or even determined. Like other culturally sanctioned structures, however, they seem at least to be naturally or historically necessary. This apparent self-evidence—be it religious or secular—poses an important challenge for postcolonial analysis.

3.1. "The Lord, Who over All Things So Wondrously Reigns"? Living in the Empire

Despite its origins, documented in the New Testament, which reflect suffering under empire and its exercise of power, postcolonial theologies show that, in colonial and postcolonial contexts, Christianity often found itself at the side of, and participated in, imperial power. Christian legitimacy of rule can even lead to a glorification of divine government, as the quote from the hymn in the title of this section suggests.[1] A transfer of this glorification to secular power was, and is, always possible.

The concept of *empire* is often used in postcolonial theologies because it metaphorically takes up the sociohistorical context of the New Testament and, to some extent, the Bible as a whole. The confrontation of the biblical authors with imperial rule, above all with the Roman Empire, has left clear traces in the texts, which are worked out in postcolonial exegeses and biblically oriented theological investigations.[2]

At the same time, postcolonial authors often refer more or less explicitly to Michael Hardt's and Antonio Negri's concept of empire.[3] These authors transform the historical conception of empire, which was always more or less based on the centralized exercise of power, into the idea that global claims to power, especially of the capitalist economic system, are no longer based on the power of a single state or its immediate sphere of domination or hegemony, but on diverse, at times contradictory, and sometimes fragile power systems that can react flexibly and dynamically to resistance and counter-movements without being centrally controlled.

The term *empire* can also be used to designate the current consequences of the historical legacies of colonialism. Using the term in this sense, the Chinese-North American exegete Benny Liew Tat Siong writes:

> The difference between imperialism and colonialism explains, for example, why many former colonies still find themselves under the indirect or informal rule of others, including, but not restricted to their former colonies.[4]

1. The second stanza of the hymn "Praise to the Lord, the Almighty" contains the text above cited; in the German original, the correspondent text reads: "Lobe den Herren, der alles so mächtig regieret."

2. See, for example, Wind, *Christsein im Imperium*.

3. See Hardt and Negri, *Empire*; "Empire—zwanzig Jahre später"; and Rivera, "Ränder," 149–57.

4. Quoted from Dube, "'Rhodes Must Fall,'" 94.

As a rule, postcolonial theological reflections in which the term plays a role also move within this wide range of meanings of biblical, historical, and postmodern notions of empire. What these different ideas have in common is that they point to global political rule that has far-reaching effects in economic and cultural areas.

A revealing example of such a theological criticism of empires is provided by Joerg Rieger's comparative historical study of the history of Christologies through the ages from the perspective of their inter-actions with the respective empires.[5] On the one hand, according to his analysis, Christology is influenced by the prevailing ideologies of domination and adopts elements from them to determine the theological significance of Jesus Christ. On the other hand, Rieger shows how Christologies were always misused to legitimize imperial power interests. Finally, however, he also refers to the power of resistance, which is always inherent in Christology and which cannot be completely absorbed and controlled by the respective empire.

Rieger first shows the extent to which the first Christologies were critical of the Empire. Paul and other New Testament authors gave the risen Christ the title of rulership: *"Kyrios"* or "Lord," which—at that time more than today—correlated with patriarchal exercise of power, but in direct competition to the power claims of contemporary lords or *kyrioi*: Those who acknowledged the *Lord* Jesus Christ and his powerless form of exercising power offered direct resistance to the *Kyrios* of the Roman Empire, the emperor, or other regional, local, and family lords. Accordingly, Paul and numerous early Christians were treated as enemies of the state.[6]

Later stages of christological development—after the first council under Emperor Constantine in 325 CE and the later rise of Christianity to become the religion of the Roman state—however, participated in strong mutual interactions in the secular, imperial power relations. Nevertheless, at every stage of this development, Rieger draws attention to how Christology, despite its involvement in political hierarchies, repeatedly developed the strength to resist empire, aided by the living memory of the historical figure of Jesus, for example by figures such as Bartolomé de las Casas, in the midst of the colonial abuse of the Christian religion and by it.[7]

5. See Rieger, *Christus und das Imperium.*

6. See Rieger, *Christus und das Imperium*, 21–52.

7. See Rieger, *Christus und das Imperium*, 134–49.

From this analysis arises the important challenge, at every stage of the development of Christology, to convert itself anew toward the people who have been oppressed by the empire and to the lived experiences of these people. This allows it to activate its potential of resistance. Otherwise, it runs the risk of fitting into and supporting imperial power structures. At the same time, it has to deal repeatedly and self-critically with the diverse interrelationships between the christological glorification of the rule of Jesus Christ and the legitimacy of imperial power.

US Native American theologian George E. Tinker similarly criticizes the use of christological titles associated with imperial and colonial concepts. The *kyrios* title, in its English translation *Lord*, is still reminiscent of the subjugation of the North American Indians by English and US American "lords":

> To call upon Jesus as lord suddenly began to strike me as a classic example of the colonized participating in our own oppression. To call upon Jesus as lord is to concede the colonial reality of new hierarchical social structures; it is to concede the conquest as final and become complicit in our own death, that is, the ongoing genocidal death of our peoples.[8]

For Tinker, therefore, it is imperative that "if theology is to make any legitimate claim to universality,"[9] it must transcend the limitations of European culture and engage in dialogue with cultures that think and speak radically differently.

Juan Bosco Monroy, theologian and biblical scholar from Peru, uses another example to demonstrate how such an approach critical of empire can fundamentally change the interpretation of Bible texts: in a traditional understanding of the story of the Tower of Babel (Gen 11:1–9),[10] the abandonment of the construction of the tower, the confusion of languages, and the scattering of people are often seen as God's punishment for human hubris.

In this case, however, Monroy first examines from a postcolonial perspective the context in which the biblical story came about: *Babel* now appears in his analysis as a symbol for the claim to imperial world domination, in which, among other things, power is optimized through the implementation of a uniform language and major projects are carried out

8. Tinker, *American Indian Liberation*, 96.
9. Tinker, *American Indian Liberation*, 62.
10. See Monroy, "Babel."

through forced labor (brick production). The bricks are also a reminder of the bondage of the people of Israel in Egypt in a biblical-intertextual reference (see Exod 1:13). God's intervention is thus experienced by the oppressed as a liberation, not as a punishment: the empire is broken, its mega construction project destroyed, and forced labor ended.

In this way, a different view of the text opens up, which also makes visible new, challenging connections to the present: the diversity of languages can then even be seen as an enrichment and not as a punishment, both *before* and *after* the confusion of the language in Babel. And in fact: The immediately preceding chapter in Genesis arranges people in all areas of the world according to their languages (see Gen 10:31). The plurality of languages is there part of the blessing of humanity, of the multiplicity of peoples that fill the space of the Earth. In the present, however, the global standardization of culture and language and large-scale imperial projects still serve to promote and secure the power of the rulers through exploitation and forced labor. The text can thus be read in the present as a symbol of hope for cultural diversity, economic independence, and political liberation.

Monroy combines a changed view of the Bible with a critical analysis of empire's current power strategies, its efforts to homogenize language and culture, and hard and alienating labor. Through his interpretation, the God of the Tower of Babel story becomes recognizable as the liberator from imperial claims to power well-known from other parts of the Bible. In a similar vein, other postcolonial theologians are questioning the close connection between Christianity and the exercise of power, and are rereading well-known texts from the Bible and tradition in order to be able to interpret them from the perspective of the subaltern as good news of liberation and empowerment.

3.2. Bought Back and Redeemed? Economic Dependence and Christian Redemption

As a rule, the declarations of independence of colonized states did not bring real economic independence with them. On the contrary, especially in the economic sphere, the structures of the exploitation of resources and people, dependence on exports, and the unjust concentration of property in the hands of a few sometimes continued seamlessly.

Mostly, only the ownership structure changed, from European to local elites, although these were often also of European descent.

The orientation of production in the now former colonies to the interests of the markets in the European states remained as a rule, as did agricultural monocultures, on which cotton or consumer goods were grown for export and not so much for personal use, and excessive mining, to enable the export of unprocessed commodities such as timber, precious metals, oil, and minerals to industrialized countries. The proceeds from these export-oriented production relationships often remained (and still remain to this day) directly or indirectly in the industrialized countries.

For these reasons—which can only be presented here in a very simplified manner—protests are being raised in many postcolonial states that the colonies have not really achieved independence from an economic point of view. Terms such as neocolonialism and "internal colonialism"[11] are used to characterize external and internal factors of ongoing dependence and exploitation affecting the former colonies and particularly individual regions within them.

In Latin America, liberation theology has drawn attention to these economic dependencies since the 1960s and has also reflected on them theologically, usually without making an explicit connection to the continent's former colonial status.[12]

Gustavo Gutiérrez, who because of his eponymous book of 1971 is considered one of the founders of liberation theology, formulated in the spirit of the dependency theory that was then emerging in the critical social sciences: "The underdevelopment of poor peoples as a global social fact . . . is a historical sub-product of the development of other countries."[13] The development of the industrialized countries is described in this dependency theory as a major cause of the impoverishment of the colonies and the postcolonial states.

In this situation, the central theological challenge for Gutiérrez can be summarized in the question: "What is the relationship between salvation and the process of human liberation in the course of history?"[14] This challenge motivated, in the following years and decades, the development of the plural and diverse movement of Liberation Theology,

---

11. González Casanova, *Sociología de la explotación*, 221–50.
12. See Kern, *Theologie der Befreiung*, 54–61.
13. Gutiérrez, *Theologie der Befreiung*, 77–78.
14. Gutiérrez, *Theologie der Befreiung*, 135.

which is still of global significance today.[15] In it, to create and fail to eradicate poverty is characterized theologically not only as "evil and . . . scandal" but as an "expression of sin."[16] This sin has a structural power that transcends the bad actions of individuals. Furthermore, economic injustice is branded in liberation theology as idolatry that must be resisted.[17] In recent years, a dialogue between liberation theologies and postcolonial and decolonial studies has deepened, in which theological evaluation of economic, political, and social oppression is related to other developments in colonial power.[18]

In other regions of the world, too, the postcolonial economic dependency on industrialized countries is subject to theological criticism. The historian and scholar of religions Ezra Chitando from Zimbabwe writes:

> Global economic actors are interested in Africa solely for satisfying their own needs and whims. Although Africa is very well endowed with oil, minerals, arable land and other resources, the continent continues to reel from exploitation of the same by greedy and cunning external players who act in cahoots with crooked internal elites.[19]

This greed for raw materials of the regions of the Global South not only describes the relationship between Europe and its colonies, but also applies in Chitando's experience to economic relations in the postcolonial times of globalization.[20] Chitando contrasts capitalist exploitation, through which someone else's property is turned into salable goods, with a biblical memory: in the story of Naboth's vineyard (1 Kgs 21:1–19) it becomes clear that it is possible to relate to the Bible—albeit an important document of the history of colonialism—to claim respect for ancestral inheritance and respect for God against colonial exploitation: "Naboth was convinced that his inheritance could not be commodified and given away, as it was from his ancestors."[21]

Chitando gives yet another example of a liberating postcolonial Bible interpretation:

15. See Silber, *Pluralität*, 58–97.

16. Gutiérrez, *Theologie der Befreiung*, 277.

17. See, for example, Sobrino, *Christologie der Befreiung*, 225–67.

18. See Silber, "Among Sisters."

19. Chitando, "Bible as a Resource," 404.

20. Chitando, "Bible as a Resource," 407.

21. Chitando, "Bible as a Resource," 404.

> Reading the narrative in John 5:1–9, the story of the man who
> needed healing and took a strategic position by the pool of
> Bethesda, can be a very empowering undertaking. The man was
> "so near, yet so far." Similarly, we as Africans have our resources
> right within our grasp, but we struggle to access them and use
> them to maximum use.[22]

In view of the economic dependency from wealthier states and international corporations, it is also important that the exploited peoples themselves can become actors and do not allow themselves to be pushed into a victim role attributed by them or by others. Biblical stories like the one about the sick man at the pool of Bethesda can be interpreted from this perspective.

German theologian Marion Grau, who teaches in Norway, shows how motifs from capitalist economics can be fused with classical theological narratives in postcolonial theologies in a defiant and even ironic new guise. She takes up an image of Gregory of Nyssa, who in the fourth century interpreted the redemption brought about by Christ on the cross as a deliberate fraud: God paid the devil with counterfeit money, because the price God paid for saving mankind, i.e., the death of Christ, was a deception, since Christ was resurrected later: God is seen as a "trickster,"[23] who even makes fun of the deceived devil.

This narrative may be interpreted in a world of capitalist dependencies as an *exception* to a valid rule that God is allowed to break in fighting (and mocking) the devil, but its validity for human economic relations is not fundamentally questioned. But it can also develop the potential to use tricksters, counterfeiters, and other violators of capitalist rules as *role models* for the liberation of those oppressed and dehumanized by those rules. The classic soteriological picture of ransom can thus lead to a political answer to the fundamental question of liberation theology about the relationship between redemption and human liberation.

As these examples show, postcolonial theologies do not only draw attention to the fact of economic oppression in their contexts through their creative transformations of biblical and traditional narratives and connect them with theological questions. They also reveal the complicity of traditional theologies with colonial economic relations and, based on the practice of anti-colonial and anti-capitalist resistance, establish new theological

---

22. Chitando, "Bible as a Resource," 408.
23. Grau, "Göttlicher Handel," 315; see 308–18.

discourses in which the redeeming and liberating power of faith can also be applied to the power structures of economic dependency.

3.3. "To Missionize Is to Colonize."[24]

The mission of the Christian churches was an integral part of colonialism. It is true that a distinction must be made between different missionary undertakings and missionary practices, depending on the region and context, denomination and colonial motherland, and through different times. There was also mission before and outside of European colonialism, and there have been missionaries who were personally very critical of colonialism and its excesses.

Nevertheless, there is such a deep connection between the two historical projects that the Christian mission almost always plays a decisive negative role, even in nontheological and secular postcolonial criticism. Musa Dube gets to the heart of this criticism with a little story that has been handed down orally in different variants and in different regions:

> When the white man came into our land, he had the Bible and we had the land. The white man said to us, "Let us pray." After prayer, the white man had the land, and we had the Bible.[25]

Dube observes that mission and land grabbing went hand in hand in the colonial experience of sub-Saharan Africans. The Bible—as a symbol for European Christianity, here in a Protestant form—is initially seen as a foreign body, but through the missionary process characterized by this story it undoubtedly came into the possession of the African people, who use it to this day as something of their own, but at the price of being plundered, so that they were no longer allowed to keep their ancestral lands as their own. "The story explains," then, "how black African ownership of the Bible is linked to the white man stealing the land of African people."[26]

24. Joseph Schmidlin, Catholic missiologist in the year 1913, quoted by Bosch, *Transforming Mission*, 306; see below.

25. Dube, *Postcolonial Feminist Interpretation*, 3; see 148–53. This story is also passed on orally in Latin America; see Hidalgo, "Im Kampf," 211.

26. Dube, *Postcolonial Feminist Interpretation*, 3; see 3–21. For the historical memory of the land theft suffered by Dube's parents in the 1950s by a white man, see Dube, "'Rhodes Must Fall,'" 85.

In this way, mission could serve the practical implementation of the conquest, but also its justification:

> Christian Missions archives are eloquent in highlighting that their work was a handmaiden of the Empire's cultural imperialism, since these services were more often than not coupled with the explicit dismissal of indigenous structures, cultures, religions, economies in the bid to replace them with Christianity, Commerce and Civilization—namely, that of their mother countries, who were colonisers.[27]

In addition, of course, missions also exercised religious power: supported by colonialism, European missionaries could decide which religion (and, in the case of Christianity, which denomination in which European cultural shape) the conquered peoples should practice. The native religions were often simply eliminated or declared a diabolical practice.[28] In other cases, the missionizing conquerors or even their European headquarters decided which elements of these religions were compatible with Christianity and which were not. In Roman Catholicism, this Eurocentric attitude often continues into the present through the hierarchical internal organization.

In the history of missions, these conditions have changed many times. The Christian mission of the present relies more on dialogue, voluntary conviction, and self-organization. However, Kwok Pui-lan rightly points out that European missionary theology only began to call for dialogue when historical colonialism was already politically over, and it had thus lost the framework of political rule and coercion that it represented.[29]

Undeniably, the Christian mission has also generated resistance to colonialism throughout its history, as exemplified by well-known figures such as Bartolomé de las Casas. However, these have largely remained a minority and from an overall perspective, ineffective. Also, it is often pointed out that the missionaries usually had a different motivation than the conquerors. Richard Hölzl, for instance, asserts that "the religious

27. Dube, "'Rhodes Must Fall,'" 86. Dube alludes to David Livingstone, who had demanded that "civilization—Christianity and commerce—should ever be inseparable." See Dube, *Postcolonial Feminist Interpretation*, 6.

28. See Dube, *Postcolonial Feminist Interpretation*, 12–15.

29. Kwok, *Postcolonial Imagination*, 202, with reference to Raimundo Panikkar. See also my critical analysis of dialogue in missionary practice in Silber, "Synodalität, Befreiung, Widerstand," 267–70.

impetus of the conversion mission"[30] cannot be fully reconciled with the practice of conquest, plundering, and so-called civilizing in colonialism.

However, with his investigation of nineteenth-century German Catholic missionaries in Africa, he also reveals a clear proximity between mission and colonialism and at the same time refers to their own racist missionary and theological arguments:

> The theological and missionary racisms of the nineteenth century explained the alleged biological and cultural inferiority by using the Bible. By characterizing the way of life of Africans as punishment from God or the work of the devil, they established the greatest theological hierarchy possible. However, they also portrayed Africans as passive victims who could be redeemed through the work of the mission and the suffering of the missionaries.[31]

With this in mind, conquest and civilization, even expropriation and enslavement, could be interpreted as the generous benefit of colonization and mission: from the perspective of so-called civilization, the people in the colonies could develop, and from a religious point of view they would be redeemed. Dube writes, "Christianizing, colonizing, civilizing, as well as enslaving, became part of the redeeming mission."[32] To oppose this mission could only be wrong from a Christian perspective (of the time). The religious and theological justification for the mission turns out to be a disguise of the actual interests of colonialism.

The targeted theological devaluation of the native religions served both colonial and missionary interests. Richard Hölzl cites the example of the already-quoted German Father Anton Horner, who in 1870 described the religions of the inhabitants of Zanzibar as the work of the devil. He made this negative valuation specific in allegations of "infanticide and desecration" in order to use them immediately to justify the conquest: "'As you can see, these souls . . . are very bruised and bowed under the yoke of Satan.' The courage to 'come to their aid' must be all the greater."[33]

In other cases, non-Christian religions are not devalued in this dramatic way, but according to the Eurocentric ideology of superiority (see above, 2.4) they are characterized as backward, primitive, in need

---

30. Hölzl, "Rassismus, Ethnogenese und Kultur," 16.

31. Hölzl, "Rassismus, Ethnogenese und Kultur," 15.

32. Dube, *Postcolonial Feminist Interpretation*, 10, with reference to Congolese anthropologist Valentin-Yves Mudimbe.

33. Hölzl, "Rassismus, Ethnogenese und Kultur," 15.

of purification, or irrational, and all kinds of negatively evaluated practices are attributed to them. Mission, which in addition to conversion
to Christianity then also implies turning away from earlier religions,
corresponds not only to an apparently religious task but also to the self-
ascribed civilizing task by which European imperialism was justified.

The close relationship between mission and colonialism can well
be summarized in the words of Joseph Schmidlin, who is regarded
as the founder of German-language missiology, and who wrote, in
1913: "To colonize is to missionize" and "to missionize is to colonize."
Schmidlin further writes:

> The state may indeed incorporate the protectorates outwardly;
> it is, however, the mission which must assist in securing the
> deeper aim of colonial policy, the inner colonization. The state
> can enforce physical obedience with the aid of punishment and
> laws; but it is the mission which secures the inward servility and
> devotion of the natives.[34]

Like all colonial structures, missionary power relations still have
an effect and continue to be transformed up to the present. This does
not only apply—as mentioned above—to the Catholic Church with
its global centralist church structure. In all Christian churches with a
colonial-missionary past, missionary, postcolonial, and clerical power
structures overlap, albeit in different ways according to denominations.
Problems of sexism and racism also play a part in the constellation of
postcolonial power structures.

Postcolonial missionary structures can become particularly delicate
when they are also associated with development projects and other financial dependencies. In 2013, the tenth General Assembly of the World
Council of Churches in Busan wrote, self-critically, in its affirmation on
mission, evangelism, and evangelization:

> In reality, however, mission, money, and political power are
> strategic partners. Although our theological and missiological
> language talks a lot about the mission of the church being in
> solidarity with the poor, sometimes in practice it is much more
> concerned with being in the centres of power, eating with the
> rich, and lobbying for money to maintain ecclesial bureaucracy.[35]

34. Both quotes from Bosch, *Transforming Mission*, 306. "Protectorates" (*Schutzge-biete*) was the technical (and euphemistic) term used in colonial Germany for the colonies.

35. World Council of Churches, *Together towards Life*, no. 48. Financial, structural,

It cannot, therefore, simply be assumed that colonial power relations based on missionary endeavors became irrelevant with the end of colonialism, with the further developed understanding of mission in the twentieth or the twenty-first century, or with the more self-critical awareness of missionaries today. From a postcolonial perspective, they must continue to be critically analyzed and accompanied, since, like all power relations in these contexts, they are characterized by an ongoing coloniality. Mission remains a question of postcolonial power.

3.4. Land Ownership and Constructions of Space

Musa Dube's little story about the Bible and land ownership, quoted at the beginning of the last section, has already drawn attention to the problem that colonization and mission were connected with the theft of indigenous land. The Australian theologian Chris Budden writes about the first meeting of European and indigenous people (Aborigines) in Australia:

> The relationship between the two peoples began in theft. The European invaders drove people from their land, destroyed their homes and sources of food, denied them access to sacred sites and their connected stories, and in the process undermined the sociality at the heart of identity. Also destroyed was people's capacity to live from the land.[36]

Regardless of whether these invaders wanted to create a military base in their colonies, set up a mission station, enable agricultural use or the settlement of people from the mother country—they always assumed the right to possess the land they apparently discovered and thus to take it away from other people. However, the amount of land stolen in fact varied depending on the type of colonization.

The methods of land grab also varied: It was not always accompanied by wars and violent displacement. Susan Healy from Aotearoa New Zealand describes various historical approaches to land grab, ranging from breaches of trust and contracts, to supposedly legal expropriation through the privileges of the conquerors, to forcible evictions and appropriation through war. Again and again she documents how missionaries and bishops in New Zealand and Great Britain promoted and

---

and personal dependencies of African churches from Europe are also described by Boniface Mabanza, *Leben bejahen*, 154–59.

36. Budden, *Following Jesus*, 20.

legitimized this procedure or practiced it themselves.[37] However, she also documents reconciliation processes in the present, in which individual Methodist communities return stolen land through agreements with authorities and indigenous communities.[38]

A further aggravating factor, in both the case of land theft and attempts to return the stolen land, is that in the conceptions of many indigenous peoples there is no such thing as land ownership in the European sense. This concept depends on a certain cultural idea or discursive conceptualization of what land is. Budden writes:

> The use of the word "land" is indicative of one of the difficulties that are inherent in this attempt to do contextual theology in this country: the struggle with language and meaning. To call this place "land" is to define it within the discourse of European colonialism. It is a discourse that leads to real estate, economic worth, measured space and ownership. It is a discourse that stands over against the metaphors that mark indigenous discourse: "mother earth," "place," "country" or "home."[39]

"For Europeans who invaded Australia, land was largely a commodity"[40] that could be bought or sold or bartered for another land. According to indigenous concepts, however, the person or community cannot simply leave the land and start a new life somewhere else: life is linked to a specific place or home, a specific territory. Budden writes:

> There was an intimate social, religious and economic connection between people and their particular place. . . . "Native people were part of the land and it was part of them. When they lost their country, they lost themselves."[41]

"In the European narrative, earth is turned into 'landscape' (something seen from the outside and from a distance, as separate from us) and 'real estate,'" Budden maintains, and explains that, in contrast,

---

37. Healy, "Settler Christianity."

38. Healy, "Settler Christianity," 94–95.

39. Budden, *Following Jesus*, 6.

40. Budden, *Following Jesus*, 20.

41. Budden, *Following Jesus*, 21, quoting indigenous author Nigel Parbury, from his work *Survival*. Susan Healy describes a very similar connection of the Maori of Aotearoa New Zealand to their specific territory. See Healy, "Settler Christianity," 73–78. A similar conception is alive in other cultures and—as is suggested by Ezra Chitando—can also be found in the Bible (see above, 3.2).

"country is not simply where people live, but who they are."[42] This close connection between land and people is also described in North American indigenous peoples. George Tinker, theologian from the Osage Nation in the USA, characterizes this connection for his Native American worldview like this:

> Every nation has some understanding that they were placed into a relationship with a particular territory by spiritual forces outside of themselves and thus have an enduring responsibility for that territory, just as the earth, especially the earth in that particular place, has a filial responsibility towards the people who live there.[43]

The Austrian theologian Michael Nausner, who teaches in Sweden, points to another peculiarity of the discursive spatial constructions of the Australian natives: In field studies, the anthropologist Sam Gill documented a conception of

> territory not as a continued area, but as land defined by the footprints and tracks all around. Less an encapsulated area than a network of tracks becomes the characteristic image of the country. The country is defined in accordance with the journeys made by the ancestors. . . . The visualized lines are not lines of division, but rather lines of connection with the ancestors and, most importantly, they are not in competition with other itineraries.[44]

Western notions that land could be marked by borders, divided up, and sold, that people could be resettled (or expelled) into another territory, or that fences could prevent people from following in the footsteps of their ancestors cannot in any way be reconciled with these fundamentally different spatial constructions. They can ultimately only be enforced by violence or by domination. Violence and domination were, conversely, legitimized with European notions of land ownership and a specifically European perception of space as a measurable and purchasable commodity.

Borders between different colonial territories could therefore be erected and shifted in the Western sense quite arbitrarily by the colonial rulers. Moreover, colonialism did not only set boundaries to mark land

---

42. Budden, *Following Jesus*, 72.

43. Tinker, *American Indian Liberation*, 72.

44. Nausner, "Heimat als Grenzland," 196–97.

ownership and colonial rule. The border between colony and not yet colonized so-called wilderness was also considered the border between civilization and barbarism, culture and nature, inside and outside, as a measure of progress and development. In keeping with a certain notion of civilized development, the colonizers also argued that expanding these borders-frontiers by stealing indigenous lands could count as progress for civilization.[45]

In addition, Postcolonial Studies fundamentally criticize the binary character inherent in the conception of borders in Western thought. Nausner criticizes the Western understanding of borders using Homi "Bhabha's analysis of borders as complex areas of negotiation rather than as thin dividing lines."[46] Borders can never hermetically separate spaces from one another; rather, they always create "an edge of hybridity where cultural differences touch one another in a 'contingent' and conflicting manner."[47]

For Nausner, this analysis even has christological consequences: It evokes "understanding Jesus of Nazareth as a frontier person. Jesus himself, I would argue, contributes to challenging the notion of a fixed or stable territory."[48] This is because Jesus is also described in the Gospels as a migrant, cross-border, itinerant preacher who stands not for land ownership but for relationships. Budden also presents theological consequences of the analysis of land ownership and land concepts:

> To talk of the location of God in Australia is to move beyond a conversation about people to the idea of "country." It is not simply to sit with people in a particular political or social space but to honor the network of humanity and world that is country. That is, seeking God in Australia forces the theologian to enter the growing conversation about ecology and God's place in the earth.[49]

The postcolonial analysis puts theology in a position to ask about the social, ecological, and spiritual connections of *country* and thus to locate the earth beyond the economy of commodities. For Budden, this means that Christian theology needs to explore and present the Trinitarian

45. See Rivera, "Ränder," 154.
46. Nausner, "Heimat als Grenzland," 193.
47. Nausner, "Heimat als Grenzland," 193. See also 4.6 below for more details.
48. Nausner, "Heimat als Grenzland," 199.
49. Budden, *Following Jesus*, 71.

relationships between the Christian Creator God and this lived reciprocity in the indigenous concept of *country*. In this way, theology develops implications not only for a reconciliatory approach to the land-theft traumas of the colonial past, but also for an ecological approach to the challenges of country, earth, and territory in the present.[50]

The South African theologian Tinyiko Sam Maluleke sums up the liberating theological intention of postcolonial theologies in dealing with land, alluding to the story quoted by Musa Dube (see above, 3.3): "use the Bible to get the land back and get the land back without losing the Bible."[51]

3.5. Insiders, Outsiders

The Cuban-born US-American theologian Miguel De La Torre uses his own experience to describe how a person's skin color depends on numerous perspective factors. He calls himself an "international cross-dresser,"[52] not with regard to fashionable gender stereotypes, but referring to this variability in his own skin color. While "the Latino/a Miami community, where I was raised, during my formative years reinforced the notion that I was 'white,'"[53] as a professor he later found that he was perceived by his students in the US as "brown."

Perceived skin color, De La Torre analyzes, appears to depend less on the actual pigmentation of the skin and more on the cultural role that someone is ascribed: "As a Latino, even though I have light skin pigmentation, I am brown in the eyes of those with the power to look and construct my identity."[54] However, this can change at any time, for example for US citizens who leave the USA to work at another university:

> To some degree, regardless of actual skin pigmentation or ethnic origins, they all become navy blue—the color of the cover of U.S. passports. The navy blue passport signifies the global imperial might of the most privileged Empire ever known in human history. . . . Those defined as nonwhite due to the

---

50. See also the considerations of ecofeminist theology, below, 5.4.
51. Cited in Ashcroft, "Threshold Theology," 5.
52. De La Torre, "Identity Cross Dressing," 75.
53. De La Torre, "Identity Cross Dressing," 75.
54. De La Torre, "Identity Cross Dressing," 76.

domestic dominant gaze become honorary whites when trav-
elling abroad to teach.[55]

De La Torre was able to observe this overlaying of the actual or assumed skin color with the symbolic value of the blue passport, which
refers to the power of the empire, not only in his own case but also in that
of a male African American student.

Attributions of identity through othering always take place—as in
this example—simultaneously on several levels that overlap. Gender, social status, and belonging to certain other dominant groups (such as the
priesthood or ordination in the church) add to the examples of race, cultural group, academic status, and nationality given here. Depending on
which social group a person differs from or relates to, their social place is
redefined, both by the social group and by the person themselves.

This example shows very well why in postcolonialism borders are
seen as places and spaces of negotiation and not as precisely definable
and dividing lines. Homi Bhabha in particular is regarded as the theo-
retician of these border negotiations. While his concept has rightly been
criticized for being "in no way . . . in keeping with the fact of the armed,
highly-controlled borders of Europe and the United States,"[56] it proves
extraordinarily helpful to understand and describe the dissolution of cultural identities and binaries at social and cultural boundaries.

Nevertheless, precisely because of the overlapping of different border areas, it is often not possible to predict how belonging and nonbe-
longing, exclusion and inclusion of a specific person in a social group or
in relation to it will be handled in each case and in a specific situation.

Despite this vagueness that adds to the complexity of the question, inclusions and exclusions are important issues and problems of
postcolonial societies. They are based on historical subordinations and
dependencies and produce similar, comparable, or completely new
social inequalities and injustices in the present. This is also evident in
ecclesiastical and theological areas.

Cecilia González-Andrieu, also a theologian born in Cuba and
teaching in the USA, describes how postcolonial constellations can lead
to social and cultural exclusion, in academic theology, too: "I would
need to do some very creative covering of the sun with my thumb to

55. De La Torre, "Identity Cross Dressing," 79.
56. Castro Varela and Dhawan, *Postkoloniale Theorie*, 260; see 261–65.

claim that theological education does not suffer from an acute problem of exclusion."[57]

She locates the problem, among other things, in the difficulties for people in the USA who come from a cultural background of Latin American migrants, especially if they cannot produce any documents. She quotes one student: "The simple fact that I do not have documents turns me into a thing. I am no longer human. I live a life of fear."[58]

To be admitted to study at the institution where she works, such people must overcome numerous hurdles: the non-inclusive US education system makes it harder for migrants, especially if they are undocumented. Then there are the tuition fees. To get one of the few available scholarships to study theology, they need not only the highest qualifications but also a lot of luck in the selection process.

For González-Andrieu, such exclusivity contradicts the values that should be taught in theology. In her opinion, it is not enough to award five scholarships a year to those most in need with the very best grades; rather, she sees this practice as a capitulation to the prevailing exclusionary system and a contradiction to "the radical inclusivity of God's love."[59]

Added to these exclusionary structural frameworks is a culture of self-exclusion that can emerge from a lifetime of experience of exclusion: even when an institution is formally or theoretically open, inclusive, or free, it is quite often not perceived so by those accustomed to being excluded.

> The aesthetics of geographical location, architectural styles, the types of people visibly in charge and present, and other more or less subtle clues contribute to the forbidding exclusivity of many cultural institutions.[60]

Even spaces that do not want to be exclusive according to their self-understanding can be perceived in this way by people who see themselves as excluded or marginal in a certain culture and in practice turn into closed, impenetrable places in which the exclusion is repeated all over again.

In this way, people can feel or are in fact excluded not only from studying theology but also from entering into a career in theological

57. González-Andrieu, "Good of Education," 63.
58. González-Andrieu, "Good of Education," 60.
59. González-Andrieu, "Good of Education," 64.
60. González-Andrieu, "Good of Education," 66.

science and thus from the academic production of theology. After all, the undergraduate course represents an important entry point for an academic career in academic theology. Academic theology under such postcolonial conditions therefore suffers from a massive problem of one-sidedness and exclusivity simply because of the unfair access conditions. The overrepresentation of certain population groups in theological teaching has structural causes.

The same applies to theological content: Kwok Pui-lan takes up a criticism from Musa Dube when she writes that Western theology often only accepts contributions from other theological contexts if they fit well into its own system and if they do not criticize this system too openly. It is not sufficient, therefore, to add only a few courses or elements on Global South theologies to the curriculum, "usually as elective courses" or to "include only perspectives and theologies from the Global South that do not present radical challenges and that can be domesticated or appropriated."[61]

In theological discourse, therefore, one should always look at who is not represented in it. How can the voices of people who are largely excluded from theological discourse for various reasons, which can be racist, sexist, economic, or Eurocentric, be made heard in it, or at the very least not forgotten?

Dutch theologian Wietske de Jong-Kumru writes: "Simply inviting other people to the table of dialogue is not enough to undo the privilege of those who already sit at the table."[62] It is always the privilege of those who already sit at the table to decide which other people with different voices should be invited. The same is true for the scholars who sit at the table of theological discourse.

It is not enough to speak on behalf of absent voices. The representation of different and missing voices is viewed quite critically in Postcolonial Studies. While in liberation theology, for example, it was considered a sensible political strategy to be the *voice of the voiceless* or to give a voice to those who have no voice, postcolonial theorists and theologians problematize speaking on behalf of others as a further strategy of exclusion and disempowerment of people who are already excluded from the discourse, as well as further privileging those who are already at the table anyway.[63]

61. Kwok, "Teaching Theology," 24.
62. De Jong-Kumru, *Postcolonial Feminist Theology*, 103.
63. See Taylor, "Subalternität und Fürsprache." This issue is addressed in more

Similar problems of exclusion and inclusion arise when it comes to participation and nonparticipation in decisions, when assessing who is visible and who is made invisible or hidden, who is allowed to speak and who is silenced (or not encouraged to speak), who runs for office, who appears suitable for a task and who does not, who appears to be of legal age, of age, mature, or qualified, and who is denied codetermination or self-determination.

In each of these very different questions, which can sometimes also overlap or intersect, discourse strategies like essentialization and othering have the effect of excluding certain people from participation or discourse, and including others. Postcolonial constellations also mean that colonial power structures can continue to have an unconscious effect in the present and can lead to a repetition, a distortion, or a targeted abuse of exclusion structures that have become influential. Theology and church must analyze these mechanisms consistently and self-critically in order to be able to overcome them.

3.6. Saved by Suffering?

The broad field of postcolonial gender relations presents many overlaps of discursive and power strategies. In very different variants, colonial and patriarchal orders still have an effect today, interrupted and transformed by the independence movements and the nativist and nationalist transformations that went with them, but still—as is so often the case in postcolonial contexts—effective and discriminatory, working often in the subconscious realm. In many cultures that are still shaped by colonialism, women are excluded or disadvantaged from political or economic participation or from education. In addition, they experience violence, rape, and murder in many places, often at the hands of men close to them.

Economic conditions play a considerable role in the development of patriarchal structures of rule. In view of the postcolonial and at the same time neocolonial international division of labor, which has since been intensified many times over by the effects of globalization, Gayatri Spivak's analysis showed more than thirty years ago that subaltern women are negatively affected in several respects: on the one hand, a dominant patriarchal work organization uses their labor power as a resource that can be obtained cheaply, but at the same time they are

----

detail below; see 4.4.

denied access to participation and consumption (of the very goods they produce!). On the other hand, their own cultural contexts do not provide the opportunities for a feminist or critical analysis of their situation: "The woman is doubly in shadow."[64]

This double marginalization as a woman in an economically exploited country is often explored in Postcolonial Studies. The short-sightedness that can be observed again and again, with which the respective non-European culture is made responsible for the patriarchal discrimination, is also criticized. Rather, the exclusion and oppression of women is seen as part of European colonialism and global capitalism, which has been intensifying ever since. For Silvia Federici, an Italian philosopher living in the USA, colonialism and capitalism are inconceivable without a "sexual division of labor,"[65] the devaluation of female work and the associated areas of life and experiences of women, and without systematic witch hunts. The double marginalization of women, with all its tragic consequences, must be seen as a legacy of European colonialism.

We can observe a particularly critical examination of theologies of suffering and redemption in postcolonial feminist theologies. Wietske de Jong-Kumru points out the christological consequences that such a postcolonial feminist critique can have. Referring to the Christology of Lisa Isherwood, she writes that the idea of Jesus being the Suffering Servant of God is "a common masculinist myth. . . . Women . . . , especially those whose lives are filled with non-salvific suffering, are alienated and victimized by this myth."[66]

A Christology in which the suffering of Christ was glorified as redeeming helped to rob oppressed and abused women of their power and resistance. Unjustified suffering, which women often experience in postcolonial contexts, was spiritualized with reference to the suffering of Jesus.

Similarly, Kwok Pui-lan warns "against a naïve glorification of suffering and sacrifice."[67] Slavery and other relationships of dependency were also justified and legitimized from the image of a meek Jesus. For women in particular, enduring unjustified suffering was stylized as a spiritual challenge instead of reminding them of their rights and

64. Spivak, "Can the Subaltern Speak?," 84, see 82–85.

65. Federici, *Calibán y la bruja*, 176.

66. De Jong-Kumru, *Postcolonial Feminist Theology*, 136, with reference to the collaborative work of Althaus-Reid and Isherwood, *Controversies in Feminist Theology*.

67. De Jong-Kumru, *Postcolonial Feminist Theology*, 137.

strengthening their dignity. "Religious language when spiritualized can be misused to camouflage oppressive reality and sacralize the pain of debased servanthood."[68]

The Korean theologian Wonhee Anne Joh, who teaches in the USA, uses the theology of the cross to describe the postcolonial and feminist problematic of the Christian doctrine of salvation.[69] According to Joh, the cross, which has become a symbol of redemption and salvation in Christianity, must also be seen as a symbol of suffering and death, of abuse of power and violence, in accordance with its original function. For her, this results in a true closeness of the figure of the crucified Christ to all those who are exposed to violence and death, torture and murder in the present.

Due to the Christian tradition of atonement theology, however, this closeness is lost sight of; the tortured body of Jesus only appears superficially as a place of cruelty, and the solidarity with the wounded today is abandoned. However, the suffering of Jesus on the cross cannot simply be pushed aside theologically: "God's love is neither an excuse nor an alibi for this human ability to harm one another."[70] The experience of resurrection or belief in salvation cannot be misused as compensation for this suffering. Rather, it is important to return to the sorrow and outrage of the witnesses of the cross. In this way the original solidarity of the suffering body of the Crucified with the bodies of those suffering today can be restored. Joh therefore relates the cross of Jesus to the dramatically increasing number of femicides in Ciudad Juárez (Mexico)—drawing here on a work by Nancy Pineda-Madrid.

> When we juxtapose the agonizing death of the one who is at the heart of our faith practices and beliefs with the deaths of, for example, the women of Ciudad Juárez, Christians face disturbing and pressing questions: What differences do we make in interpreting experiences of suffering? Whose bodies really matter? Which suffering inspires outrage and sadness, and which does not?[71]

68. Kwok, *Postcolonial Imagination*, 184; see de Jong-Kumru, *Postcolonial Feminist Theology*, 137.

69. Joh, "Trauer und der Anspruch," 161–70; see de Jong-Kumru, *Postcolonial Feminist Theology*, 144–47.

70. Joh, "Trauer und der Anspruch," 165.

71. Joh, "Trauer und der Anspruch," 168–69.

Joh is convinced that the indignation and sadness felt by the disciples of Jesus in view of his tortured death can also incite Christians to outrage and sadness today, remind us of our vulnerability and our hope, and motivate us to practice in community.

In this way, according to Joh, believers "get a broader picture not only of the direct victims of torture and terror, but also of those who were involved in carrying out the orders of the Empire."[72] By acknowledging responsibility, complaining, and expressing outrage, witnesses to violence can encourage each other to come together and organize as a community to prevent future violence and death. "So here, too, in this resistance rising up from the ruins, resurrection is happening."[73]

In view of those who are suffering today—and from the feminist perspective, this is precisely the suffering women—the Christian theology of the cross, suffering, and redemption can not only be freed from alienating elements that intensify oppression but also convert itself to its original function of solidarity with the suffering and the experience of resurrection in specific community action. In a broader postcolonial perspective, the view can also expand to other forms of violence, suffering, and death.

In this way, theology is guided by the critical questions of postcolonialism to contribute to overcoming unjust patriarchal and neocolonial structures. To do this, however, it must be able to look self-critically at its own tradition, its complicity in the use of violence and its being abused to legitimize suffering.

3.7. Out of Sight, Out of Mind

In the previous sections and chapters, it has already been mentioned several times that postcolonial structures, power relations, and discourse strategies are often hidden and invisible. The proverb that serves as the heading for this section applies here in many respects: what does not immediately catch the eye goes unnoticed and is considered nonexistent. What is not discussed remains untouched. This applies to structures of subordination, exploitation, and exclusion as well as to those responsible and those who benefit from these conditions: they remain invisible and

72. Joh, "Trauer und der Anspruch," 167.
73. Joh, "Trauer und der Anspruch," 168.

are kept secret. Namsoon Kang writes: "We live in a world where the center/colonizer/oppressor is often invisible and camouflaged."[74]

Postcolonial power asymmetries are usually not even actively hidden or concealed, but are taken for granted through colonial history in such a profound way that they are no longer perceived as injustice. However, they can be uncovered through analysis and criticism and in this way made accessible to change.

The hiding of unjust structures happens in everyday life in many ways. For example, a few years ago, if you opened the official website for tourism of the city of Buenos Aires, the first thing you would find was the headline that Buenos Aires is *la ciudad de todos los argentinos,*" i.e., "the city of all Argentinians."[75]

Such promises of inclusion deliberately ignore the internal distortions of such a megacity and of a large and diverse country. Neither all citizens of Argentina nor all residents of the capital can actually claim that Buenos Aires is their city: the large number of Bolivian and other migrants often live there without basic civil rights; many residents of the city with Argentine citizenship are also cut off or excluded from water and electricity, work and education, health and transport. Moreover, many people in other parts of the country, who often feel marginalized and neglected by the capital, will consider a phrase like this a mockery.

Headlines like "the city of all Argentinians" obscure the actual differences and inequalities. Such strategies are often found in postcolonial settings. A claimed universality as in the above example can make marginalizations and exclusions invisible.

A comparable strategy is to generalize the way of life of a group of people for a larger community and, for example, to make it a model for a supposed dominant culture. Thus, in postcolonial contexts, Western cultural patterns, middle-class life, or the imaginary world of men, whites, or city dwellers often become the yardstick for culturally and materially very different realities. In countries with indigenous populations, they are often viewed as a backward or underdeveloped part of an allegedly homogeneous national population, and their cultural properties are thus made invisible.

74. Kang, "Jenseits," 74.

75. See Silber, "Laboratorios de culturas," 51. The Spanish original even only contains the masculine form of all Argentinians. The corresponding page is now advertising with other catchphrases: https://turismo.buenosaires.gob.ar/es.

Other strategies consist of tabooing or deliberately concealing certain social groups. In many global societies, this affects the internally very diverse queer community, and in the postcolonial space it still often affects indigenous communities, and across all social groups the life experiences of women and girls. The naming of social groups can also make them visible or invisible: In Bolivia, in the wake of the 1952 revolution, members of indigenous peoples were considered *campesinos*, peasants (or, mostly unnamed, also *campesinas*, peasant women), and only through increased pro-indigenous policies of nongovernmental organizations, and later also governments, were indigenous cultures and people brought back into the public eye.[76]

In this way, hidden, secretive, and invisible reverse sides can be detected in postcolonial societies. The openly propagated view of tourism portals and reports of economic success cover up the diverse and internally devalued dark sides of reality, whose problems are linked in different ways to colonial legacy. Not only the people who live in these reverse sides but also their attitudes to life, their values, their knowledge, and their hopes are overshadowed by these obscure structures of invisibility. In postcolonial theologies, on the other hand, attention is drawn to the fact that it is precisely at these unknown and suppressed peripheries that God can be experienced and wants to be discovered.[77]

In a commentary on the parable of the good Samaritan (Luke 10:29–37), the Ghanaian theologian Mercy Amba Oduyoye uses the double meaning of the English word neighbor as the starting point for a reflection on neighborliness, community, and exclusion. For her, the neighbors or "the people next door"[78] are not only a code for the neighbors in the parable but also very specifically for the people who live right next door, but who are often not recognized or treated as neighbors.

Oduyoye does not take an explicitly postcolonial stance in this text, but the description of the context in which she places her biblical commentary makes it clear that the problems she characterizes, which lead to the fact that neighborhoods are divided, are also the results of colonial history. Because neighbors cannot recognize each other as neighbors if "race, class, religion, or whatever is the name of the fence we have erected to mark our in-group"[79] separates people from one another.

76. For a more contemporary example, see Silber, "Fragmented Identities," 323–25.
77. See Silber, "Laboratorios de culturas"; *Pluralität*, 230–41.
78. Oduyoye, *Beads and Strands*, 54; see 45–56.
79. Oduyoye, *Beads and Strands*, 54.

Gender differences can also have the consequence that people are not seen as neighbors, as fellow human beings. In the case of sex tourism, Oduyoye charges that women are not considered "neighbours, they are tools, instruments, objects for feeding the ego of the neighbour who can 'pay' for the services of others who have no bargaining power."[80]

In addition, Oduyoye also addresses people who are no longer in sight. They remain invisible because their existence is perceived as a burden for the community. They are in need, homeless, or displaced, they are hungry, sick, or housebound, children, or people with disabilities. Such people are hidden or simply no longer noticed,

> when we do not acknowledge the existence of the other. The people next door become invisible and inaudible to us. The many isolated and hidden persons whom we simply ignore or actively marginalise are put beyond the bounds of our neighbourliness. When we pass by on the other side, we cannot even tell who it is we are avoiding. We simply deny their existence. . . . They are persons we do not need and who, in our view, are dispensable.[81]

However, according to Oduyoye, it is these apparently superfluous people that determine whether we are able to put Jesus' message to work and life in the present. Postcolonial analysis of the concealment and secrecy of certain social groups and individuals is therefore very important in the tracking down of the power relations that characterize postcolonial contexts.

It represents a far-reaching challenge, especially from a global perspective. In Europe and in other highly developed countries and contexts, it is easily possible to simply ignore the vast majority of people on the planet and make them invisible for daily communication. The life experiences of the majority of people are also regularly absent in the public sphere of the universal Church and in theological production worldwide. The study and discussion of postcolonial theologies is therefore an important way of counteracting this structural invisibility.

---

80. Oduyoye, *Beads and Strands*, 54. Oduyoye's formulation that women "have no bargaining powers" could be interpreted as victimization. I understand it here as a clarification or specification of the refusal of the most elementary humanity by the customers.

81. Oduyoye, *Beads and Strands*, 54; see 54–55.

3.8. Coloniality of Power: Conclusion

Quijano's term *coloniality* has already been briefly introduced (see 1.2 and 1.4 above). It can be used here as a summary of this chapter and at the same time as a link to the previous one. The *coloniality of power* in Quijano describes the continuity of various power structures from the colonial past to the neoliberal present, and also points to the fact that epistemic and discursive coloniality enables and legitimizes this continuity.

According to Pablo Quintero and Sebastian Garbe, Quijano's concept of coloniality of power describes "a specific structural power pattern of modernity that arose from the conquest of America and the subsequent global hegemony of Europe."[82] Quintero then describes in more detail the two central axes of power that are related to one another in Quijano's concept of coloniality:[83] on the one hand, the basic racist differentiation and separation of people serves the political structures of domination and oppression, which, on the other hand, enable the economic exploitation of resources and labor power. This system of colonial power is guaranteed by a fundamental Eurocentrism. Other cultural and discursive factors that support these two central axes would also have to be mentioned.

In this way, the coloniality of power enables a historical and structural continuity between colonial and globalized neoliberal exploitation and domination. According to Quijano's analysis, power structures that prevail in the present are deeply shaped by the beliefs that legitimized the conquest of America and colonialism. He considers the idea of European superiority, reinforced by racism, to be a central element.

There are clear connections between the topics of this chapter—such as the criticism of the Empire and economic exploitation—and those of the previous one, which dealt with othering, Eurocentrism, and racism, among other issues. Further cross-connections become clear when some further developments of Quijano's concept of coloniality are considered.

Argentine philosopher María Lugones, who has taught in the USA, applies Quijano's concept to the realm of gender relations. At the same time, she criticizes Western feminism insofar as it does not analyze the effects of colonialism on gender relations and, on the other hand, decolonial thinking that does not take sexism into account. Quijano's concept needs to be corrected and expanded in this regard. Just as racism is

82. Quintero and Garbe, "Einleitung," 10.
83. Quintero, "Macht und Kolonialität," 59–65.

fundamental to the coloniality of power, she criticizes the transformation of gender relations from precolonial cultures to the present day as *coloniality of gender*. She writes:

> It is important to understand to what extent the imposition of this gender system was as constitutive of the coloniality of power as the coloniality of power was constitutive of that gender system. The relationship between the two follows a logic of mutual constitution.[84]

Edgardo Lander, a Venezuelan sociologist, extends Quijano's notion to the *coloniality of knowledge* and focuses his decolonial analysis on the discursive and epistemic side of the coloniality of power. Colonialism also changed what could count as knowledge in colonized societies in favor of narratives that served exploitation and domination. Although this knowledge is transformed again by the end of the colonial epoch, its form of power remains in the sense that it continues to serve the interests of the rulers. Here, too, the influence of Eurocentrism is decisive: what is considered normal in Europe is also regarded as the norm in the colonies, even stylized into something obvious. It loses the status of a specific, context-bound social construction and becomes something seemingly self-evident, universal, or even natural. In this respect, Lander can speak of a coloniality of knowledge:

> A form of organization and being of society is transformed into the "normal" form of humans and society by this colonizing instrument of knowledge. Other forms of being, other forms of organization of society, other forms of knowledge are transformed not only into different [forms], but also into defective ones, into archaic, primitive, traditional, pre-modern ones.[85]

The apparent normality of Eurocentric knowledge therefore corresponds to the devaluation and marginalization of other, non-European and alternative forms and practices of knowledge in Lander's *coloniality of knowledge*.

Nelson Maldonado-Torres, a Puerto Rican decolonial theorist, interprets the concept of coloniality as the "coloniality of being."[86] As a result, coloniality is to be experienced not only in knowledge or in individual social power relations, but in everyday life and in all areas of life.

84. Lugones, "Colonialidad y género," 68.

85. Lander, "Ciencias sociales," 10.

86. Maldonado-Torres, "Sobre la colonialidad."

The entire human experience, all references and relationships are shaped by and reproduce coloniality. With this comprehensive understanding, attention can be drawn to the fact that coloniality actually encompasses many areas and relationships at the same time and therefore requires a profound and diverse analysis and that, if it is to be overcome, it must be worked on at numerous levels at the same time. Albeit, of course, such a generalization always harbors the dangers of abstracting from the specific individual experiences of the coloniality of power.

Through these extensions, transformations, and corrections of Quijano's concept of the coloniality of power, it becomes clear that discursive and power configurations in postcolonial contexts are not distinct or separate problems. Rather, they are closely related. Discursive strategies are used to legitimize, obfuscate, and take for granted power constellations. Power asymmetries that have become culture in this way in turn produce discourses, narratives, and epistemologies shaped by colonialism. Aspects of these relationships interact individually, in bundles, or in networks.

It is one of the most important features of postcolonial and decolonial thought that, ideally, many of these different aspects of the coloniality of power can be analyzed and revealed in their relation to one another. The fact that this is not always the case is shown perhaps most impressively by the necessity with which postcolonial feminism has to deal critically with other feminisms and other currents in postcolonialism. Feminist-postcolonial theory, which at the same time uses anti-racist and intercultural methods to critically examine other axes of coloniality, must also repeatedly justify this multiplication of methods, perspectives, and networked thinking.

Conversely, feminist and anti-racist arguments within the postcolonial spectrum are repeatedly accused by other theorists of distracting attention from the apparently most important postcolonial challenges with seemingly secondary identity problems. What counts as important in such allegations can be very different. Viewed from a comprehensive perspective, however, it becomes apparent that it is precisely the entanglement and mutual complementarity of different intersectional approaches to postcolonial issues that do them justice best.

The methodological distinction made in the last two chapters between discursive and power strategies repeatedly gives rise to discussions and mutual demarcations in postcolonial debates, depending on whether someone is more interested in the political and economic or in the cultural challenges of coloniality. However, the multifaceted possibilities for interdisciplinary and intersectional work represent an important resource with the help of which postcolonial theories (and also theologies) can analyze contexts shaped by coloniality. The different axes of the coloniality of power do not have to be played off against each other if they are considered in their mutual interdependence and processed in their manifold references.

In addition to these diverse axes, religious, theological, and ecclesiastical aspects of coloniality also appear in postcolonial theologies. Especially through the history of missions, these aspects are present in practically all postcolonial contexts—and hence almost everywhere in the world. They were or are often directly connected to colonial power relations and discourse strategies, since theology provided legitimization, content, and methodologies for mission and for colonization. The coloniality of power is thus also an important topic for theology and the church.

While in the past, colonial power relations were often provided with sacred claims, and conquest, submission, cultural destruction, and exploitation—not infrequently even murder and genocide—could be religiously and theologically legitimized, today in many theological areas the conviction prevails that God is to be found on the side of the powerless, the suffering, the excluded, and the mute, and that the church must also move to that side. Despite this reorientation, it can still be demonstrated in many areas that the coloniality of power has also led to a coloniality of theology. Conflicts in theology can be traced in part to the struggle to uncover the colonial legacy in theology and its underlying epistemology. Postcolonial theologies are therefore—and they have this in common with postcolonialism as a whole—not an automatic process of self-purification, but lead to conflicts, resistance, and arguments.

This path of conflict is mapped out by postcolonial theory, because it is obvious that powerful coloniality does not want simply to allow this well-disguised power to be contested. Aníbal Quijano therefore calls for a fundamental critical examination of content and methods, starting with epistemology, which can also be regarded as a program for a renewal of theology:

> The alternative, then, is clear: the destruction of the coloniality
> of world power. First of all, epistemological decolonization, as
> decoloniality, is needed to clear the way for new intercultural
> communication, for an interchange of experiences and mean-
> ings, as the basis of another rationality which may legitimately

pretend to some universality. Nothing is less rational, finally, than the pretension that the specific cosmic vision of one partic-ular ethnic group should be taken as universal rationality, even if such an ethnic group is called Western Europe because this is actually pretend to impose a provincialism as universalism.[87]

The following two chapters will first deal with ways and methods of resistance with which the coloniality of power can be challenged and—in Quijano's wording—destroyed, and then with the alternatives he suggests, i.e., the "new intercultural communication . . . as the basis of another rationality."

87. Quijano, "Colonialidad y modernidad/racionalidad," 19–20.

4.

Resistance

THE RECOGNITION AND ACKNOWLEDGMENT of the formative power of coloniality in our present and the analysis of its diverse and interwoven effects call postcolonial scholars to take a stand: the postcolonial discourse is, therefore, not only about uncovering and questioning the effects of colonialism beyond the formal declarations of independence, but also about considering how they can be transformed in order to render their destructive consequences as little injurious as possible. In postcolonial thought, the profound analysis of power and discourse structures compels to also reflect on the resistance to the coloniality of power and the question of possible practical and theoretical alternatives to it.

An important element of this reflection is the resistance that those affected by colonialism already put up in colonial history and are still practicing in the present, even if it is often not practiced consciously or identified as active resistance. However, Postcolonial Studies show that those affected by colonialism are not simply passive victims in need of being empowered, but that their relationships to power are varied. On the other hand, the perpetrators, those in power, in the past and in the present, can also be—in very different ways—part of resistance practices. A simple perpetrator-victim schema conceals the diversity of these relationships, and the agency of the assumed victims, that is or can be perceived in different forms of resistance.

In the analysis of resistance practices, frequent changes of perspective are needed in order to detect these different aspects of resistance. In the Eurocentric postcolonial world, however, the willingness to change one's perspective is in itself an act of resistance, because in the humanities and sciences, the European perspective claims universality and uniqueness. However, the variety of postcolonial experiences and the different constellations of coloniality can only be considered if there is a fundamental willingness to change perspectives. It is certain that there are privileged perspectives which allow the experiences of the subaltern to emerge more clearly. The search for these preferred perspectives requires openness to plurality and a profound determination to change perspectives if necessary (4.1). Resistance and changing of perspective can also include a complete departure from certain traditional theological perspectives (4.2). This turning away can be accompanied by an explicit turn to alternative experiences of life (4.3). The dangers of paternalism and of patronizing excluded subjects arise from this attention (4.4).

One particularly fruitful strategy in postcolonialism proves to be the discussion of borders and spaces. Borders and spaces are seen as particularly creative places to forge and negotiate relationships, to connect the disparate, to overcome differences, and to undermine power structures. Borderlands and interstitial spaces are therefore seen as important tools for the resistance to colonialism and the search for alternatives both in metaphorical and in material terms (4.6). Borderlands are also identified as places of dialogue and negotiation between different perspectives (4.5).

The theological examples in the following sections often fall back on the analysis of discourse practices and power relations and at the same time already point to possible alternatives that become visible in them. As always in this book, to present them as examples of *resistance* only serves the didactic purpose of bringing many singular aspects of postcolonial theological practice to the fore. This chapter focuses on the strategies and tools of resistive practice in postcolonialism, which are often very different from and opposed to traditional theological approaches. From the point of view of traditional theologies, however, such an approach may seem rather undisciplined (4.7).

4.1. Changing Perspectives

During the colonial period, theology, faith, and Bible interpretation were understood as matters for Europeans, who—due to the missionary constellation—were held as the self-evident experts on Christianity. The centralization of church structures, reinforced by financial dependence on the North, contributed to the fact that this self-evidence often continues to this day. The European and Eurocentric perspective is still seen by many as normative and authoritative. Even if it is becoming increasingly evident in the present that there are diverse and contradictory perspectives in Europe, a certain dominance and higher legitimacy of each of these European perspectives over native perspectives remains palpable.

However, a change of perspective can help to make the hidden visible and uncover misinterpretations. This also applies to fundamental epistemological and methodological questions: seen exclusively from a European perspective, many facts, relationships, and concepts of non-European cultures simply cannot be adequately recognized, since European epistemologies have different prerequisites. Non-European cultures often remain simply incomprehensible to Europeans.

The postcolonial scholar Laura Donaldson from the US points out that every perception depends on the perspective one takes. In order to gain better insight, it is therefore necessary to move and take on different perspectives. With this idea, she distinguishes herself from a Eurocentric way of thinking, in which an abstract, seemingly objective perception of things appears possible, even regardless of perspective. Donaldson points out that non-European thought, such as Native American philosophy, relies on changing perspectives. She quotes indigenous theorist Gregory Cajete of the Tewa Nation:

> The idea of moving around to look from a different perspective, from the north, the south, the east, and the west, and sometimes from above, below, or from within, is contained in the creative process. Everything is like a hologram; you have to look from different vantage points to understand it. In the Indigenous causational paradigm, movement is relational, or back and forth in a field of relationships, in contrast to Western science's linearity (A to B to C and so on). Indigenous logic moves between relationships, revisiting, moving to where it is necessary to learn or to bring understandings together.[1]

1. Donaldson, "Native Women's Double Cross," 106. Quote from Cajete's book

The cognitive process must itself be changed in order to approach reality more appropriately. Linear, abstract, and generalizing approaches, such as those prevalent in European epistemology, are not so easily capable of these shifts in perspective, because they universalize a certain perspective or simply ignore the perspectivity of perception by declaring one's own epistemology to be objective.

Moving from one perspective to another in the cognitive process, returning and bringing the findings from the different perspectives into dialogue with each other can enrich and improve the process of perception and understanding. Postcolonial theologies rely in the same way on this strategy of (frequently) changing perspectives.

Laura Donaldson herself cites an instructive example of this fundamental shift in perspective: she picks up on a colonial report by a French missionary in North America in the seventeenth century, who describes encounters with a woman from the Mi'kmaw nation. This Native woman possessed a cross of indigenous design, which featured patterns, figures, and symbols from her indigenous religion but was also revered by her as a Christian symbol and kept in a special place in her wigwam. During the encounters,

> she placed it usually between her and the French, obliging them to make their prayers before her cross, whilst from her side she made her own prayers, according to her custom, before her King of Hearts and her other Divinities.[2]

Donaldson refers to the "*double cross*" of the Mi'kmaw woman: the "double cross" is also a "double deceit"[3] because from her perspective, the cross, which is furnished with indigenous symbolism, is a place of indigenous religious practice. The Mi'kmaw woman makes the French missionaries and/or colonists, who kneel in front of it to pray according to the Christian concept, kneel at the same time *in front of her*, because the cross is placed between them. Through the shift in perspective, Donaldson is able to articulate the ambiguity and resilience of the Mi'kmaw woman's approach.

Such reactions to colonial proselytizing can often be uncovered when there is a change in perspective. Indigenous people, writes Donaldson,

---

Native Science.

2. Donaldson, "Native Women's Double Cross," 100; Donaldson quotes Chrestien le Clercq from his *New Relation of Gaspesia*.

3. Donaldson, "Native Women's Double Cross," 100.

have assumed the names and gestures of their enemies, but have
held on to their own, secret souls; and in this there is a resistance
and an overcoming, a long outwaiting. When Jesus came, the
Corn Mothers did not disappear; they just took in another son.[4]

Such changes in perspective are still practiced in the present. In a
study, Musa Dube evaluates qualitative interviews with women who hold
leadership positions in African Independent Churches (AIC). AIC are
independent Christian churches founded in Africa, often led by women,
who develop distinct interpretations of Christianity that may also include
indigenous traditions. For the study, these women were asked questions
about the version of Jesus' encounter with the Canaanite woman in Matthew (Matt 15:21–28). Dube also analyzed their sermons.[5]

Dube's own interpretation of the text takes a critical look at the
evangelist's endorsement of a gentile mission and correlates the naming
of gentile people as "dogs" in the text with the missionaries' devaluation
of Africans. In contrast, the women from the AIC emphasize the appreciation that Jesus has for the Canaanite woman and her faith. They see
no contrast between Israel and Canaan, but relate the Canaanite woman's
faith, praised by Jesus, to the promise of milk and honey flowing in the
land of Canaan, which the people of Israel longed for.[6]

The encounter described in the Gospel of Matthew is read by the
women from the AIC as a healing story and a path of reconciliation, on
which the evils of colonization can be treated and corrected. Dube understands the positive and empowering interpretation of the text made
by these women as an expression of their resistance and refusal to be
victimized. According to her interpretation, the legacy of African traditions comes into play here:

> Historically born in imperial times when people were robbed of
> their cultural and religious integrity by the promotion of Chris-
> tianity as a universal religion, the AIC undermine this imperial
> strategy. They reject the imposition of Christianity as the one
> and only valid religion and freely harvest from both religious

---

4. Donaldson, "Native Women's Double Cross," 96. Corn mothers are mother and
fertility deities in various North American indigenous traditions; often used in the
singular.

5. Dube, *Postcolonial Feminist Interpretation*, 184–95.

6. Dube, *Postcolonial Feminist Interpretation*, 193.

cultures whatever wisdom these traditions offer for the better-
ment of life and the promotion of difference.[7]

Dube also refers to the rich variety of interpretations that have
arisen from the different changes in perspective: The diverse interpretations of the Matthean story made by the women from the AIC cannot
simply be standardized or systematized, but testify to the ongoing creativity of African women in their dealing with colonial patriarchy and
their resistance to it.

The theologian Fernando Segovia, who originates from Cuba and
teaches in the US, also draws attention to the fundamental importance of
such a change of perspective. He emphasizes that, according to Cultural
Studies, every "flesh-and-blood reader . . . is always positioned . . . and
interested."[8] Whoever reads the Bible—and this could be extended to any
other form of interpretation of the Christian tradition—represents their
own cultural position and their own political interests. With the distinction between position and interest, it is possible to indicate the breadth
and complexity of what is considered here as perspective: while Segovia
uses the word *position* to refer to the relative stability of cultural influences,
the political interest is directed toward the intention to change something,
i.e., on what a person wants to achieve through their actions.

However, in postcolonial contexts, both position and interest are
shaped by coloniality: neither the cultural situation in which readers find
themselves nor their political interests in relation to this situation can be
perceived without relation to colonial history and the fight for independence. Position and interest therefore not only characterize the reading of
the Bible (and tradition), but are themselves marked by coloniality. In this
way, colonialism influences the reading of the Bible in many ways.

In addition, readers differ from each other both in terms of their
position and their interests, so that their interpretations of the same biblical text can also differ greatly from one another. This influence of interests and positions—and thus of coloniality—on the interpretation of
biblical texts can even be seen in biblical scholarship. One consequence
of this problem could therefore be to actively seek a variety of interpretations from different perspectives and to bring them into dialogue. In this
way, they can not only enlighten each other but also reveal the interests
and positions shaped by colonialism and coloniality.

7. Dube, *Postcolonial Feminist Interpretation*, 193.
8. Segovia, "Grenzüberschreitendes Interpretieren," 88.

4.2. Turning One's Back

A radical form of change of perspective consists in turning away from or, as it were, turning one's back on the familiar interpretations of a biblical or theological text. Laura Donaldson calls in a biblical role model for this reading strategy: Orpah, the other woman from Moab who, unlike her sister-in-law Ruth, does not migrate to Bethlehem with her mother-in-law Naomi, but goes back to her own mother (see Ruth 1:6–14).[9] Donaldson interprets (with others) the Hebrew root of Orpah's name referring to the "neck" or the "back" and thus to the action of turning away. Orpah is presented in the biblical story as the one who turns her back and returns to her mother, her relatives, her culture, and her homeland.

Donaldson reads the Ruth story as the tale of a woman (Ruth) who transcends cultural boundaries. In her reading, however, she contextualizes the relationship between Moab and Israel as hostile and belligerent, as is indeed the case in much of the Bible. Furthermore, according to Donaldson, Moabite women are portrayed in Bible texts "as a hypersexualized threat to Israelite men,"[10] based on the biblical genealogy of the Moabites in Gen 19:30–38, in which the origin of Moab is traced back to an incest between Lot and his daughters. The relevant narrative of the unfaithfulness of the Israelites in Num 25:1–3 (see Ps 106:28–31), in which sexual relations with Moabite women and idolatry are intertwined, is not even mentioned by Donaldson.[11]

This alleged hypersexualization was also ascribed by male interpreters to the two Moabite women in the story, Ruth and Orpah. Furthermore, at the time of the conquest and colonization of North America, white men compared this alleged sexual behavior of Moabites with the sexual activity of Native American women. Donaldson cites the second US president, Thomas Jefferson, as a not insignificant witness, who also attributes the alleged hypersexuality of Native American women to an alleged sexual reluctance on the part of Native men, thereby revealing

9. See Donaldson, "Sign of Orpah."

10. Donaldson, "Sign of Orpah," 134.

11. Jione Havea expressly contradicts such a negative characterization of Moab: this should not simply be transferred from other biblical stories. In the book of Ruth, the country of Moab (and its inhabitants) is described as hospitable and helpful. See Havea, "Stirring Naomi," 116. For Donaldson, however, the traditional interpretation of the book of Ruth by white Americans is also significant. In my view, this discussion is a striking example of the necessity and the validity of different perspectives in postcolonial interpretation of the Bible.

his own male fears. She writes: "Both [North] American indigenous and Moabite women exist as agents not only of evil and impurity but also of men's sexual frigidity."[12]

From a North American indigenous perspective, Donaldson interprets Ruth as a character who crosses hostile cultural boundaries to submit to domination in the alien (but more powerful) culture and thus benefit from it. While she could have returned to her mother's house when she left Moab, she chooses life in patriarchy, in the house of Boaz, and as the mother of a male-patriarchal royal dynasty (Ruth 4:17–22). Donaldson compares this narrative to stories from the North American colonial era that have gained strong influence in popular culture: Malinche, the interpreter of Hernán Cortez in the conquest of Mexico, and Pocahontas as the example of the *good Indian* in US culture. Both are also considered traitors to their people from an indigenous point of view.

Against this background, Donaldson concludes, it is not surprising that indigenous readers of the book of Ruth today react with sadness and indignation. Due to the concrete historical and contextual conditions under which this reading takes place, the interpretation is too obvious that here, once more, a story is being told in which "yet another relative has succumbed to . . . a hegemonic culture."[13] She evaluates this text as one of several that have become "unreadable" for North American indigenous people.[14]

From this perspective, the other Moabite woman who "turns her back" on this fate, Orpah, is the true heroine of the story, at least in Donaldson's eyes. She summons up the courage to resist the threatening colonial and patriarchal hegemony and returns to her mother's home. "To Cherokee women, for example, Orpah connotes hope rather than perversity, because she is the one who does not reject her traditions or her sacred ancestors."[15]

In Donaldson's example, the change of perspective corresponds to an unequivocal rejection of a misinterpretation of biblical texts and its misuse for the purpose of colonialist othering of subjected people. Criticism of this abuse goes so far as to *turn the back* on the text itself—in this case the tale of Ruth—and give preference to the story's counter-heroine,

12. Donaldson, "Sign of Orpah," 135.

13. Donaldson, "Sign of Orpah," 141.

14. Donaldson, "Native Women's Double Cross," 107. See 5.1 below for the theoretical background.

15. Donaldson, "Sign of Orpah," 143.

Orpah. The reason for this is that this misinterpretation has deep roots in the contemporary postcolonial cultural context, as the comparison with Malinche and Pocahontas makes clear.

Donaldson uses a term coined by indigenous poet Kimberly Blaeser to describe this fundamental departure from traditional interpretations of the Ruth narrative—and thus even from those traditions that are *not* based on sexism and racism—as an expression of the *"response-ability"* of indigenous readers, who rise to the need to "reconsider, reevaluate, reimagine what [religious] terms might mean or have meant for Indian people as well as what they might come to mean for all people."[16]

While Laura Donaldson's example focuses on a misinterpretation of a Bible text deeply rooted in postcolonial culture, the Colombian theologian Juan Esteban Londoño points out that there are also texts in the Bible that need themselves to be read critically, even *rebelliously*: With reference to the South African Bible scholar Itumeleng J. Mosala, Londoño speaks of the "rebellious reader" of the Bible.[17]

Mosala cites Deut 6:10–11 as an example. In these two verses, land grabbing and the appropriation of foreign cities, houses, and farms are presented as a promise from God. According to Mosala, from a South African point of view, the text cannot be separated from the interpretation of those who used this and similar Bible texts to justify colonialism and land theft in Africa. But he is not satisfied with exegetical explanations of the text either: He neither agrees with the conservative interpretation of the Israelite's conquest as a punishment for the sins of the Canaanites, nor does he find the liberal search for any liberating and humanizing aspects of the text convincing; the rebellious reader rebels directly against the author of this biblical text, because it is this author who legitimizes, on a narrative level, the land theft as a promise of the biblical God. Londoño comments:

> The rebellious reader tries to understand the scriptures exegetically. He doesn't want to hermeneutically transform the texts so that they say something liberating, because there are actually texts that are not liberating. What he does then is read and

16. Donaldson, "Sign of Orpah," 43. Quote from Blaeser, *Pagans Rewriting the Bible* (brackets in the original).

17. Londoño, "Hermenéuticas postcoloniales," 154. The term *lector rebelde*, rebellious reader, apparently stems from Londoño and not from Mosala; see Mosala, "Implications," 136.

interpret, but that doesn't mean he has to say "Amen" at the end
of the reading: he doesn't agree, he doesn't obey.[18]

The reason for this lies in the diversity of the Bible, the biblical texts,
and the biblical authors. The polyphony of the Bible itself is taken seriously, even in its contradictions and sometimes conflicts, without questioning the authority of the Holy Scriptures fundamentally. It is possible
that on a narrative level biblical texts—due to reasons of the cultural,
political, and social contexts of its various editorial phases—justify attitudes and practices that from today's perspective are perceived as unjust
and contrary to other biblical traditions. The rebellious reader can also
name such injustices as such and does not have to interpret them away:

> The great value of this postcolonial reading is hermeneutic
> honesty. It is not about disguising the text or making it easier
> for believers to digest. You go directly to the text and, if neces-
> sary, against the text. The Bible is a rich store of memory that
> contains not only the voices of the oppressed but also those of
> the oppressors.[19]

The rebellious reader thus claims the authority not only to uncover
and reject the misuse and misinterpretation of the biblical texts in colonial history, but also to rebel against oppressive attitudes in the biblical
text itself, with the help of sound exegetical support, and to choose not
to obey. Londoño and Mosala do not forget that the rebellious reader is
also shaped by their own cultural context. The criticized Bible texts are
therefore not dismissed as non-biblical. Rather, the rebellious reader
rebels in a concrete, context-bound reading act against a certain interpretation of the text that could promote oppression (land grabbing,
theft, murder . . .) and allows the different voices of the Bible to enter
into a dialogue with one another.[20]

Another vivid example of such a rebellious reader was presented in
chapter 1: The Chinese woman who used a needle to remove verses from
the Pauline epistles because they were misogynist in her interpretation,
also—in her own way and by her own means—rebelled against these biblical texts and refused to obey them.

Musa Dube also warns against biblical texts (and the argument could
well be extended to other theological traditions) that harbor the seeds of

18. Londoño, "Hermenéuticas postcoloniales," 154.
19. Londoño, "Hermenéuticas postcoloniales," 156.
20. See also 5.1 below for the theoretical background.

dangerous misinterpretation. She cites the composition of the speech in
Matt 23 as an example. In this text, which she interprets as "a unique creation of the author of the Gospel of Matthew,"[21] she draws attention to the
condemning, unforgiving language with which the text is directed against
the Pharisees. According to Dube, the evangelist uses sharp words to dis-
tinguish himself and his group of Jews who believe in Jesus from another
Jewish group. However, the destructive and divisive power of Roman imperialism, acting simultaneously in the same context, is largely neglected
in the Gospel of Matthew, according to her interpretation.[22]

From her postcolonial perspective, however, such a one-sided view
of interwoven conflicts should not be taken. At the same time, she recognizes in this text written by the evangelist structures of colonial conflicts,
in which those who use a similar exclusive and divisive language could
invoke the language of the Bible. She acknowledges that Matthew, in his
context, was interested in the protection and survival of his own group.
"But his strategy of survival was primarily dependent on disqualifying
the other groups."[23] Dube considers dramatic metaphorical wording
such as "snakes" and "brood of vipers" (v. 23), which contain a dehu-
manization of the opponent, to be characteristic of Christian polemics
in contexts of colonialism and gender up to the present. For Dube, the
biblical model of such defamatory language becomes "a loaded gun that
can always shoot—with deadly consequences":[24]

> As long as such loaded texts remain unpacked, they retain the
> potential to explode and kill whenever any reader decides to
> pull the trigger of such a text. It, therefore, seems essential, that
> such killer ideologies underlining and pervading some scrip-
> tures, should always be identified and marked as dangerous by
> all liberation interpreters as a first step towards arresting the
> ideology of oppression and domination.[25]

The precise exegetical analysis of the intention of the text and of
the contexts of the evangelist must therefore uncover and—if necessary—criticize the ideologies and rhetorical strategies hidden in a text.
At the same time, Dube places a counter-text from the same Gospel

21. Dube, "'Liberating the Word,'" 425; see 425–35.
22. See Dube, "'Liberating the Word,'" 418.
23. Dube, "'Liberating the Word,'" 434.
24. Dube, "'Liberating the Word,'" 435.
25. Dube, "'Liberating the Word,'" 436.

alongside the "loaded text," which enters into a dialogue with it and can thus neutralize the threatening effects of the text: love of enemies (see Matt 5:43–44) opens up to the otherness of the opponent and captures his humanity. In this way, the loaded text is disarmed and can no longer easily be used as a weapon in the present.

Loaded guns, rebellious readers, and turning away like Orpah are powerful examples of resistant Bible reading, which stands against the misuse of the Bible for the exercise of power experienced during colonialism. They draw attention to the dangers of an uncritical use of the Bible in the church in the face of the challenges of coloniality working under the surface. They are just examples of the variety of postcolonial criticism of Christian traditions, but they point out that this criticism can also contain an element of disruption. With this rupture as a possible strategy of resistance, postcolonial subjects seize agency and gain the freedom to turn to other subjects and their experiences.

4.3. Turning toward Someone Else

Turning your back on someone and turning away are often associated with turning to someone else at the same time. Postcolonial shifts in perspective therefore not only evade the hegemony of dominant perspectives, but also intentionally turn to other, different perspectives. They turn precisely to those perspectives, places, and subjects that are neglected, faded out, or silenced by hegemonic discourse and put them in the focus of attention.

The South African exegete Gerald O. West develops a strategy of changing perspectives under the keyword "ordinary readers."[26] He characterizes these as nonprofessional, non-exegetically trained Christians who are socially, politically, and culturally disadvantaged or oppressed. *Ordinary readers* bring their own tools for the interpretation of the Bible to bear and can contribute something new and decisive in a dialogue with critically trained Western Bible scholars. The perspectives of ordinary readers are themselves diverse and different from each other. An example of a successful Bible project on this basis is the South African Tamar campaign.

Beginning in 2000, the Ujamaa Bible Center at Kwa Zulu Natal University in South Africa ran the Tamar Campaign, a large-scale biblical

---

26. West, *Academy of the Poor*, 10; see Akper, "Role."

education project that simultaneously raised awareness of and sought to help overcome sexual and gender-based violence. West describes the history and development of this campaign.[27]

The story of Tamar's rape by her half-brother Amnon in 2 Sam 13:1–22 plays an important role in the wide-ranging narrative arc of King David's succession. At the same time, however, it is also a story about arguments, protests, complaints, and a woman's silence in the face of the violence that is being done to her. The family context, the disrespect of the no, the mechanisms by which a woman in a patriarchal society becomes silent and passive, and the shifting of attention away from the woman and toward the male protagonists—both by the characters of the story and by the narrator themselves—make Tamar "someone whose story is still very modern," as Pamela Cooper-White writes.[28] The American theologian comments:

> In Tamar's story we find a *rape* which combines elements of *incest* and *domestic violence*. There is a *conspiracy* of men aiding and abetting the perpetrator of the crime and a male conspiracy of silence after the act. Finally, there is a raw form of *retribution* in the end but this brutal act of revenge is done quite apart from the victim. All power to act or even to speak is taken away from Tamar.[29]

The "ordinary readers of the Bible (whether literate or not),"[30] to whom the text was read in three languages during the course, reacted with surprise and recognition from the start: here they got to know a text that they would not have expected to find in the Bible, and which in many ways reflected their postcolonial patriarchal experiences.

With well-directed questions and plenty of time for discussion in small groups, which were separated according to women and men (who were clearly in the minority), not only were exegetical details of the story worked out, but above all a dialogue was guided between the narrative and the experiences of the readers. In the women's groups, personal experiences of sexual violence, but also of solidarity and loss of solidarity, were addressed. Empowered or transformed by the Bible text and the group discussion, women expressed their willingness to take up the fight

27. West, "Wir werden nicht," 164–68.

28. Cooper-White, "Rape of Tamar," 27.

29. Cooper-White, "Rape of Tamar," 26 (emphasis in the original).

30. West et al., "Rape," 36.

against silence in the face of sexual violence in their communities and to show solidarity with the victims.[31]

In the groups of men, the readers also identified with the various male characters in the story: above all with Amnon, his friend Jonadab, his half-brother Absalom, and their father David. The group around West deepened these experiences by later reading this text with groups consisting only of men, and worked out specific questions for these male groups.[32]

The biblical text, which had emerged many centuries earlier in a completely differently structured patriarchal culture, unfolded a critical and transformative potential by creating opportunities to recognize and name one's own share of structural and cultural responsibility and guilt. In this way, current patriarchal and postcolonial power structures, mechanisms of repression, and taboos could be addressed and overcome. It is by no means self-evident to have an open and self-critical discussion among men about sexual violence and ideals of masculinity, as West notes: "Across all age groups of male participants, there was a real willingness to talk about these things, which was surprising even for the men themselves."[33]

The change of perspective to that of the ordinary reader enables diverse identifications with the Bible text and its individual protagonists. The real-life experiences of people in postcolonial contexts can be addressed with the help of the Bible text and brought into dialogue with the biblical narrative. In this way, the experiences of violence spoken of in the biblical text can also be examined from different contemporary perspectives. In the hands of postcolonial subjects, the Bible thus becomes an instrument of resistance against the real gender and violent constellations of their context.

A biblical text that is deeply characterized by violence, exclusion, and silence does not have to be considered a loaded gun in the wording of Musa Dube (see the last section), even if of course it could assume this function in a different context and among other subjects. By being confronted with the real-life experience of the ordinary reader and from their perspective, its potential is transformed toward resistance and healing. It is crucial that this change of perspective also includes a change of actors: the ordinary readers are themselves subjects of their

31. See West et al., "Rape," 39–41.
32. See West, "Wir werden nicht," 168–70.
33. West, "Wir werden nicht," 170.

interpretation of the Bible; the professional biblical scholars switch to the roles of listeners and learners. This enables a dialogue in which both sides can hear and learn. What is fundamental, however, is that not only the perspectives change but also the subjects.

The Brazilian theologian Cleusa Caldeira describes and analyzes another example of how a change of perspective and subject in postcolonial contexts can change the view of church and faith and also have a liberating effect through identity processes: "the church of holy black women."[34] This church in both senses of the word—a church building that is also supported by a church community—was an initiative of fourteen black women who lived in a Brazilian favela. Caldeira writes:

> It is perhaps the first church liberated from patriarchy and racism. It represents by far the most original Afro-Brazilian spiritual resistance experience in the bosom of Catholic Christianity.[35]

The church of holy black women grew out of the regular meetings of women—since the 1960s—who cooked, talked, worked, and prayed together in a barrack. This closeness to the everyday life of the poor black women is still one of the most important characteristics of the church today. In resistance to "the clerical patriarchal power,"[36] the women achieved the construction of a church building, whose iconographic design is the second important characteristic of the church: the fresco that covers almost the entire interior shows images of various scenes from the lives of Jesus and Mary, almost all represented by black people,

> for the church itself is indeed black. The painting relates the fourteen black women who planted the church to the life of Mary, the mother of Jesus. There are fourteen scenes that are assigned to the seven sorrows and the seven joys of Mary. The church wanted to tell the story of terror combined with the story of hope.[37]

Surrounded by these pictures, the community's black women can now "assert themselves as *imago Dei*, the image of God, an image that the racist system has tried so hard to distort."[38] The third characteristic of this church is the specific spirituality and liturgy, in which

34. Caldeira, "Theo-Quilombismus," 59; see 58–60.
35. Caldeira, "Theo-Quilombismus," 59.
36. Caldeira, "Theo-Quilombismus," 59.
37. Caldeira, "Theo-Quilombismus," 59.
38. Caldeira, "Theo-Quilombismus," 59.

Catholic-Christian forms are related to the spiritual heritage of Africa. In this way, too, it is possible for the women to identify intensively with this community, with this building.

This church helps black people "become black." This is not something that can be taken for granted in a racist and postcolonial society: "So becoming a black woman and a black man represents the hard work of giving birth to the Afro-Brazilian identity. And this cannot be construed as a pre-conceptualized identity."[39] In Caldeira's opinion, liberation is possible through this process of identity formation, even if it represents "hard work" and has to assert itself in the resistance against racism, patriarchy, and clericalism.

4.4. Option for the Subalterns?

Turning away from colonialist interpretations of Christianity and turning to excluded and oppressed perspectives—this implies a conversion in the realm of theological method that can be compared to the *Option for the Poor* in Liberation Theology.[40] This option, which was theorized in depth in the 1970s, involved a fundamental epistemological preference for the perspective of the poor, which was at the same time characterized by a real change of location toward the poor, a deep solidarity with their lives, and concern for their empowerment and agency. This option has proven to have consequences for content and method in all areas of theology.

The option for the poor is simultaneously problematized, criticized, and expanded in postcolonial theologies. While the concept of the option for the poor is hardly ever used outside of liberation theology and its current developments, a similar methodological reversal can be identified within postcolonial theologies, which, however, often appears to be more complex and self-critical. The American theologian Mark Lewis Taylor illustrates this reversal and its inner difficulties using the concept of the subaltern and an analysis of Gayatri Spivak.

For Taylor, the term *subaltern* denotes two important aspects that complement each other: the Latin *sub* refers to the subordination and subjection of the subalterns, while the second part of the term—*alter*—connotes their otherness, difference, and internal plurality.[41] The

---

39. Caldeira, "Theo-Quilombismus," 57.
40. See Kern, *Theologie der Befreiung*, 36–43; Silber, *Pluralität*, 18–21, 69–74.
41. See Taylor, "Subalternität und Fürsprache," 284–87.

poor, who in early liberation theology were understood primarily as the economically poor and socially excluded, are also *different*: they are defined by their culture, ethnic and social affiliations, religion, gender, sexual practices, etc. They are an internally very diverse group and, at the same time, find themselves subjugated by various flexible power constellations, so that a pure socioeconomic analysis is not sufficient to do justice to their everyday reality.

At the same time, for Taylor, the concept of the subaltern also indicates that the *others* are also *poor*: the diversity of their cultures and social relationships must not be misused in a postmodern "celebration of difference and play."[42] Taylor speaks here of a "fetishization"[43] in the discourse on difference, which is misused when difference, diversity, play, and celebration are viewed as a positive plurality per se, isolated from oppressive and repressive relationships. In this understanding, it is not only that the subalterns are diverse and different, but that with the prefix *sub* it is possible to denote and analyze their social role and the potential for injustice that is inherent in cultural diversity.

For Taylor, the turn toward the perspective of the subalterns is crucial for a theology that wants to have a liberating effect in postcolonial contexts. Only from this perspective can cultural and social differences, as well as poverty and oppression, be described in such a way that they can transform theology so that it enables the liberating and life-giving message of the gospel to become a reality in a specific context. Taylor calls this turn to the subaltern a "liberating *a priori*," meaning "the ways in which the desire and drive for total, structural freedom can haunt the deep places of our thought, action, and life."[44]

Taylor, however, also problematizes this crucial turning point which he describes as the practice of people who are not themselves subaltern. They are people

> who have access to empowerment that others do not have, usually because of group affiliation (class, ethnicity, gender, educational experience, political position) or some combination of those affiliations.[45]

42. Taylor, "Subalternität und Fürsprache," 282.
43. Taylor, "Subalternität und Fürsprache," 281.
44. Taylor, "Subalternität und Fürsprache," 283.
45. Taylor, "Subalternität und Fürsprache," 277.

For these people—and here Taylor takes up an argument by Gayatri Spivak—it is not easy to effectively hear the subaltern speak. In her
important essay "Can the Subaltern Speak?,"[46] she examines the problems of the representation of the subaltern by a "benevolent *Western*
intellectual."[47] This benevolent intellectual, when speaking *about* the
subalterns, differs only slightly in his attitude from that of a benevolent
colonist who, in his own opinion, only wants what seems to him to be
the best for the subalterns he has conquered or displaced. Both speak
for and *about* others, and both represent someone who apparently cannot or is not allowed to represent themselves.

Representation, Spivak explains with recourse to Karl Marx and
Michel Foucault, can have two related meanings: "representation as
'speaking for', as in politics, and representation as 're-presentation', as
in art or philosophy."[48] The two meanings must not be confused, even
if they are related to each other. However, according to Spivak, neither
type of representation of the subaltern leads to their voice being really
heard. Rather, the representation means that the voice of the subaltern is
also interpreted, transformed, and, in the worst case, falsified by the "benevolent intellectuals." "The subaltern cannot speak,"[49] concludes Spivak
provocatively on the last page of her essay, thereby expressly distancing
herself from Foucault, who considers such speaking to be possible if the
conditions for it could be created.

For Mark Taylor, this problem is also virulent in postcolonial theologies when they are pursued by people who are not themselves subalterns.
He links the problem with the discussion about the question of whether
the option for the poor of liberation theology is not also an option of
Western or Western-influenced intellectuals *for* people who are not so
privileged due to global constellations. So the problem of representation
also applies to the option for the poor, by which people (at worst) are
silenced by those who mean to speak *for them*. He writes:

> Thus it is that the benevolent intellectual, even when writing
> as a critic demanding liberation, is caught in a bind: how is it
> possible to hear and acknowledge the voice and language of the

46. See Spivak, "Can the Subaltern Speak?"; Kerner, *Postkoloniale Theorien*, 104–6;
Castro Varela and Dhawan, *Postkoloniale Theorie*, 72–77.

47. Spivak, "Can the Subaltern Speak?," 87 (italics in the original); see Taylor, "Subalternität und Fürsprache," 277.

48. Spivak, "Can the Subaltern Speak?," 70.

49. Spivak, "Can the Subaltern Speak?," 104.

> subalterns without engaging in the exercise of control, which
> reinforces the fact that they do not have a voice?[50]

The problem here is, of course, formulated from the perspective of
"benevolent Western intellectuals"—for postcolonial theologians, who
come from subaltern biographical contexts, the situation is quite different. In this book, I am interested in a discussion of this problem from a
Western, in fact *German*, perspective, so that the problem of the criticized Western (and hopefully benevolent) intellectuals applies.

Mark Taylor proposes strategies for the solution of the dilemma he
has described. The first step proposed by him is *acknowledging* that the
problem exists. For Taylor, without this critical self-awareness, no way
out of the problem is conceivable: "We can never avoid the fact . . . that
'academic knowledge is a practice that actively produces subalternity.'"[51]
If it is not possible to avoid this problem, it should not be concealed or
glossed over.

Only with a self-critical acknowledgment of the entanglement in
postcolonial, patriarchal, racist, and other global and local structures of
injustice can Western theologians attempt to make the concerns of the
subaltern their own—without already succeeding in overcoming this
entanglement by acknowledging the problem. This acknowledgment
includes the self-critical awareness that Western intellectuals are not
themselves the subalterns they wish to speak for, and that their knowledge of the life realities and experiences of the subalterns is only mediated and therefore very limited.

As a second strategy of solidarity with the subalterns, Taylor names
participation in their resistance, specifically not only in the locations
where the subalterns themselves resist (or experience exclusion), but also
in the lives and works of Western intellectuals. Taylor is referring not only
to globally oriented solidarity, which is directed against global economic
structures, for example, but also to concrete local resistance to injustice
and exploitation in the personal context of Western intellectuals.

A third strategy for resolving the representational dilemma is to
develop a critical self-awareness that advocacy for the subalterns is not
just about them, but also about the challenge, advancement, and *vulnerability* of the benevolent intellectuals themselves. These are not the

---

50. Taylor, "Subalternität und Fürsprache," 290.

51. Taylor, "Subalternität und Fürsprache," 291; Taylor quotes John Beverley, *Subalternity and Representation*.

heroic, selfless, and successful saviors of the subalterns, who supposedly cannot help themselves. The Western intellectuals also need to be freed and converted from their own entanglements in colonial, Eurocentric, racist, and patriarchal stereotypes. They must therefore allow themselves to be challenged and changed by the criticism, resentment, and even resistance of those for whom they want to work.

Then the fourth strategy can also come about, which Taylor calls "delirium,"[52] using a term coined by Jacques Derrida. In this *delirium*, the intense and reciprocal relationships between the represented and the representer are revealed. Both are understood as being dynamically related to each other, so that they double as the inner voices of the intellectual and, so to speak, begin an inner conversation. Taylor deliberately formulates this fourth strategy very vaguely, because he wants to describe a precarious delirium that does not emanate from the initiative of the intellectuals but rather to which they submit in order to resist objectifying the subalterns in the process of advocating for them.

An important point, which I think Taylor does not sufficiently explore, is the importance of subaltern *resistance to the solidarity* and advocacy of benevolent intellectuals. This resistance, which is often perceived as annoying, disruptive, and counterproductive, shows the power of their subjectivity and their ability to be resilient. At the same time, this resistance points to the fact that these intellectuals, who want to stand up for solidarity, liberation, and justice, are themselves part of a global postcolonial structure and also share responsibility for the reproduction of these structures through their (self-)critical academic work.

Through this resistance—as unproductive as it may appear in detail—the subalterns destabilize the self-evidence of postcolonial hierarchies and in this way enable self-reflection and the transformation of liberating and solidarity strategies. Resistance to any kind of Western interference (including that of benevolent intellectuals), to any form of encounter with Christianity (including its liberating versions), or even to invoking human rights (as formulated in the West) has an important meaning here for the reconfiguration and reconstruction of liberating Western practices. The self-critical respect for the resistance of the subaltern against the solidarity of the benevolent intellectuals is therefore a very definite part of the attitude and practice of this solidarity itself.[53]

52. Taylor, "Subalternität und Fürsprache," 295. The term is quoted from Spivak's work.

53. See my reflections on the subject in the field of missiology: Silber, "Synodalität," 267–70.

Another important strategy for consciously avoiding the pitfalls of representation, which Taylor also does not name as such, is proposed by the Peruvian church advisor and activist Juan Carlos La Puente Tapia, who lives in the USA: the *cultivation of friendship* and fellowship with subaltern people. He believes an "epistemic change" is possible if the actions and lives of the people concerned are taken seriously. He writes: "Listening to the voice of the victims is crucial to the question of how we recognize ourselves in other people's forms of resistance."[54]

According to La Puente, this results in the need to create and cultivate real relationships and friendships in order to be able to listen to, learn from, and correct one another. Finally, especially in church contexts, there are also important *spiritual connections* that can contribute to deepening and changing the common and friendly engagement with and for one another:

> Including other people in the web of our resistance and involving them deeply becomes a powerful invitation, in which we find ourselves involved with our open and offered wounds: body and blood, symbolized by bread and wine, which, offered in fellowship, announce and realize the messianic banquet.[55]

4.5. Contrapuntal Reading

Postcolonial theories identify specific methods to show how different perspectives can be brought into dialogue with one another. Especially in literary studies, which was an important area of discourse for the emergence and development of Postcolonial Studies, various methods were developed that not only serve to analyze power relations in discourses and narratives, but also enable resistance to the prevailing perspectives, by opening spaces that were closed by colonialism.

Edward Said, who was not only a literary scholar but also a musician and a music critic, developed the method of *contrapuntal reading*. He named it after a composition technique of European baroque and classical music called *counterpoint*, in which a musical theme or several different themes answer to one another (respectively to itself) in different voices, thus constructing a musical dialogue. They can complement

54. La Puente Tapia, "Widerstand," 74.
55. La Puente Tapia, "Widerstand," 78.

each other in tension, dissonance, and/or harmony and interpret each other reciprocally.

Similarly, Said suggests combining, as in counterpoint, colonial literature or texts about the colonies with other texts that bring into play experiences, views, or characters that are hidden or distorted in the first text. In this way, different perspectives are brought into dialogue with each other and can thus—analogously to musical counterpoint—be interpreted reciprocally:

> Let us begin by rereading the cultural archive not as a univocal phenomenon, but *contrapuntally*, with an awareness of the simultaneity of the metropolitan history being told and those other histories against which (and in concert with) the discourse of domination acts.[56]

An important aim of this reading strategy is to "expand the reading of the text to include what was once forcibly excluded,"[57] not in order to exclude now the literature that used to exclude violently subaltern experiences, but in the way of a dialogue, using the juxtaposition of the counterpoint. Said's proposition is "to read what is there and what is not there."[58]

Such reading is a practice of resistance, since the context, expanded to include the experiences of the marginalized, changes the original meaning of the text and can alienate it to the point of contradiction. It destabilizes, disrupts, challenges colonial narratives. But it also shows connections, overlaps, blurred boundaries, and hybridity. Biblical scholar Rasiah S. Sugirtharajah writes:

> To read contrapuntally means to be aware simultaneously of mainstream scholarship and of other scholarship which the dominant discourse tries to domesticate and against which it speaks and acts.[59]

Contrapuntal reading thus not only brings up the colonial perspective *and* the resistance to it but also puts each into dialogue with the other; their mutual entanglements can be analyzed and uncovered.

---

56. Said, *Kultur und Imperialismus*, 92.

57. Said, *Kultur und Imperialismus*, 112.

58. Said, *Kultur und Imperialismus*, 148.

59. Sugirtharajah, "Postkoloniale Untersuchung," 126.

Sugirtharajah takes up Said's concept of contrapuntal reading to criticize the "deep-seated Eurocentric bias" he observes in biblical scholarship, according to which "anything theologically worthwhile can only be provided by Greek-Jewish traditions."[60] To this end, he refers to studies of comparative religious studies in which New Testament and Buddhist writings are analyzed for their "textual and conceptual affinities"[61] and thus enter into a dialogue with one another.

To illustrate the influence of Asian spiritual traditions on the formation of the New Testament, Sugirtharajah quotes Canadian religious scholar Roy C. Amore, who examines the importance of Buddhist thought in the formation of the Q source:

> There are several indications that Luke and Matthew were relying on a source or sources that, in addition to statements about the end of time, also contained statements that were actually Judeo-Christian versions of Buddhist teachings. The Sermon on the Mount contains the greatest accumulation of these Buddhist sayings.[62]

Amore also reads the New Testament statements about Jesus' preexistence, incarnation, birth, and ascension in contrapuntal terms with Buddhist avatar concepts and suspects that the dialogue between Judeo-Christian beliefs and Buddhist views helped early Christianity to gain a foothold in the pluralistic religious milieu of Greco-Roman antiquity.

As well as Amore, Sugirtharajah cites other authors who read New Testament texts, especially from the Gospels, in contrapuntal terms together with Buddhist texts from different traditions. Neither he nor the authors presented are concerned with asserting a direct literary dependence of the New Testament texts on Buddhist texts. Rather, the idea of the New Testament as a purely Western text is to be deconstructed in order to gain a more diverse and hybrid idea of the origin of the New Testament and thus also of Christianity. The Jewish and Hellenistic contextualizations of the biblical texts are each preserved, but are complemented by a description of their hybrid and intercultural character.

From a postcolonial perspective, it is crucial for Sugirtharajah that the duality between Christianity and Buddhism is dissolved in this way.

60. Sugirtharajah, "Postkoloniale Untersuchung," 138.

61. Sugirtharajah, "Postkoloniale Untersuchung," 139.

62. Sugirtharajah, "Postkoloniale Untersuchung," 140. Sugirtharajah quotes from Amore's book *Two Masters, One Message*.

Christianity is losing its character as an exclusively Western religion that would be alien in Asia and would have to assert itself *against* Buddhism and other religions and religious traditions. Rather, it is possible to understand the New Testament as a hybridized Judeo-Hellenistic *and* Buddhist as well as a Western *and* Asian text.

The contrapuntal reading of the Bible as a basic text of European colonialism, which appeared in connection with the Christian mission in Asia, and Buddhist scriptures as a possible representation of Asian religiosity, can make visible the overlaps, touches, harmonies, and dissonances of both religious traditions. According to Sugirtharajah, historical scholarship can also reveal how these agreements and hybridizations came about:

> The Christian faith arose in a cultural and literary milieu that has indeed been influenced by Indian, Buddhist and Hindu thought patterns. Trade relations between India and the Mediterranean Roman Empire were more intense than is often believed. Along with the merchandise, religious ideas traveled both to and from the Mediterranean world.[63]

Ancient documents provide information about the presence of Buddhist monks in West Asia and North Africa. The Indian emissary Zarmanochegas, who set himself on fire in Athens shortly before the turn of the century, and whose story Paul may have known, has already been mentioned above (see 2.5). Even if both Buddhism and Christianity have developed further in many respects since that time, these historical facts make a historical and substantive relationship between the two religions plausible.

Similar processes of contrapuntal reading have already been presented in earlier sections without designating them by this term: Thus, numerous examples of postcolonial resistance from this chapter also demonstrate that biblical texts, but also Christian symbols (such as the cross—see 4.1 or a church building—see 4.3) and theological concepts (e.g., redemption—see 3.6), can be brought into dialogue with the experiences of the subaltern through contrapuntal reading.

To do this, it is not necessary to assume a direct historical connection with the New Testament or Christianity, as is the case with the Buddhist texts in Sugirtharajah's example. Rather, according to Said, contrapuntal reading is a strategy by which texts, symbols, and structures,

---

63. Sugirtharajah, "Postkoloniale Untersuchung," 139.

which in their traditional sense represent the power of colonialism, can be brought into dialogue with texts, symbols, and traditions that represent the experiences of those silenced, ridiculed, misrepresented, or even killed by colonialism. It is therefore also possible to contrapuntally read texts that originally had no connection with one another, but which illuminate one another in the face of colonialism. Contrapuntal reading thus emerges as a powerful strategy of resistance to the misuse (and allegedly legitimate use) of biblical, Christian, and theological texts, symbols, and concepts for the purposes of colonialism.

4.6. Contact Zones

The idea of static identities, which postcolonial theories extensively criticize (see 2.1 and 2.2 above), is often countered with the concept of *contact zones*. Boundaries between different groups, identities, and concepts are seen less as barriers than as fields of relationships in which spaces for contact, exchange, and hybridization open up. This more differentiated view of identities and the relationships between them is used in postcolonialism as an important tool of resistance.

The term *contact zones* is usually attributed to the US-American linguist and literary scholar Mary Louise Pratt. She coins it to refer to

> social spaces where disparate cultures meet, clash, and grapple with each other, often in highly asymmetrical relations of domination and subordination—like colonialism, slavery, or their aftermaths as they are lived out across the globe today.[64]

In this contact, the violent nature of which is not neglected by Pratt, but emphasized, the cultural groups do not remain unchanged, but experience different mutual transformation processes in which they approach each other, distance themselves from each other, subjugate one another, imitate one another, learn from one another, etc. Borders are not viewed as insurmountable barriers, but as places or spaces that make diverse forms of contact both necessary and possible.

The term is expanded beyond the purely spatial meaning of borders. Contact zones can also be identified in the boundaries between people and groups with different identities. In the first place, this description of contacts and relationships makes identities less distinct

---

64. Pratt, *Imperial Eyes*, 7. See Donaldson, "Native Women's Double Cross," 97; Kwok, *Postcolonial Imagination*, 82.

and separate. Rather, their kinships, similarities, and interwovenness, as well as their relationships of domination, violence, and resistance, step into the foreground.

The analysis of these interrelationships is presented as an act of resistance to the rigid and domination-oriented binary structure of opposing identities. Pinning people down to their roles of perpetrator and victim can be avoided by means of describing their multiple characteristics, including their different responsibilities in a colonial conflict. Within the group of white, colonial masters, there is space for the analysis of (e.g.) social and gender relations (and conflicts), just as within the group of oppressed people, specific forms of concrete oppression can be highlighted. Resistance inside the ruling group and collaboration on the part of the subjugated can also be addressed in this way.

But there is an obvious danger in this: Through this differentiated approach, an existing conflict can also be talked down and veiled. The obvious exploitation of the colonized by the colonial masters is not eliminated by drawing attention to cases of collaboration and participation by individuals from the group of the exploited. Such an approach can even lead to an attempt to blame the victims themselves for the conflicts and thus relieve the perpetrators of their responsibility.

A careful analysis is therefore required here, which also asks about the epistemological interests of those who make these differentiations in each case: Should the responsibility for colonialism be shifted off by looking at native collaboration, or does it serve to describe the plurality of colonial forms of rule more precisely? Can hidden elements of resistance also come to light in the concrete forms of collaboration, which point to the fact that the subjugated are not to be seen in a purely passive role as victims? Any differentiation in the analysis of the contact zones must keep in mind the conflictual nature of colonial power relations *and* of their analysis.

Without referring to the work of Mary Louise Pratt, Homi Bhabha presents a very similar interpretation of the phenomenon of the border, which, however, points even more strongly to the fact that borders should not be thought of as lines, but as spaces (see 3.4 above). Although borders appear as lines on a map (or in other discursive areas), they actually represent a web of relationships, negotiations, and power relations. Homi

Bhabha calls them a "Third Space,"[65] from which the identities on both sides of the border take on a new meaning.

It is a space of negotiations in which active and passive roles are not predetermined, even if conflicting power structures suggest that they are. Rather, Bhabha works out how these power structures are constructed and changed in the negotiations between the participants. In his study *The Location of Culture* he describes imitation or mimicry, ambivalence, *sly civility*, and other phenomena of these negotiations that can unsettle and destabilize the static identities of those involved. The border opens up a space for negotiations and resistance.[66]

In postcolonial theories and theologies, these considerations are often taken up with concepts such as *intermediate space, threshold area, liminal space, in-between, edges, margins,* etc. What these concepts usually have in common is that they break up the static, essentialist duality of identities and their demarcation from one another and liquefy them in favor of a diverse, lively, and dynamic conceptual interdependence. The conflictive character of the border is transferred into a more precise analysis of the (conflictive and plural) interplay between domination, resistance, negotiations, and all their nuances.

Bhabha's concept of *hybridity* must not be viewed in a biological sense as crossbreeding, as something which would result in the production of a new identity. In his conception, it stands for a description of "complex cultural formations that arise in a colonial and thus clearly hierarchized, asymmetrical constellation and, at the same time, destabilize this constellation."[67] Processes of hybridization are constantly being transformed and reinterpreted. The space of colonial rule in which they occur brings it about that they are constantly being renegotiated, since they cause insecurities and thus the reorganization of the colonial space.

The Bolivian sociologist Silvia Rivera Cusicanqui names such hybridizations with a term from the Aymara language *"ch'ixi."*[68] *Ch'ixi* means a texture or structure that appears to be of gray color but is composed of tiny dots of black and white (or other colors): the overall impression is that of a mixture; however, the individual color dots retain their specific identity. For Rivera Cusicanqui, this term shows better

65. Bhabha, *Verortung der Kultur*, 56; see Kerner, *Postkoloniale Theorien*, 125–31.

66. See Castro Varela and Dhawan, *Postkoloniale Theorie*, 239–71.

67. Kerner, *Postkoloniale Theorien*, 126.

68. Rivera Cusicanqui, *Sociología de la imagen*, 295; see Rivera Cusicanqui, *Mundo ch'ixi es posible*.

than the concepts of hybridity and *mesticism* (preferred in Latin American cultural theories) that traditional identities are preserved in cultural mixtures and are not simply replaced by a new, hybrid identity. In this way, it is also possible to describe constellations of power and resistance that are transformed in hybridizations.

Such forms of resistance at the contact zones are also taken up in postcolonial theology. In the words of Daniel Franklin Pilario, this theology

> opts for a hermeneutics of resistance, that is, to read not only how the colonial powers construct the colonized but also how the subaltern subverts the same power used to dominate them. It attempts to highlight the ways "how the invaded, often caricatured as abused victims or grateful beneficiaries, transcended these images and wrested interpretation from the invaders, starting processes of self-discovery, appropriation and subversion."[69]

The Puerto Rican theologian Mayra Rivera describes the biblical figure of Sophia/Wisdom as someone who makes contact zones her living space and ambivalence her identity. Much like Latinxs[70] in the United States—people of Latino or Caribbean origin—Sophia lives on the frontier line, "at the crossroads"[71] in a cultural and often literal sense. Rivera points out that even in biblical scholarship, it has not been conclusively clarified whether Sophia—the biblical personification of wisdom—originates from Egypt, from Israel, from Babylon, or from a region that transcends borders and cultures. "Is the language of Israel your native language?" asks Rivera,[72] in a nod to the bilingualism of Latinxs in the United States.

Sophia also shows her independence and hybridity in the biblical text: Unlike the praised housewife from Prov 31, who tends the house while her husband stays in the city gates and sits in the council there (v. 23), Sophia—wisdom—stands herself in the streets and in the squares, and speaks herself at the city gates (Prov 1:20–21; 8:2), instead

---

69. Pilario, "Mapping," 49, with a quote from R. S. Sugirtharajah, from *Bible and the Third World*.

70. This spelling avoids the pair "Latinos and Latinas" that is possible in Spanish; while at the same time trying to include persons beyond the gender binary.

71. Rivera, "God at the Crossroads."

72. Rivera, "God at the Crossroads," 193.

of making herself useful in the house.[73] Sophia claims for herself a role that the book of Proverbs otherwise attributes to a contrasting figure, the dangerous strange woman (see Prov 7:5) who should be avoided: like the strange woman, Sophia can be found on the streets and on the squares, lurking on every street corner (Prov 7:12).[74]

Sophia crosses borders, leaves the role ascribed to her by patriarchal gender relations, and is nevertheless recommended to the (male, reading) youth as a role model to be followed: "Everything you might desire cannot be compared to her" (Prov 8:11).[75] Through this interpretation of Mayra Rivera, contemporary Bible readers can also find in Sophia a model for overcoming borders and ascribed identities.

The German theologian Dietmar Müßig also describes an interesting example of negotiations in religious contact zones with the *Jungfrau im Silberberg* (i.e., the Virgin in the silver mountain).[76] Using a painting from colonial Bolivia depicting the Virgin Mary in the form of the silver-mined mountain of the colonial Bolivian city of Potosí, Müßig shows how both pre-Hispanic and colonial religions were infused into the image's iconography through ambivalent mimicry or imitation, in the terminology of Bhabha. The painter of the picture succeeded in anchoring important elements of precolonial religiosity in this image of the Virgin Mary and at the same time veiling them, so that they could be read by members of the indigenous cultures, but remained hidden from the Spanish-Christian view.

Using postcolonial methodology, particularly that of Homi Bhabha, Müßig visualizes the interrelationships of power and resistance, the visible and the hidden, identity and hybridity, through which the creator of the picture was able to develop a resistant, hybrid indigenous theology in pictorial form. While in the past this image was interpreted primarily in terms of its intercultural significance, as a document of the merging and mutual adaptation of cultures and religions, in Müßig's postcolonial analysis, the dimensions of submission and resistance and the importance of negotiations in this contact zone of the rule of Spanish conquerors over the indigenous population become evident.

Understanding borders as contact zones already contains the germ of resistance, as these examples make clear. It also makes it possible to

73. See Rivera, "God at the Crossroads," 193.
74. Translations of the biblical quotes by the author.
75. See Rivera, "God at the Crossroads," 196.
76. Müßig, *Jungfrau im Silberberg*.

uncover, in the Bible, church history, and tradition, the resistance and creativity that came to fruition in the various contact zones of history. This perspective can also shape the church's attitude toward borders in the present, as Catherine Keller, Michael Nausner, and Mayra Rivera write in the introduction to their book on *Postcolonial Theologies*:

> A theology that decolonizes the between-spaces of our inter-dependence will shift its task from boundary-protection to boundary-crossings: hardly an "alien" metaphor for Christianity. The task of a postcolonial theology will not be to shore up the barriers between the Christian and the non-Christian, the holy and the profane, the church and the world, the ethical and the immoral, even the Creator and creation. Nor will it be simply to demolish them. We will want instead to pay careful attention to what happens in all these in-between places.[77]

4.7. Indiscipline: Conclusion

Indiscipline and being undisciplined do not sound like virtues. In connection with the postcolonial resistance against the hegemonic coloniality of power, however, the term can be associated with liberation from the disciplinary power of colonialism, which is expressed, among other things, in the Western definitions of scientific disciplines and their methods. The decolonial theorists Catherine Walsh, Freya Schiwy, and Santiago Castro-Gómez therefore write in the foreword of their book *Indisciplinar las ciencias sociales* (*Undisciplining the Social Sciences*):

> Our use of *to undiscipline* [*indisciplinar*] refers to the need to make evident the disciplining [*disciplinamiento*], the discipline [*disciplina*], and the disciplinary formations [*formaciones disciplinarias*] that have been constructed in the social sciences since the nineteenth century, but particularly in their institutionalization in Latin America in the twentieth century, and to highlight their colonial legacy. It is reminiscent of Foucault's disciplinary power—a power which not only punishes but also rewards, a power that works on offenders from within, consolidating the ranks of the "normal."[78]

What is said here for the social sciences applies to academic theory and practice as a whole, and also to theology: the demarcation of the

---

77. Keller et al., "Introduction," 14.
78. Walsh et al., *Indisciplinar*, 13 (emphasis in the original).

disciplines and subjects, their canon, their content, their methods, what counts as scientific and what doesn't; the forms of teaching, research and academic career paths—all of this developed and consolidated in Europe at around the same time that Europe was trying to export its own culture to the big cities of the world through colonialism. Academic scholarship in most parts of the world is therefore still shaped by this European scientific culture, and it is not surprising that it is perceived and criticized as colonial in postcolonial countries.

To undiscipline oneself means pushing back at the disciplining imposed by the coloniality of science. With their use of the term *discipline*, Walsh et al. not only allude to the scientific disciplines but also connect them with Michel Foucault's *disciplinary power*. Foucault understands discipline as a "technique of exercising power"[79] that makes it possible to control society and individuals. Discipline is that aspect of the exercise of power that aims directly at controlling the individual as the smallest element of society, but which has society as a whole in mind. Foucault also includes the common understandings of discipline—e.g., in sports, in the military, in the monastery, in health care, etc.—in this form of power strategy.

For Walsh et al., the scientific disciplines and their internal power structure represent another example of such an exercise of power, which in the postcolonial context is also shaped by coloniality. In order to resist this disciplining in science, various steps of undisciplining are necessary:

> *Undisciplining* means unbinding the frontiers of the social sciences . . . . It implies the acknowledgment of other forms of knowledge, particularly local knowledge generated from colonial difference and the dialogic intersections and flows that can occur between them and disciplinary knowledge.[80]

So the point is not to reject Western colonial scholarship, but to criticize and question it, to uncover its coloniality and to engage it in a genuine critical dialogue with alternative forms of knowledge, especially those that have been repressed, appropriated, or distorted by colonialism. To do this, however, it is also necessary to question its *absolute* authority and its claim to universality.

Walter Mignolo summarizes this questioning of the authority of Western knowledge traditions under the concept of *epistemic*

---

79. Ruoff, *Foucault-Lexikon*, 120.

80. Walsh et al., *Indisciplinar*, 13–14 (emphasis in the original).

disobedience.[81] This disobedience aims at the basic premises of Eurocentric and colonial knowledge, namely its modes of knowledge. Mignolo argues that the coloniality of knowledge is already effective from an epistemological point of view, and that for the decolonization of knowledge, it is necessary to break away from this mode of knowledge. Mignolo therefore proposes a double method of epistemological decolonization: "detachment and openness."[82] The *detachment* from Eurocentric ways of thought corresponds to the *openness* to alternatives that draw from the diverse cultural traditions of humankind, not only on the level of content, but also in questions of methodology and epistemology.

It is obvious that for Mignolo, too, detachment from European paradigms and disobedience to them does not imply an absolute rejection or complete abandonment of Western academic methods. After all, he himself is part of the Western academic network and also uses European authors in his writings. However, Mignolo postulates a fundamental freedom from the premises, ideas, and academic standards of European scholarship in order to create space for resistance and for openness to alternative forms of knowledge. In this way, creative *third spaces* can open up at the disciplinary boundaries, which can develop into areas of contact with forms of knowledge and can go beyond Western scientific standards.

The principle of shifting perspectives discussed in this chapter represents an important postcolonial strategy of resistance. With dynamic, sometimes surprising and unpredictable changes in location and perspective, it is possible to complement, debunk or—in some cases—overcome European perspectives. Turning away from colonial perspectives goes hand in hand with turning to the perspectives of the marginalized and excluded.

In Latin America, historically, this concerns primarily the indigenous peoples. The Mexican theologian Carlos Mendoza-Álvarez points out that resistance to colonialism has a history that is as old as colonialism itself. The indigenous resistance represents for Mendoza-Álvarez— similar to every other individual resistance—a

> point of reference for many other forms of resistance of vulnerable and *resilient* groups in the face of systemic violence, such as women, queer communities, forced migrants, communities

---

81. See Mignolo, *Epistemischer Ungehorsam.*
82. Mignolo, "Pensamiento decolonial," 25. See also below, 5.7.

of African descent, and many other groups that *transform their own exclusion into a principle of the transformation of the world.*[83]

Resilience is an important keyword in understanding the forms and motivations of decolonizing resistance. Juan Carlos La Puente Tapia gives examples of how resistance often appears irrational or inefficient on the outside, but expresses dignity and self-assertion on a personal level.[84] Such resistance may then be based on the refusal to allow oneself to be degraded, to give up a last remnant of personal autonomy, or to lose one's group-related identity. Building on this refusal, which may not seem constructive, it is possible, as quoted by Mendoza-Álvarez, to make one's own exclusion the "principle of the transformation of the world."

Another form of theological *indiscipline* can also be seen in a fundamental ecumenism that can be found in postcolonial theologies. The denominational church affiliation plays at most a secondary role for most authors. Occasionally, thematic peculiarities can be identified that can be assigned to individual Christian denominations, such as reflections on Marian piety or theology of the cross. As a rule, however, theologians receive information from one another across denominational boundaries and work together on specific projects, without there being any discernible methodological or hermeneutical difference between members of different Christian denominations. An important aspect of this interdenominational cooperation may be that postcolonial theologians currently occupy a minority position in all Christian churches.

The decisive factor in the post- and decolonial analyses of resistance practices is their non-dualistic conception: resistance is interpreted as a process of negotiation, as a creative design of the contact zone, as alienation and hybridization. It is not a resistance that would only accept one or the other, but one which opposes othering, dualism, and the making invisible of the different. Its goal is not the annihilation of the oppressor or the oppressive philosophy of science, but a profound critique of them and their creative transformation. This sometimes requires turning away, detachment, and disobedience.

The construction of new binary opposites can be a temporary strategy to overcome these opposites. It can be associated with the "strategic use of essentialism"[85] advocated by Gayatri Spivak: by this she under-

---

83. Mendoza-Álvarez, "Entstehung von Rationalität," 55 (emphasis in the original).

84. La Puente Tapia, "Widerstand," 72–73.

85. Spivak, *Post-Colonial Critic*, 109; see Castro Varela and Dhawan, *Postkoloniale*

stands a purposeful, temporary use of essentialist attributions in an activist or political context, which serves the possibility to address people collectively. However, this use must take place with a self-critical attitude that is aware of the danger of such essentialist assignments.

For this reason, the Argentine theologian Nicolás Panotto also calls for an "attitude of confrontation," but at the same time calls for change and transformation. For him, the goal is

> creating other ways of doing theology. The change calls us to take a critical theological stance on established forms and discourses, in search of the construction of other languages, other spaces, other institutionalities and other practices. We cannot achieve transformation of these elements without an epistemological suspicion about how we define the divine economy. Therefore we need a process of mutual relations between *practice*, existence in public space, *kenosis*, as an example of self-purification, self-criticism and constant deconstruction of discourses, worldviews and practices, and *perichoresis*, which includes the "in between" of existence, that is, all the elements needed to speak of God constantly deconstructing the processes of self-assertion.[86]

Mendoza-Álvarez also speaks of "an anti-hegemonic theological—better still: a kenotic—rationality that is suitable for entering into dialogue with those who have been made invisible by hegemonic thought."[87] Resistance to traditional epistemological elements of theology, which are criticized as being afflicted with colonialism, is not a sufficient transformation strategy if it is not accompanied by attention, a new dialogue, a search for theological alternatives, and the construction of decolonized, counter-hegemonic theologies. Such theological practices merit a high theological appreciation according to Mendoza-Álvarez: "These messianic acts, breaking down the walls of hatred, make possible the original experience of salvation that comes from the living God."[88]

Theorie, 201–3.

86. Panotto, *Descolonizar o saber teológico*, 76 (emphasis in the original).

87. Mendoza-Álvarez, "Entstehung von Rationalität," 57.

88. Mendoza-Álvarez, "Entstehung von Rationalität," 57.

5.

Alternatives

POSTCOLONIAL THEOLOGIES DO NOT limit themselves to criticism of and resistance to the coloniality in church and theology. They also show that there are theological alternatives to colonialism and coloniality. These alternatives existed and still exist beyond the reach of both historic colonialism and its contemporary aftermath. In addition, postcolonial theologies refer to newly created alternatives in theology, and even create them themselves.

These theological alternatives can affect the areas of both method and content of theology. In this way, a diverse and broad panorama of postcolonial theologies emerges and presents itself, which is difficult to sensibly systematize. Due to the *indiscipline* of postcolonial theologies described in the last chapter, they even actively resist any systematization.

In this chapter, therefore, some examples of these alternatives will be presented in order to show the bandwidth of the postcolonial theological spectrum. In addition, it will become clear how the search for and the openness to alternative methods, epistemologies, subjects, areas of experience, linguistic worlds, power relations, and discourse practices lead to a transformation of theology on many different hermeneutical and methodological levels. The examples from the last three chapters already have made it clear that postcolonial theologies are not about a new theological method (or fashion), a further discipline in theology, or an additional contextual theology, but that they are about a fundamental critique, revision, and transformation of the European theology of the past five hundred years.

As has already become clear, the cosmovisions and systems of thought of those cultures that have been marginalized, devalued, and neglected by colonialism are of central importance. Non-European ways of thinking around the world were often condemned, ignored, or openly opposed by colonial ideology. This affected, among other things, indigenous cultures, popular religiosity, non-Christian religions, and Christian communities that were once characterized as heretical but continued to exist outside the Roman Empire. Many of them have not been completely destroyed and are now seen as an experiential, methodical, hermeneutical, or epistemic framework for thinking, formulating, and living Christian theology differently. Many creative movements in postcolonial theologies feed off the dialogue with them.

The aim is not to return to a precolonial religiosity or culture. Even if this could be unequivocally reconstructed from historical documents or contemporary memories (which is not possible in the vast majority of cases), it would be necessary for this supposedly reconstructed culture to enter into a dialogue with the circumstances of the present, or—to use the postcolonial expression—enter into negotiations. The reconstruction of a supposedly pure precolonial culture is an anachronistic undertaking that would devalue this reconstruction into a sterile museum piece if it remained excluded from the dialogue with the present.

Postcolonial alternatives to the coloniality of theology therefore usually represent creative and dynamic negotiations of power relations and discourse practices on the borders and fringes of colonial theologies. They engage in creative forms of resistance to the coloniality of theology by negotiating hybridizations between different European and non-European, between hegemonic and oppressed, between dominant and resistant reflections on the Christian faith.

Depending on the perspective from which these negotiations are carried out, which methods and discourses predominate and which forms of colonial oppression and exclusion are specifically addressed, they can—as is practiced in this chapter—be classified as indigenous (5.2), syncretistic-subaltern (5.3), ecofeminist (5.4) or queer (5.5) theologies without excluding their use of and relationships with other perspectives and methodologies.

What all these alternative theological drafts have in common is that, under the conditions of coloniality, they can be characterized as resistant negotiations or as resistance through negotiations. They are aiming at both a liberated theology and the liberation and improvement of the living conditions of the people from whose perspective they are formulated. A special focus in this chapter is on alternative biblical readings (5.1), while finally the fundamental question is examined whether the taking up of alternative knowledge by theology should perhaps itself be criticized as a form of neocolonialism (5.6). In summary, postcolonial theological alternatives are recognized as a creative and constructive form of border transgression (5.7).

Daniel Franklin Pilario distinguishes this postcolonial theological strategy from the nativism occasionally practiced in postcolonial scenarios: "Unlike the nativist projects of romantic return, postcolonial theology 'enlists' hybridity into the service of theological construction."[1] In the epoch of independence of the African states, such a return to an imagined native—or originally African—culture had been encouraged by some independence movements. However, this had proved to be unfeasible in the practice of national independence and in the confrontation with postcolonial problems. The proclamation of a return to precolonial religions and theologies turns out to be another form of resistant negotiation under the ideological guise of nativism, which at the same time blocks numerous approaches to liberating transformations.[2]

The freedom and radicalism with which postcolonial theologies also take up traditions of thought that have been rejected for centuries or simply appear alien often cause great difficulties in understanding for theologians trained in a European tradition. Wietske de Jong-Kumru invites us to see these difficulties as a positive challenge:

> For Western readers, unfortunately, this inclusion of non-Western sources may make it somewhat difficult to deal with postcolonial writings. But maybe that should be seen as a positive side effect. The use that Dube, Kwok, and others make of non-Western knowledge is capable of confronting Western readers with the limitations of their own epistemological horizons.[3]

Finally, she argues, it is usually taken for granted that theologians worldwide must engage with the entire European tradition of thought. Western theologians should therefore not consider it an impertinence if

---

1. Pilario, "Mapping," 49.
2. See López Hernández, *Teología India*, 103–7.
3. De Jong-Kumru, *Postcolonial Feminist Theology*, 103–4.

they are to engage in non-Western knowledge under the conditions set by the bearers of this knowledge themselves.[4]

5.1. Different Ways to Read the Bible

In various sections of this introduction it has already become clear that it is an essential concern of postcolonial theologies to read the Bible differently: from diverse perspectives, with different eyes, alternative questions and approaches. Postcolonial interpretations of the Bible have become so widespread and complex that it would be worth writing a separate introduction to just this specific area of postcolonial theology.[5] In this section, the aim is to reflect specifically about the alternative methods of postcolonial reading and interpretation of the Bible.

Citing Fernando Segovia, Kwok Pui-lan emphasizes that an important starting point for the development of postcolonial biblical studies was the adoption of literary criticism and other methods of cultural studies toward the end of the twentieth century. As a result, "the universal, objective reader is gradually replaced by the interested, local, and perspectival reader."[6]

> The addition of Western women, men and women from outside the West, and also of non-Western minorities in the West, has resulted in a diversity of method and theory, an expansion of scope of inquiry, and an explosion of interpretive voices.[7]

Through the practice of no longer ignoring the voices of these previously excluded subjects of Bible reading, and of bringing them into a dialogue with Western biblical scholarship (in this sense the "addition" from the quote can be interpreted in a way other than as a patriarchal act of patronizing) the biblical text was enabled to enter into a dialogue with numerous different contemporary contexts. From these contexts and through these subjects, however, the questions that were brought

4. See de Jong-Kumru, *Postcolonial Feminist Theology*, 103–4.

5. See the important anthologies by R. S. Sugirtharajah, *Voices from the Margin* (1991), *Postcolonial Biblical Reader* (2006), and *Still at the Margins* (2008), as well as the authors represented therein; see also Moore and Segovia, *Postcolonial Biblical Criticism*.

6. Kwok, "Verbindungen herstellen," 324, with reference to Segovia, *Decolonizing Biblical Studies*. This approach from the perspective of the reader touches on the exegetical perspective of reception aesthetics.

7. Kwok, "Verbindungen herstellen," 324.

forward toward the text and the context in which it was produced became very different ones.

Musa Dube shows that readers from African Independent Churches (see above, 4.1) justify their own reading perspective with an authority that they derive from both biblical Christian and traditional African roots: by basing their Bible interpretation on the dialogue with the Spirit and giving it an African name (*moya*, "spirit") and attributes from African tradition, they resist the European and academic claim of correct and universal interpretation of the Bible. From this spirit (*se-moya*) that stands for prophecy, healing, fertility, and vitality, these readers interpret the Bible in their own way and for their own context. These *semoya* qualities are also recognizable in the interpretation of biblical texts from the point of view of these readers.[8] This reader orientation widens the limits of biblical hermeneutics for alternative interpretations and modes of understanding. Dube writes:

> I try to innovate, other ways of reading: divination, storytelling, reading with primary readers, which for me is a conscious, subversive way of reading, independent of Western scholarship. . . . I [ask] my students to take a Bible text to the church and read it with four or five people, and then write an essay about how the grassroots people read that text. . . . We need to deconstruct the notion that there is only one right way to read the Bible.[9]

In postcolonial contexts, the orientation toward the perspective of the readers brings a multitude of postcolonial questions to the Bible texts, be it discourse strategies, power constellations, or resistance to colonial rule. These postcolonial critiques concern both contemporary and historical interpretations of the Bible. Postcolonial biblical scholarship also asks about the power relations that are reflected in the text of the Bible itself, because they determined the culture of the authors of the biblical books at the time they were written.

R. S. Sugirtharajah thus characterizes *three main levels of postcolonial biblical criticism*:

> 1. It seeks to situate colonialism at the center of the Bible and biblical interpretation. The Bible emerged as a literary product of various colonial contexts—Egyptian, Assyrian, Persian, hellenistic, and Roman. Postcolonial criticism tries to look at

8. See Dube, *Postcolonial Feminist Interpretation*, 40–41; 115–17; 186–87; 192–93.

9. Dube, "'To push the boundaries,'" 163.

these narratives and investigate them for colonial assumptions, imperial impulses, power relations, hegemonic intentions, the treatment of subalterns, stigmatization of women and the marginalized, land appropriation, and violations of minority cultures. In reading these texts, it endeavors to revive and reclaim silenced voices, sidelined issues, and lost causes.

2. It seeks to scrutinize biblical interpretation and expose the ideological content behind its apparent claim to neutrality. What postcolonial biblical criticism does is focus on the whole issue of expansion, domination, and imperialism as central forces in defining both biblical narratives and biblical interpretation.

3. It seeks to reread the Bible in the light of postcolonial concerns and conditions—plurality, hybridity, multiculturalism, nationalism, diaspora, refugees, and asylum seeking. The Bible is appropriated not because it has prescriptions for problems which arose in the wake of colonialism. Rather, it is to see whether it can lend itself and evolve as an appropriate Word of God in response to issues that were not the primary concern of these narratives.[10]

Sugirtharajah's characterization reveals the diverse range of postcolonial biblical studies, not only in terms of subject matter, but above all in their historical depth, because according to his interpretation, colonial interpretations of the Bible are not only misinterpretations from the time of European colonialism but can also be found at the present time. Moreover, they point to roots in the context in which the biblical writings themselves came into being. It might not be appropriate to call those biblical contexts *colonial*, as Sugirtharajah does, because the term *colonial* is very much geared toward the concrete development of European colonialism over the past five centuries. In the empires of the biblical period, which Sugirtharajah mentioned above, however, it can be shown that discourse and power structures display parallels to the coloniality of the present that have left their traces in the narratives of the biblical writings. In Sugirtharajah's view, it is precisely these historical imperial contexts that are all too often overlooked or neglected by contemporary exegesis.[11]

In the practice of colonial and postcolonial Bible interpretation, the three historical levels of the context of origin, colonial interpretation,

10. Sugirtharajah, "Postcolonial Biblical Interpretation," 67. See a more detailed, somewhat different description with individual examples, in Sugirtharajah, *Bible and the Third World*, 250–59.

11. See Sugirtharajah, "Postcolonial Biblical Interpretation," 68.

and the present overlap. The different contexts and their respective uses of the biblical text can therefore lead to conflicts in the contemporary confrontation of postcolonial Bible readers with the texts. These conflicts may not seem to do justice to the biblical text and its historically and critically researched meaning.

To give an example, the North American Indigenous literary and cultural scholar Robert Allen Warrior of the Osage Nation reads the biblical story of the Exodus (and conquest) from the perspective of a people conquered and driven out by a foreign people. He writes, "I believe that the story of the Exodus is an inappropriate way for Native Americans to think about liberation."[12] Warrior acknowledges the liberating importance that the same text had in the immediate past for the Black liberation movements of the 1960s in the United States and for Latin American liberation theology exercised in the 1970s and 1980s. But it is not possible for him to read the text other than from the perspective of the Canaanites. In his opinion, the historical experience of his own indigenous people finds too strong an echo in the role that is ascribed, in this narrative of land theft, to the inhabitants of Canaan.

Warrior explains that the misuse of the texts by "Puritan preachers"[13] in the days of the North American conquests only reinforces this identification. However, the experience of land grabbing is already inherent in the narrative of these texts and can only be partially eliminated or mitigated through academic study of the texts. Because, Warrior observes, the narrative remains: "Yahveh [sic] the deliverer became Yahveh the conqueror."[14] Read from a North American indigenous perspective, for him, the text remains trapped in this interpretation and cannot unfold its liberating meaning: "With what voice will we, the Canaanites of the world, say: 'Let my people go and leave my people alone?'"[15]

Postcolonial Bible interpretation does not attempt to resolve such contradictions and bottlenecks, but instead draws attention to them and in this way makes it clear how problematic it can be in the present to transfer biblical interpretations from one culture to another, even if as in the case

---

12. Warrior, "Native American Perspective," 236. This text was first published in 1989.

13. Warrior, "Native American Perspective," 240.

14. Warrior, "Native American Perspective," 237.

15. Warrior, "Native American Perspective," 241. "Let my people go" approvingly alludes to the Black civil rights movement's use of the Exodus narrative.

here—the example of Black and indigenous liberation movements in the United States—they are very close and related issues.

Moreover, the results of historical-critical exegesis cannot easily be applied to any context. Even if the achievements of historical criticism and other biblical methods developed in Europe are recognized (and used) in postcolonial biblical criticism, their universality and general applicability are questioned. On the other hand, postcolonial critics also ask—as shown above in 2.4—about the historical presuppositions of critical European biblical studies and their interconnectedness with colonialism.

Postcolonial exegesis therefore insists on confrontation with the current context and its inquiries into the text. Through this dialogue it is possible to discover those aspects of the biblical text that can have an alienating, oppressive, liberating, or healing effect in this context. Accordingly, the interpretation of the text can bring one aspect or another to the fore and must clarify or neutralize other aspects.

The Old Testament scholar Archie Lee from Hong Kong describes this postcolonial exegetical dialogue by comparing the texts of Trito-Isaiah (Is 56–66) with his own context, the perspective of the so-called return of the British colony Hong Kong to the People's Republic of China at the end of the twentieth century. The point of comparison is the encounter associated with the return as coming-home (Isaiah) or return as been-given-back (Hong Kong) of two communities that had developed culturally and politically separately over decades, their risks and their promises. He calls his context his own text, which enters into a crosswise dialogue with the biblical text:

> When the two texts are brought together and read cross-textually, one makes crossings between the two and seeks to integrate them creatively. One text will act as the context from which the other is read. The horizon provided by one text will enlighten the other, and a fusion will be achieved for the enrichment of the reader's understanding.[16]

The proximity to Said's concept of *contrapuntal reading* (see above, 4.5) is obvious. Biblical text and current context unfold new meanings through this dialogue. This does not invalidate the traditional meanings of the biblical text, and the newly created meaning cannot claim universality for all present and future contexts of interpretation of that

16. Lee, "Returning to China," 284.

text. But this postcolonial cross-reading of two texts can shed light on the contemporary understanding of a biblical text, enabling the text to re-spell the good news of the Bible in today's postcolonial contexts. At the same time, the Bible text can open up new clarity about the meaning of concrete contemporary (post)colonial contexts. This dialogue has the potential to uncover colonial discourse practices and power relations so that resistance to them becomes possible. In this way, the Bible and its current context can be read with new eyes, differently.

5.2. Indigenous Theologies

In preparation for the commemoration of the five hundredth anniversary of Latin America's conquest in 1992, the region's indigenous movements have gained an increased self-awareness about their colonial history and their own nation states. Since then, a theological current has developed, which takes dialogue with the indigenous cultures and religions as its starting point.[17] It is called (in Spanish) *Teología India*, literally "Indian theology," but I prefer the expression of *Indigenous Theology*. It is often associated with indigenous theologies of North America and other postcolonial regions.[18] It is by now possible to speak of indigenous theologies on every continent outside Europe and in many cultural regions of the world, even if they are generally not as well organized and documented as in Latin America. A few examples in this section will illustrate this diversity.

Indigenous theologies emerge from negotiations between indigenous spirituality, religion, culture, and life experience on the one hand and Christianity in its European form on the other. Each indigenous culture has its own fundamental set of views of the world and of life, which can only inadequately be described with various European terms such as philosophy, cosmovision, worldview, wisdom, ontology, episteme, etc. What is crucial, however, is that in each case it is a matter of looking at and evaluating the world, life, and people in a way that

17. See López Hernández, *Teología India*; Estermann, *Apu Taytayku*; Weiler, *Gut leben*; on the history of the *Teología India* in Latin America, see Caero Bustillos, "Für Christen ist es ein Vorrecht." There has been a similar movement in North America, which I didn't follow in detail at the time. This is the reason why I allude here mostly to the Latin American indigenous theologies.

18. There are also regional terms such as "Andean theology" (especially in Bolivia and Peru), "Maya theology" (in Central America), and the like.

differs from Western perspectives. Indigenous theologies therefore often fundamentally question the Western way of doing theology, also from a methodological and epistemological point of view, and practice alternative forms of theological construction.

The indigenous worldviews of the present are no longer the same as they were before the colonial era. Cultures continue to develop, especially in contact with other cultures, but also, for example, through internal historical processes and the confrontation with natural conditions. Colonialism, as an intensive, violent, and threatening form of cultural contact naturally also changed the structures and values of indigenous cultures. Nevertheless, indigenous ideas can still be described today that are fundamentally different from Western thought, oppose it, and present themselves as an alternative to it.

In this respect, indigenous theologies are, by their very existence, a project of resistance against coloniality and an alternative to it. They oppose colonial devaluation and alienation of indigenous cultures and peoples. They value what is their own, which was devalued, changed, and othered by colonial Christianity. On the other hand, they understand their own Christian-indigenous spirituality as something alive and dynamic that can contribute to liberation and decolonization.

Due to their close relationship to local cultures, they see themselves as contextual theologies and consequently as quite diverse. However, they enter into dialogue with each other and with other Christian theologies in order to learn from and stimulate one another. There is a lively exchange between different indigenous theologies, especially in Latin America, but now also worldwide.

These are hybrid theologies, theologies in the contact zone, which draw on indigenous spiritualities and religious convictions and at the same time enter into critical and creative negotiation processes with traditional European Christianity, from which new religious forms, ways of thinking, and contents emerge.

A nativist return to precolonial forms of indigenous religions is usually dismissed as illusory, unhistorical, and inappropriate to the intercultural dynamics of cultures.[19] Rather, one associates the construction of indigenous theologies with ideas that correspond to the *negotiations* of Bhabha, the *contact zones* of Pratt or the *ch'ixi of* Rivera Cusicanqui (see above, 4.6). Nicolás Panotto speaks of a "symbolic negotiation" with

---

19. See López Hernández, *Teología India*, 103–7.

regard to indigenous theologies: "The amalgamation with Christianity does not erase the indigenous cosmovisions, but rather preserves them and gives them a new meaning."[20] This also entails

> a reinterpretation of various elements of the Christian cosmovision. For example, the figure of Jesus is understood as someone with whom one walks in everyday life, . . . he stands for the protection of the house, safety on the way, one owes him thanks for the harvest, food, rain, wisdom.[21]

The construction of indigenous theologies is never just about the freedom to choose alternatives, but always also about a critical-constructive dialogue that strives for the transformation of Christianity in its various European cultural forms. In this respect, they have a fundamentally critical postcolonial character trait.

The preparatory phase before the Catholic Synod of Bishops for the Amazon region in 2019 made this clear: During the consultation process, communities and individual representatives from more than 170 indigenous peoples of the Amazon took part in the consultations. Their requests to the bishops were evaluated in the synod's final document as a theological and spiritual challenge: "Listening to the cry of the earth and the cry of the poor and of the peoples of the Amazon with whom we walk, calls us to a true integral conversion," the bishops write in their final document of the synod.[22] In other words, the bishops confess that they themselves feel called to conversion in the face of the requests that are addressed to them by the indigenous peoples of Amazonia, among others, and are no longer advocating the conversion of the colonized peoples, as in previous centuries.

Indigenous theologies address differences in power, past and present oppression, and discourse practices that serve them. At the same time, feminist indigenous theologies are organizing themselves in order to bring the questions of injustice in gender relations and other specifically feminist issues into this dialogue.[23]

It may be said that indigenous theologies represent postcolonial alternatives to European theological traditions in four respects:

---

20. Panotto, "Descolonizar lo divino," 149.
21. Panotto, "Descolonizar lo divino," 149–50.
22. Synod of Bishops, *Amazon*, no. 17; see Silber, "Synodalität," 262–65.
23. See Chipana Quispe, "Relationale Wissensbestände," 48–50.

- At the level of **epistemology**, they take up different perspectives on the world, humans, and communities than the philosophies and sciences imported from Europe. In doing so, they formulate alternative theological statements about the relationships between God and humankind, community and creation, guilt and redemption, etc. These differences at the substantive level are often incomprehensible if the fundamental differences at the epistemic level are not considered.

- Further alternatives can be found on a **methodological** and formal **level**: Indigenous theologies reach far beyond the spectrum of scholarly methods, places, and subjects that is considered regular in European theology. People outside academic theology and outside the university can also be recognized as subjects of theology. Likewise, the methods that are traditionally available to these people, such as storytelling, song, wisdom teaching, ritual, dance, etc., are taken up for the development of indigenous theologies.

- This creates a broad spectrum of alternative **content** in the indigenous theologies, which relates to the contextually and culturally determined everyday life of the people, but also to resistance and resilience in the face of colonialism.

- Finally, indigenous theologians make a different **claim** with regard to their theologies: they neither claim that their theology is universally valid for all people and all cultures nor do they pretend to design an unchangeable theology that is valid for all times. Indigenous theologies claim a transitory, contextually, and culturally constrained theological meaning for people seeking to further develop and enhance theological expressions in their context. They reject and critically examine theology as knowledge produced and dominated by power, criticizing both colonial Christianity and their own theological productions.

Two examples should now make these considerations even more tangible, while the first is located in the epistemic area, and the other on the level of methods. Numerous other examples can be found in the various sections and chapters of this book.[24]

---

24. See, e.g., 2.5, 2.6, 2.7, 3.1, 3.4, 4.1, 4.2, 5.1, 5.4 for examples from different regions of the world.

In many indigenous cultures of the world, a fundamental belief in the deep interconnectedness of all things can be demonstrated. It manifests itself as relatedness, correspondence, reciprocity, complementarity, or in some other way. During the period of colonial conquest, this worldview was often regarded as magical and was fought against as incompatible with Christianity. In that time in Europe, a similar holistic or organic way of thought was still active from medieval times, which was severely opposed by humanism and incipient enlightenment as a fight against witchcraft.[25] This conflict may have played a role in the colonial opposition against supposed paganism in the Americas, occurring at about the same time.

In the indigenous worldview of the Bolivian and Peruvian Andes, the interrelatedness of everything is a central element.[26] Not only are all living beings considered interrelated and interconnected, but so are all things of inanimate nature, ancestors, and local spiritual beings. This universal relatedness is difficult to capture with European concepts. A dynamic harmony prevails in these diverse networks of relationships, which is repeatedly thrown out of balance by climatic, astronomical, and tectonic events, as well as by human actions. Rituals, narratives, memories, pilgrimages, offerings to local divinities or spirits, and other cultural practices can serve to restore balance, as can political and judicial decisions to restore justice within the indigenous community. Politics and justice are conceived as being intimately related to ecological and cosmic balance.

Indigenous theologies in the Andean region therefore also aim to bring these traditional practices of searching for harmony and justice into dialogue with the Christian message of salvation and redemption, in order to make the everyday reference of these Christian terms contextually tangible. Similar considerations can be shown in the adjacent Peruvian Amazon region.[27]

Jione Havea, biblical scholar from Tonga, sheds light on a very similar basic epistemological attitude for the area of the Pacific islands: he describes the cultural idea of *tapu*—from this term our colloquial *taboo* has developed—as the healthy, harmonious connection between

---

25. See Federici, *Calibán y la bruja*; and, theologically, Merchant, *Tod der Natur.*

26. See Silber, *Kirche*, 188–97; Bascopé C., *Espiritualidad originaria*, 11–16; Estermann, *Apu Taytayku*, 66–73.

27. See Weiler, *Gut leben*, 35–59.

land and sea, human and nature, the individual and the community.[28] Without *tapu* nothing grows, nothing flourishes, everything is threatened. Therefore, this healthy mutual relationship between all that exists must be protected and preserved. Traditional practices capable of maintaining *tapu* also include prohibitions, which is what we think of as taboo, but more than that.

An important communal ritual practiced in the countryside of Tonga, while a part of the community is at sea catching sharks, consists in the long-running, uninterrupted communal narration of traditional stories. This community of storytelling must not be abandoned. If it is, difficulties and perils may arise in the open sea, or fishing may end unsuccessfully. Such a communal narration can last all day—like the catching of fish: "A ritual that takes a whole day, in island time, is not time wasted."[29]

Havea develops a theological ethics of dealing with climate change from such and similar traditional indigenous ideas. Likewise, in the various indigenous theologies, alternative epistemologies repeatedly enter into debates with current political and theological issues. Because of the different worldviews from which they start, they often arrive at different solutions to the problems than those that would be possible within European paradigms.

The community of storytelling described by Jione Havea to stabilize the *tapu* leads to the second example that is intended to explain the difference between indigenous theologies and theologies of European tradition: it is about the importance of narrative theology. Havea resists the colonialist devaluation of the story:

> Story-telling and oral cultures are unfairly romanticized and discredited in academic circles, when scholars draw hard distinctions between story and history, speech and writing, orality and textuality, and so forth. There is also a tendency to racialize story-telling and oral cultures, especially when people uncritically assume that those are activities of illiterate brown, coloured or black folk.[30]

On the one hand, he finds that the concepts of insufficient education and illiteracy are always dependent on the question of which culture and in which language someone has received more or less education.

---

28. See Havea, "Politics of Climate Change," 347–51.

29. Havea, "Politics of Climate Change," 349.

30. Havea, "Politics of Climate Change," 346.

On the other hand, he also emphasizes that *talanoa*, the Pacific culture of storytelling, "should not be confused with what some westerners understand as story-telling, which in their eyes has to do with the re-telling of stories in so-called oral cultures."[31]

Talanoa is a creative and dynamic process of retelling that involves the story itself, the practice of storytelling, and the listeners' response in equal measure. None of the three elements can be omitted. In *talanoa*, the stories are adapted to the present moment and commented on creatively, critically, and ironically by the listeners. *Talanoa* can and should provoke and call into question. From a biblical perspective, Havea emphasizes that this can also be the case with biblical narratives. The culture of *talanoa* can therefore easily enter into dialogue with biblical thought.

Laura Donaldson also highlights the importance of storytelling in her own North American indigenous cultural tradition.[32] The possibilities of taking different points of view in a story or of constructing variations, deviations, and different narrative processes or even results when retelling a story anew allow for contradiction and criticism, creativity and surprise, reflection and discussion in a completely different way than in the Western, rationally shaped discourse. Storytelling can therefore be a practice of resistance and can creatively construct liberating alternatives to deal with changing contexts and situations. Donaldson quotes African American theorist Barbara Christian:

> I am inclined to say that our theorizing (and I intentionally use the verb rather than noun) is often in the narrative forms, in the stories we create, in the riddles and proverbs, in the play with language, since dynamic rather than fixed ideas seem more to our liking. How else have we managed to survive with such spiritedness the assault on our bodies, social institutions, countries, our very humanity?[33]

In an indigenous version of the Christmas story according to Luke, Donaldson argues, the animals might play an even greater role, taking the place of the angels in proclaiming the birth of the Messiah. This would reflect the close relationship between humans and animals in Navajo

31. Havea, "Politics of Climate Change," 346.

32. Narrativity is also a practice that theology in other cultural regions likes to take up. Mercy Amba Oduyoye associates it with traditional women's crafts such as weaving and beadwork; see Oduyoye, *Beads and Strands*, 102–9; see also the title of a book co-edited by Havea: Brett and Havea, *Storyweaving*.

33. Donaldson, "Native Women's Double Cross," 103. Quote from *Race for Theory*.

culture, while also expressing this: "humans only learn about this special event through knowledge communicated by the animals."[34]

Storytelling is just one example of the multitude of practices that indigenous theologies are taking up to construct alternatives to a theology that was experienced as alienating and oppressive under colonialism and still suffers from the consequences of colonialism today. Other forms of practice that go beyond European rationality, such as theater, performance, dance, song, painting, etc., should also be mentioned, as well as questions of the political and economic organization of the community and the design of the year according to the agricultural cycle.

Indigenous practices that can be directly linked to a non-Christian concept of God, such as rituals, prayers, the use of masks, figures, etc., are not excluded from this creative theological dialogue from the outset. In many cases, they are also integrated into the negotiations. But this is not understood and tolerated by all members of the traditional Christian churches. Romi Márcia Bencke, general secretary of the Brazilian Council of Churches, writes about the intolerance shown by Christian fundamentalism in Brazil:

> This incursion of the buried gods and goddesses is not without tension and conflict. Instances of religious intolerance have increased significantly, particularly towards indigenous and Afro-Brazilian religions. . . . This indicates how easy it has become in Brazil to fuel a discourse of delegitimization and public annihilation of the other in the name of God or Jesus.[35]

On the other hand, she advocates an ecumenical opening to the various forms of Brazilian syncretistic religious practice, because

> faith in Jesus Christ is dynamic. He is not frozen over time; his message is constantly updated. Therefore, theological action must not be conditioned by doctrine, dogma, and institutional power.[36]

34. Donaldson, "Native Women's Double Cross," 112. Donaldson takes up a Christmas narrative by a young Navajo girl, Lori Tapahonso, recollected in a poem by her mother, Luci Tapahonso (from *Breeze Swept Through*).

35. Bencke, "Irruption des Sakralen," 173–74.

36. Bencke, "Irruption des Sakralen," 177.

5.3. Subalternity and Syncretism in Religion

In secular Postcolonial Studies, religions are widely dismissed as alienating. Christianity in particular, which mostly came from outside in connection with colonialism and is still considered a Western or European (and therefore foreign) religion in many parts of the world, is suspected of never having given up its complicity with colonialism. Despite the critical attitudes that representatives of Christianity have shown toward colonialism throughout the centuries, its liberating potential is not valued very highly.[37]

Postcolonial theologies, on the other hand, are not concerned about religions in general,[38] but rather about the concrete consequences that certain religious practices and beliefs have for the lives of the subaltern. They point to both alienating and liberating aspects of religion, including Christianity. The question therefore arises as to the real effects of the concrete practice of religion:[39] Does it lead to devaluation or to the exclusion of certain people? Does it contribute to violence and impoverishment? Does it enable resistance and liberation? Does it promote self-confidence and respect for one's own dignity? For postcolonial theologians, these questions about the right practice usually develop a higher priority than questions about an orthodoxy determined by religious authorities.

Because of this direct approach to the experiences and practices of the subaltern, postcolonial theology also has a high regard for the religious constructions of the subalterns themselves. The subalterns often create their own religious beliefs, practices, and even institutions, albeit short-lived and transitory, but always dynamic and changeable. Such subaltern religious practices were and are ridiculed, despised, or actively opposed as popular piety, syncretism, superstition, or magic.

In many cultures worldwide, the subalterns understand themselves primarily as religious people and practice religion in different forms. These are often hybrid or mixed forms; or practices of different religious systems are practiced side by side. This understanding of the subaltern of themselves as religious people is taken up by postcolonial theology and opposed to the fundamental rejection of religion by other postcolonial theorists. By

---

37. See Castro Varela and Dhawan, *Postkoloniale Theorie*, 62–72.

38. For the difficulties that the use of the concept of religion itself entails, see above, 2.5.

39. See Silber, *Pluralität*, 109–33.

recognizing the religions of the subalterns, they should be freed from the devaluation of the past and, in this sense, be decolonized.

The people who were (and are) devalued by colonialism and coloniality come into particular focus with their religions and religious forms of expression. These religious practices are viewed as postcolonial religious alternatives that already exist, and not as deviations from an imagined or claimed pure form of a religion. It is not about folklorizing this religiosity or simply celebrating a desired diversity, but about recognizing the religious dignity, creativity, and subjectivity of the people who are affected by the devaluation of their religious practice.

Postcolonial theologians find a weighty argument for this practice of recognition in church history. The diversity, hybridity, and capacity to change of Christianity can already be found in the times of the New Testament. At that time, Christianity was integrated not only into the Hellenistic context but also into Syrian, Egyptian, and Asian cultures, as the US theologian William Dyrness points out. In this way, very different forms of expression of Christianity emerged, which could even differ in central issues such as Christology. Dyrness attributes these differences to cultural and contextual realities:

> These differences reflected significant local differences and cultural expectations, not ignorance and unbelief. Moreover, their oppression caused divisions that were to prove harmful to the advance of the Gospel.[40]

For Dyrness, at the time, the search for doctrinal unity led to division in the communion rather than dialogue and better understanding of Christianity. In his (self-critical) analysis, "this insistence on unity and intolerance of diversity . . . was a particularly Western characteristic"[41] of the Roman as opposed to the Byzantine Church. Christianity was weakened by this rejection of diversity and difference. Diversity, however, continued to live outside the confines of the Roman Empire, as pointed out by Lai Pan-chiu, who traces ancient Christianity in China and Southeast Asia, in a form which was considered heterodox.[42] For Lai, the survival of archaeological and symbolic traces of early Chinese-Nestorian Christianity points to a centuries-old Christian character of Chinese culture that goes back beyond colonialism. Chinese cultures thus have a possibility

---

40. Dyrness, "Listening for Fresh Voices," 34.
41. Dyrness, "Listening for Fresh Voices," 35.
42. See Lai, "Teaching Global Theology," 92–95.

of identifying with Christianity without colonialism. On the other hand, these traces make visible the fundamental diversity inherent in the different cultural forms of Christianity:

> A theology that was rejected or condemned as heresy by the Western Churches is not necessarily wrong or false. This is because this kind of condemnation might be based on misunderstanding or miscommunication, and might have been influenced by church politics, political ideology, and/or even racial biases. It is thus problematic to privilege the Western theological tradition against other theological traditions in a globalized world.[43]

This fundamental historical plurality of Christianity in different cultures and contexts goes hand in hand with the fact that it must be viewed as a religion that has always been hybrid and syncretistic, that has absorbed and transformed different religious traditions.[44] Even the European branch of Christianity has gone through a syncretistic and diverse history of development. In principle, today's syncretisms and hybridizations can expect the same respect and appreciation as the Christianity that has historically grown and is anchored in Europe, and must not be devalued as a deviation or falsification.

Two examples will help to broaden the idea of popular piety and syncretic religions to include the phenomena of dynamic and flexible expansion and reinterpretation of traditional religions. The first stems from US Hispanic Christianity and is presented by New York-born Latinx theologian Carmen Nanko-Fernández: "Flickering candles, prayer graffiti, plastic saints, and artificial roses, images of Guadalupe and assorted vírgenes all mark this unusual space as holy ground—an accident investigation site on a heavily trafficked Chicago thoroughfare."[45]

This "holy ground" is the space in front of a concrete wall in Chicago. On this wall in April 2005 "an apparition or a stain" became visible "depending on your perspective."[46] This apparition of the Virgin Mary began with the prayer of a young Latinx woman who was unable to attend church because of the double burden of school and work, but who wanted to enlist the Virgin's help with her final exams. This developed

43. Lai, "Teaching Global Theology," 94.

44. See Sugirtharajah, "Postkoloniale Untersuchung," 138–41; see above, 2.5.

45. Nanko-Fernández, "From Pájaro to Paraclete," 14. The letter x in the self-designation *Latinx* stands for gender-appropriate linguistic inclusion. The Spanish word *vírgenes* denotes figurines of the Virgin Mary.

46. Nanko-Fernández, "From Pájaro to Paraclete," 14.

into a lively pilgrimage business with prayers and miracles, holy images and candles. The graffiti attack of a Latinx Protestant who wanted to assail the Catholic faith in miracles, but was arrested by the police, and the subsequent overpainting executed by the transport authority triggered another Catholic grassroots action by a pair of professional cleaning personnel who restored the original apparition (or stain).

Nanko-Fernández interprets these expressions of popular piety as typical elements of Latinx spirituality: faith and religion can be experienced personally and are present in everyday life, be it as a perceptible accompaniment by the sacred, or through the interruption, the miraculous intervention of the sacred, which can be hoped and prayed for. Religion and spirituality not only belong in places of worship and other officially sacred spaces but are also effective in everyday life and help to be resilient and resistant.

For Nanko-Fernández, Latinx spirituality is characterized not only by the fact that it is popular piety but also by its very realistic reference to a challenging and dangerous everyday life. And this apparently applies not only to its Catholic variant. Nanko-Fernández uses a quote from Elizabeth Conde-Frazier, from an article on "Hispanic Protestant Spirituality," that "could just as easily apply to popular Catholicism":

> A distinctive emphasis of Protestant Hispanic spirituality is that it belongs to the people or the laity, as opposed to the ordained or professional clergy. It is not leisurely contemplation, but rather, the tools of survival and struggle for those who are part of the busy rhythms of work and life.[47]

Religious expressions of the subaltern may not only be "tools of survival and struggle" in a complex and hostile cultural context. Marcella Althaus-Reid shows how certain developments in Latin American popular religiosity can also be used as a means of political demonstration, representing not only political but also religious values. She describes the voluntary self-crucifixion of two Paraguayan hospital workers in the early twenty-first century.[48] Such self-crucifixions are used again and again for political purposes, not only in Latin America.

> Given that theology (and hermeneutics) are always contextual, popular crucifixions in Latin America are a twenty-first century complement to the gospel. . . . This does not diminish the

47. Nanko-Fernández, "From Pájaro to Paraclete," 13.
48. See Althaus-Reid, "Schlimmes Sterben," 524.

mystery and cruelty of the crucifixion, rather it brings us much closer to Calvary as a place of death and despair.[49]

In this way, death and despair can gain greater visibility in postcolonial society. At the same time, the act refers to the holiness of the victims of the present and to the hope they place in the silent God, but also in the "divine gestures of solidarity by and among the poor."[50]

Such drastic actions have their basis in a widespread and lived subaltern spirituality that feeds dynamically from hybrid sources. These include colonial Christianity as well as indigenous and Afro-American religions, globalized spiritualities of the New Age and non-Christian religions that are encountered, for example, through the media, as well as creative confrontations with current cultural and political challenges that require new religious and spiritual transformations.

The subaltern religions integrate these and other forms of spirituality and religion and transform themselves in an ongoing process of dialogue with the challenges of their contexts. As a result, they also develop some malformations and are susceptible to manipulation, exploitation, and alienation. Nonetheless, some expressions of these religions are quite capable of creating habitats and providing means for political struggle through hybridization, mimicry, and other strategies of resistance and resilience. Not only in anti-colonial struggles of liberation, but also in numerous postcolonial processes of change in everyday life, some of these phenomena prove to be spiritual paths that offer ways out of the shackles of coloniality using traditional cultural means.

5.4. Ecofeminist Theologies

Ecofeminism and theologies that refer to it cannot in every case be regarded as a postcolonial current or as a postcolonial theological alternative. However, ecofeminist theologies that arose in contexts affected by colonialism and its aftermath often incorporate post- and decolonial thinking. Often they also integrate Indigenous, Afro-American, and syncretistic notions, as discussed in the last two sections, and connect them with ecological and feminist concerns. Their explicit reference to ecofeminist theories and theologies is the reason for me to characterize them as an independent theological alternative in postcolonialism. Kwok Pui-lan

49. Althaus-Reid, "Schlimmes Sterben," 524.
50. Althaus-Reid, "Schlimmes Sterben," 524.

points out that there is a close similarity between ecofeminist thinking and ecological considerations in Gayatri Spivak's recent work that should—in her opinion—be further explored theologically.[51]

Ecofeminist theories have been discussed around the world since the mid-1970s.[52] They combine ecological and feminist theories and emphasize that both the depletion and destruction of nature and the oppression and exploitation of women have their roots in the same patriarchal attitude. Ecofeminisms of the Global South add to this the exploitation through colonialism and more accurately characterize the criticized patriarchy as a European-colonial mindset. With the German ecofeminist Maria Mies,[53] one can speak of "white man's three colonies"[54] or a triple colonization, the axes of which are interwoven and intertwined: the colonization of the South, of women, and of nature.

The British sociologist Mary Mellor distinguishes two basic currents in ecofeminism (without wanting to separate or oppose them): one of them works with a spiritual and cultural emphasis on a more profound understanding of human characteristics identified as feminine, while the other focuses on politics and socioeconomics and is interested in fundamental societal change. Although both currents criticize each other, they also demonstrate the breadth of ecofeminist approaches, which fundamentally encompass spirituality, culture, politics, and science.[55]

Ecofeminism generally opposes different kinds of dualism in European worldviews: antagonisms between culture and nature, humans and nature, male and female, reason and emotion, Europe and the rest of the world prevail widely. These dualisms are always accompanied by hierarchization and subordination. The perspectives of white, European, supposedly rational men on nature, on women, and on the colonies present structural similarities: the *other* is perceived as subordinate, inferior, in need of help, and destined to be exploited. In the view of ecofeminism, sexism, colonialism, and the exploitation of nature can only be overcome together, since they have common roots and multiple overlaps.

51. Kwok, "What Has Love to Do with It?," 35.

52. On ecofeminist theory and its history, see, e.g., Mellor, *Feminismo y ecología*, 58–94; Graneß et al., *Feministische Theorie*, 268–303; Gebara, *Intuiciones Ecofeministas*, 17–27.

53. See Graneß et al., *Feministische Theorie*, 285.

54. Mies and Shiva, *Ökofeminismus*, 70.

55. Mellor, *Feminismo y ecología*, 64.

Ecofeminist authors oppose these dualisms with the principle of interrelatedness, which has already been presented as an example of indigenous thought (see above, 5.2). The multiple reciprocal relationships between all things, between nature and humans, between people of different genders and different ethnic and cultural backgrounds is seen as a resource and an opportunity for growth. Postcolonial ecofeminist authors in particular often resort to existing indigenous narratives and concepts in order to illustrate the principle of interrelatedness using local means.

The Brazilian theologian and nun Ivone Gebara develops her ecofeminist theology from observing the intersections of patriarchy, colonialism, and the destruction of nature. According to her analysis, colonialism led not only to the subjugation of people, especially women, and to the exploitation and destruction of nature in the colonies, but also to alienation of the colonized people from their traditional worldview, not least through Christian mission.[56] The traditional communion with ancestors and the lively exchange with the rest of the natural world was given up in favor of a dualistic and apparently rational attitude of use and exploitation.

She contrasts this attitude with the belief in the interconnectedness and interdependence of all things, which she finds in both traditional indigenous worldviews and ecofeminism:

> The central point of ecofeminist epistemology is the interdependence between all elements that touch the human world. This is a statement . . . that comes from our own experience. It is enough that we pay close attention to what is happening to our body, for example, when we feel some kind of sharp pain. It seems that [then] even the most ordinary things are difficult to achieve.[57]

Gebara locates this interdependence not only in the world connected with humans but also in the rest of nature and in the entire cosmos: even inanimate nature, even the space where something or someone is located, are included in this connection; instead of separation between subject and object, which is one of the bases of Eurocentric rationality, there is an ecological community of everyone with everything.

Gebara also traces this ecological-cosmic commonality in anthropology. Everything in relation to the human being is connected with

---

56. Gebara, *Intuiciones Ecofeministas*, 83.

57. Gebara, *Intuiciones Ecofeministas*, 74.

everything else: body and spirit, soul and body, male and female, rational and emotional. Every subordination, every exclusion endangers this
reciprocal connectedness. Gebara therefore pays particular attention to
both human emotionality and the relationship between people in the
community.[58]

In addition, Gebara connects cosmic and anthropological interdependence: The unity and intensive connection of mankind and every
human being with all of nature must not be endangered by subordination
or objectification. She therefore writes about ecofeminism:

> It emphasizes the idea that we (all of creation) are one sacred
> body. Patriarchal systems, on the other hand, separate our social
> bodies into distinct parts, each ruling over the other.[59]

She even connects this comprehensive "sacred body of the earth
and the cosmos"[60] to God. A conception of God that describes God
as separate from the world and in contrast to humans, creation, or the
cosmic body must be overcome, according to her conviction, because
otherwise it would legitimize the human dominance of one over the
other or over nature. Rather, God is thought of as a power present in
creation, which also flows through human beings and pushes toward
the interconnectedness of all things. This power can be experienced as
"the God of everyday life."[61]

For Gebara, ecofeminism also has fundamental consequences for
theological method: she challenges the rigid, self-assured traditional
model of theology, that ultimately serves patriarchal rule, as the representation and explication of "eternal truths,"[62] and subjects it to a fundamental critique with the help of alternative theological methods. In the
foreword to the Spanish-language edition of her book on ecofeminist
theology, she writes:

> I dare to use the classical terms of "learned" science mixed
> with the everyday sighs, the trivial things of life, my observa-
> tions and thoughts. So do not expect to find clear and distinct
> concepts in perfect dialectics, nor discourses of exceptional

58. See Gebara, *Intuiciones Ecofeministas*, 86–87, 111–14.

59. Gebara, "Ökofeminismus," 422; Gebara, *Intuiciones Ecofeministas*, 74–77.

60. Gebara, *Intuiciones Ecofeministas*, 76.

61. Gebara, *Intuiciones Ecofeministas*, 143.

62. Gebara, *Intuiciones Ecofeministas*, 60; see 60–69.

rationality, with many quotations from classic, modern and postmodern authors.[63]

In addition to the "everyday sighs," like other postcolonial theologians, she also includes poems and stories, spontaneous interviews with neighbors, newspaper reports, and other everyday experiences in the elaboration of her theology.

Chammah Kaunda, an African theologian who teaches in South Korea, develops an "ecogender theology"[64] on the basis of ecofeminism, which integrates the experiences not only of women but also of men from a postcolonial perspective. He does not see this as a criticism of or opposition to ecofeminist theology, but as a meaningful addition that is necessary from an African point of view. Colonialism also alienated men from their relationship to nature, through patriarchal concepts of God: "By colonizing African ideas of God, the European missionaries and colonizers managed to introduce a different model of human relation to the environment."[65]

This colonial model entails the notion of a single God, detached from creation, who is also detached from the human being. As the alleged crown of creation, the human being in turn represents the sovereign God over against creation and detached from it. In the precolonial African world view, however, the conviction that all things were related to one another prevailed. Colonialism's devaluation of this worldview not only included African women in the dualistic devaluation on the part of the colonial masters but also alienated African men from their ancestral connection with nature:

> It is clear here that both women and men were involved and interconnected with the environment, which was not perceived as a self-sufficient entity on which human beings were to impose themselves but as a family member who took care of human beings and *vice versa*.[66]

Kaunda therefore interprets colonialism as "a ferocious attack on the essence of African humanity,"[67] on their cultures, religions, and their

---

63. Gebara, *Intuiciones Ecofeministas*, 15.

64. Kaunda, "Towards an African Ecogender Theology."

65. Kaunda, "Towards an African Ecogender Theology," 182.

66. Kaunda, "Towards an African Ecogender Theology," 191.

67. Kaunda, "Towards an African Ecogender Theology," 180.

lively "environmental kinship"[68] with everything in the world around them. Using two examples, he explicates how colonialism alienated men from agriculture and their living relationship with creation and obliged them to work in the mining industry, so that even food security was ultimately called into question.[69]

For Kaunda, however, it is possible to overcome the burden of colonialism through a postcolonial ecogender theology:

> The objective of constructing an African ecogender theology is to enable African women and men to understand some African present realities as continuation of colonial matrices of power.[70]

Kaunda is not concerned with anachronistically restoring a holistic relationship to nature that may have existed in the past. Rather, he advocates a hybridizing learning process in which the experiences and contexts of the present can enter into a constructive dialogue with the wisdom and worldview of the ancestors. For Kaunda, too, this has significant consequences for the Christian image of God. God can no longer be understood as someone who stands above creation, but rather "God is a member of the community of life":[71] "God is not above creation but through the Holy Spirit is within creation and with creation as an expression of unconditional love."[72]

5.5. Theology as Transgression: Queer Alternatives

What I wrote about ecofeminist theologies is also true for queer theologies: not all of them work in a postcolonial perspective, and, conversely, not all postcolonial theologies are queer theologies. However, there exist significant overlaps between the two perspectives, and these are the focus of this section. They show that the legacies of colonialism also include a devaluing of human sexuality manifested in practices other than heterosexual and that, conversely, this devaluation can be amplified under the influence of coloniality. This applies not least to ecclesiastical and

---

68. Kaunda, "Towards an African Ecogender Theology," 180.
69. See Kaunda, "Towards an African Ecogender Theology," 183–92.
70. Kaunda, "Towards an African Ecogender Theology," 180.
71. Kaunda, "Towards an African Ecogender Theology," 195.
72. Kaunda, "Towards an African Ecogender Theology," 196.

theological contexts, in which gender dualism and the higher valuing of heterosexual practice have a long tradition.

Stefanie Knauss and Carlos Mendoza-Álvarez note that, in the present, queer theories have expanded their methodological and content orientation

> from the focus on gender and sexuality in the West to the epistemic South to include ethnicity, race, class, disability and other categories used to classify and marginalize individuals in their intersectional interactions within the broader context of the decolonial project.[73]

They make this affirmation in their introduction to an issue of the journal *Concilium* under the heading "Becoming the queer body of Christ," which is dedicated to queer theologies and which is worth reading as a whole.

Queer theories go well beyond classical studies on homosexuality.[74] They not only criticize the devaluing of nonheterosexual practices but also analyze the social construction of sexuality as a whole and ask about the power interests that become visible behind essentializations of gender. Surpassing gender theories, queer studies criticize not only the cultural construction of social *gender*, but also that of biological *sex* and of concrete sexual practice. These categories are theorized as fundamentally plural, dynamic, and fluid properties; every definition or explanation of gender and sexual properties is challenged as to the concrete interests in power behind.[75] The Brazilian theologian André Musskopf writes of the term *queer* that it represents

> a theoretical perspective that surpasses and breaks away from the binary identity categories constructed and maintained by social movements and academics. It is not restricted to the process of the construction of identities related to sex, gender and sexuality, but is concerned with the multiple intersections of those with other markers, such as race and ethnicity, class, belief etc.[76]

---

73. Knauss and Mendoza-Álvarez, "Queer-Theorien," 493–94.

74. See de Jong-Kumru, *Postcolonial Feminist Theology*, 104–14; 149–52; Althaus-Reid, "Queer-Theorie," 90–91; Musskopf, "So queer," 498–503.

75. See Althaus-Reid and Isherwood, "Introduction," 5.

76. Musskopf, "So queer," 499–500.

In addition, this fundamental critique of gender constructions develops into a deep cultural critique that opposes processes of essentialization and othering, and resists exclusion and devaluation in many areas of society, in a fundamentally intersectional method of analysis. It is therefore understandable that there is a great openness to postcolonial theories that use similar means. This is also true of many theologies that are based on queer theories. Marcella Althaus-Reid and Lisa Isherwood therefore write:

> Queer theology is, then, a sexual theology with a difference: a passion for the marginalized. That passion is compassion, but also a commitment to social justice because there is a wider understanding of the human relationships involved.[77]

In the case of Althaus-Reid, Latin American and European feminist and liberation theological, postcolonial, and queer perspectives combine to form a very creative and sometimes explosive theology. For example, she also criticizes the practice of the Jesuit missionaries in the colonial settlements called *reductions*, which is usually viewed positively in history and in missiology. Her reason is that the Jesuits enforced strictly European ideas of heterosexual marriage and broke up polygamous and close family relationships to do so. She considers the traditional transgression of these strict rules by members of the indigenous population of the reductions not only as a legitimate resistance but as an alternative theological practice:

> It is important to reflect on this gesture of sexual defiance by the colonies as a challenge to Christian theology, because through it we can see how people perceived that Christian dogmas were to be destabilized by rebelling against the imposition of monogamy or heterosexual affective contracts. There is a methodological issue there, because that was the people's theology at the time, dismantling oppressive structures of the Church not by arguing about the Trinity, but by delegitimizing the Christian sexual project.[78]

In this case, the close connection between religious authority, colonial power, and sexual violence could be seen as a lever of resistance against oppression and alienation. Similarly, Althaus-Reid argues, that at the present time, opposition to rules of sexual propriety and

77. Althaus-Reid and Isherwood, "Introduction," 6.
78. Althaus-Reid, "Queer I Stand," 102.

transgression can be read in relation to opposition against religious, political, and social authority.

This trespassing or transgression is not a one-off affair, but takes on a fundamental character in queer theory and theology: newly achieved practices or newly constructed realities also require renewed transgression, otherwise they run the risk of essentialization. In this way, achieved goals of a queer practice can also lead to new oppressions and exclusions if they are not *queered* or transgressed again. André Musskopf therefore writes with reference to theology:

> In the production of queer theologies there is no fixed place, no closed space, no stable belonging. In each step, the condition of foreigner is evident, the condition of the one who is not in their place and who makes each place their own, open to communication, hybridization, entanglement, syncretism.[79]

The Mexican anthropologist and performance artist Lukas Avendaño uses an example from his own experience to show that cultural realities can be read both postcolonial and queer. In his interpretation, both perspectives are helpful and necessary for liberation and justice. Avendaño describes and theologically analyzes his own experience as a *muxe*, as a member of a "third sex."[80] In the Zapotec culture, since precolonial times, there has been a group of people who are neither male nor female; they take on important and specific roles and tasks in the community, are recognized by it in their sexual identity, and cultivate it themselves. Avendaño is aware that this is a geographically and contextually bound identity: "Muxe-ness, outside the isthmus of Tehuantepec, is 'polygamy,' 'incest,' 'desecration,' irrationality, superstition, paganism, idolatry, sodomy, and heinous sin."[81]

He regards his own being a *muxe* as a practice of resistance against colonial, capitalist, and religious exclusion. It has a broad social and personal meaning and is not limited to a sexual practice or identity. Through the Spanish concept of *gracia*, Avendaño connects this practice with both *gracefulness*, as a community-recognized value, and theological and religious *grace*. Precisely in its theological meaning as a *gift* or as a *mercy*, this grace can serve as an element of resistance

---

79. Musskopf, "So queer," 503.

80. See Avendaño, "Brief eines Indios." See also for a similar example from Asia: Culbertson and Maliko, "G-String-Tanga"; see also at the end of this section.

81. Avendaño, "Brief eines Indios," 527.

against merciless capitalism, which relies on competition and exchange value.[82] However, while colonialism and Christianity could not destroy the cultural form of being *muxe*, it is precisely now the encounter with the globalized LGBT community that threatens the cultural and sexual identity of the Zapotec *muxe* at present times.[83]

Gerald West (see above, 4.3) and the religious scholar Charlene van der Walt, who also teaches in South Africa, use queer methods to show that biblical narratives both contain queer elements themselves and release new aspects of meaning when they are read in a queer way.[84] They also do so from an African postcolonial perspective. In the Joseph story, therefore, what stands out from this combination of perspectives is Joseph's colorful coat and nondominant masculinity, which his brothers perceive as *different* and to which they respond with violence. In a queer interpretation of the creation of man and woman in Gen 2, they point out that it is not God, but the human being who decides whether one of the animals or the woman is a suitable companion for them, and wonder what would have happened if this first created human being had decided differently, or what this means for the case if a human being today takes the liberty to decide what his/her *suitable companionship* is.[85] Given the story of Sodom in Gen 18–19, they were asked by *ordinary readers* (see above, 4.3), if the text could not "be read as a story about the acceptance and welcoming of homosexuals into our churches."[86] It turns out that the texts can be read from these perspectives against the grain and in a certain way transgressively, thereby allowing for interpretations that can have a liberating and empowering effect.

Marcella Althaus-Reid gives another example of how the traditional theology of sin, grace, and redemption needs to be critiqued from both postcolonial and queer perspectives. In Althaus-Reid's interpretation, the colonial mission brought with it the definition of the sins from which it then purported to offer redemption. What was considered sin in the ecclesiastical-imperial center could be considered right by the people

---

82. See Avendaño, "Brief eines Indios," 526.

83. See Graul, "Dritte Geschlecht," 70–73. The abbreviation LGBT (lesbian, gay, bisexual, transgender) is used by Graul to refer to a plural and diverse global current of people who understand their sexual orientation as not heteronormative.

84. See West and van der Walt, "Queere (Eröffnung)."

85. West and van der Walt, "Queere (Eröffnung)," 587.

86. West and van der Walt, "Queere (Eröffnung)," 589.

who were to be colonized.[87] On the other hand, missionary theology could not recognize and acknowledge the holiness and closeness to God of the people it addressed, because it lacked the linguistic and methodical means to do so. "The paths of holiness outside the decent orders of imperial Christianity are meant to suffer the absence of God."[88]

Something similar happens with the "paths of holiness" of queer Christianity, which is also outside the "decent order." With the means of traditional theology, it cannot be recognized as a space of grace, but on the contrary, is considered a place separated from God:

> Queer spirituality is an affirmation of agency and a de-colonization process in itself. It can claim that God the Stranger amongst our community of strangers may have declared us, made us, irredeemably lost in the eyes of the church and Christian ethics, yet it is not we who are lost.[89]

Those declared "irredeemably lost" in this way regain the ability to act, to recognize, and to explain their closeness to God. In doing so they transcend the boundaries of seemingly decent theological language, and find a new mode of expression in which they fill the concepts with new life. For example, the theological abstraction of grace can become a "physical, concrete, sensual experience of faith" "that one cannot have in sermons and university courses."[90]

The language itself is stretched to its limits (and sometimes beyond) by the transgressivity of queer theologies. "This play, twist, pun with words and expressions is part of the epistemology and method" of queer theologies, writes André Musskopf.[91] Through alienations, distortions, caricatures, and other linguistic means, transgression is also practiced in the language itself in order to break through the habits to which traditional theologies cling and to question doctrines that are taken for granted. In this way, new theological spaces can open up, in which different rules apply and therefore other human and spiritual experiences can also be discussed.

---

87. See Althaus-Reid, *Queer God*, 164–66.

88. Althaus-Reid, *Queer God*, 165.

89. Althaus-Reid, *Queer God*, 165.

90. Althaus-Reid, "Gnade und Anderssein," 426.

91. Musskopf, "So queer," 497.

Philip Culbertson (USA) and Tavita Maliko (Samoa) dare a striking experiment in theological imagery after an anthropological-theological exploration of the *fa'afafine*, people of the third sex in Samoa:

> What could we understand of God, if we would speak meta-
> phorically of the Divine *Fa 'afafine*, the dweller in the interstices,
> instead of Father and Lord or Mother God? . . . The Divine
> *Fa 'afafine* could appear in men's or women's clothing, depend-
> ing on their whim, and we would be perfectly fine with that.
> . . . The Divine *Fa 'afafine* would haunt our churches, . . . sing-
> ing soprano in the choir and . . . rearranging the furniture, but
> also regularly being reviled from the pulpit because our human
> and cultural prejudices and expectations would get in their way.
> . . . In heaven, . . . he/she might meet Ninawaki, the woman
> with a man's heart who—according to the tales of the Blackfeet
> tribes—enjoys politics, likes to tell dirty jokes and owns horses.
> And then everything, everything would be fine.[92]

5.6. Postcolonial Neocolonialism?

An important form of self-criticism can often be found in Postcolonial Studies, when one's own discursive attitude is critically examined: With what right do non-indigenous scholars represent the worldviews and the wisdom of indigenous peoples in Western academic discourse? Can the reference of postcolonial intellectuals to non-Western knowledge itself take on colonial traits? Aren't postcolonial theologians who adopt theological alternatives from non-Western churches guilty of a kind of neocolonialism? Must we see a structural similarity between the use of indigenous epistemic resources by Western intellectuals and the exploi-tation of material resources by colonialism?

This self-critical question is a consequence of the difficulties raised by the concept of representation in postcolonialism (see 4.4 above). The problem is that taking sides with the subaltern, assuming their world views and learning from them, representing their interests in foreign forums and discourse contexts, and speaking on their behalf can turn into an overbearing, paternalistic claim to representation, which again sentences the subaltern to silence. Therefore, the question must also be asked at this point whether the assumption of alternatives, which is presented in this chapter as a postcolonial strategy, does not in fact

92. Culbertson and Maliko, "G-String-Tanga," 59–60.

represent an alienation and appropriation of the traditional intellectual property of a colonized people.

Ramón Grosfoguel, a sociologist from Puerto Rico who teaches in the United States, reviews an interview by Naomi Klein conducted with sociologist Leanne Betasamosake Simpson of the Mississauga Nishnaabeg indigenous people, both from Canada, to discuss this problem.[93] Grosfoguel (like Simpson) compares the appropriation of indigenous knowledge by non-indigenous people with the exploitation of natural resources under colonialism. They describe this exploitation of raw materials and its consequences under the keyword of extractivism, i.e., the destructive mining of these resources with the aim of appropriation and self-enrichment. This (neo)colonial extractivism is based on the Western idea of dualisms between humans and nature, center and periphery, colonized and colonizers, economy and environment, raw materials and industrial products, etc., which make it possible to ruthlessly exploit everything that is understood as the inferior part of these dualisms.[94]

Similarly, Simpson and Grosfoguel denounce "cognitive" (Simpson) and "epistemic extractivism" (Grosfoguel)[95] in cultural domains. Grosfoguel quotes a lengthy description of this type of exploitation from Simpson:

> When there was a push to bring traditional knowledge into environmental thinking . . . in the late 1980s, it was a very extractivist approach: "Let's take whatever teachings you might have that would help us right out of your context, right away from your knowledge holders, right out of your language, and integrate them into this assimilatory mindset." It's the idea that traditional knowledge and indigenous peoples have some sort of secret of how to live on the land in a non-exploitive way that broader society needs to appropriate. But the extractivist mindset isn't about having a conversation and having a dialogue and bringing in indigenous knowledge on the terms of indigenous peoples. It is very much about extracting whatever ideas scientists or environmentalists thought were good and assimilating it. . . . put it onto toilet paper and sell it to people.[96]

93. Grosfoguel, "Del extractivismo." Klein's interview with Simpson, titled "Dancing the World into Being," appeared in the *Yes!* magazine in 2013.

94. See Grosfoguel, "Del extractivismo," 35–38.

95. Grosfoguel, "Del extractivismo," 38.

96. Cited by Grosfoguel, "Del extractivismo," 38.

Grosfoguel comments that, similarly to industrial extractivism, indigenous ideas are taken out of their context in order to be able to adapt them to the interests of those in power. In this way, they lose their "political radicalism"[97] and the critical-alternative potential with which they could actually change the relationship between humans and nature in industrialized countries. Instead, they only serve to enrich a few and to increase the efficiency of a destructive way of life.

Grosfoguel denounces similar exploitative attitudes among some representatives of post- and decolonial thinking. Referring to the work of Bolivian sociologist Silvia Rivera Cusicanqui, he adopts her criticism of Walter Mignolo, who—according to Rivera—took over numerous ideas from other scholars in Asia and Latin America and from the indigenous peoples, without citing these sources, in order to use them in a depoliticized way and under his own name.[98] Grosfoguel not only quotes these allegations but also confirms them from his own experience of working with Mignolo. At the same time, he draws a fundamental conclusion that goes beyond Mignolo: "This reminds us that epistemic extractivism can occur even among authors who speak in the name of epistemological decolonization."[99]

Urgent questions arise concerning criteria and methods by which such unauthorized appropriation can be avoided and prevented. Grosfoguel once again quotes Leanne Betasamosake Simpson, who calls for

> a shift in mindset from seeing indigenous people as a resource to extract to seeing us as intelligent, articulate, relevant, living, breathing peoples and nations. I think that requires individuals and communities and people to develop fair and meaningful and authentic relationships with us.[100]

In this way, there can be an exchange that takes place more or less on an equal footing. "The alternative to extractivism is deep reciprocity,"[101] says Simpson. Whether that reciprocity can exist or how it can be established in practice are quite different questions, that, however, arise immediately, following these considerations. Especially in

97. Grosfoguel, "Del extractivismo," 38.

98. Grosfoguel, "Del extractivismo," 39; he refers to Rivera's 2010 book *Ch'ixinakak utxiwa: una reflexión sobre prácticas y discursos descolonizadores.*

99. Grosfoguel, "Del extractivismo," 40. See also a consideration below in section 5.7.

100. Cited by Grosfoguel, "Del extractivismo," 41.

101. Cited by Grosfoguel, "Del extractivismo," 41.

postcolonial contexts, relationships based on "deep reciprocity" are the exception rather than the rule.

Jione Havea discusses examples of the difficulties that arise when this "deep reciprocity" comes into play in the context of climate change and its effects on the people of Oceania, whose habitat, the islands, is threatened by rising sea levels. Havea observes critically that the interests of these people are not really represented at international conferences, because often they are not even themselves invited to these conferences. Their interests are represented by others who have a different worldview than they do and therefore cannot really represent the attitudes of the islanders. In recent times, for example, the ocean has often been viewed and feared "as enemy" or as a threat and not—as in the oceanic-indigenous understanding—"as context, home and who we are."[102]

However, living together with the ocean for centuries, the inhabitants of the islands have developed mutual relationships that do not have to turn into hostility simply because of a new climatic situation. Rather, for many indigenous people in this region, "the ocean is also a place of refuge and survival."[103] On the other hand, Havea makes the critical observation that islanders, when able to attend international conferences, all too often represent the interests of their sponsors and that "this means that they consequently neglect the interests, voices and faces of their own people."[104]

The "deep reciprocity" that Simpson rightly demands, the equal footing desired by Grosfoguel that could liberate us from the danger of cognitive extractivism are—as in these examples—themselves threatened by the prevailing global economic inequality and by coloniality, which make it difficult or impossible for indigenous people to speak for themselves. Postcolonial scholars and theologians must ask themselves all the more self-critically, in which cases our taking up of non-Western alternative epistemic and theological concepts and programs lacks respect for the authors and owners of these alternatives and becomes extractivism. Because, as Leanne Simpson says: "Actually, extracting is stealing. It is taking without consent, without thought, care or even knowledge of the impacts on the other living things in that environment."[105] This is related to both the exploitation of natural resources and cognitive extractivism.

102. Havea, "Politics of Climate Change," 352–53.
103. Havea, "Politics of Climate Change," 353.
104. Havea, "Politics of Climate Change," 353.
105. Cited by Grosfoguel, "Del extractivismo," 42.

In this context, postcolonial theory uses the concept of cultural appropriation. While in anthropology this term largely describes the mutual appropriation and transformation of cultural facts and objects when different cultures meet, in postcolonial contexts it usually describes processes of the unjustified, illicit, and ruthless takeover of cultural elements by the more powerful party.[106] Such processes of cultural appropriation are often at the service of the commercialization of cultural products; in part, however, they can also serve other purposes, such as the stabilization of rule or the devaluation of the subjugated culture, for example through their folklorization.

Cognitive extractivism and cultural appropriation are dangers in postcolonial practice, which are critically and self-critically reflected in particular by theologians who deal with the consequences of the centuries-old practice of subjugation, alienation, and exploitation associated with colonization and mission. Adopting theological alternatives to colonialism can itself contribute to the exploitation, disenfranchisement, and marginalization of the subaltern.

Whether it is possible to avoid cognitive extractivism in dialogue with alternative forms of knowledge can be guaranteed neither by adhering to certain methodical steps nor by observing certain criteria. Rather, the question whether epistemic extractivism is present or not will always be disputed and the subject of negotiations. The critical and contentious discussion of this question can be part of a negotiation process in which possible epistemic alternatives intervene in and transform the learning process of academic theologies.

The dialogue in "deep reciprocity" intended by Simpson and Grosfoguel can also be conflictual if the institutional framework conditions produce inequality, as is regularly the case in postcolonial contexts. Even allowing for and dealing with such conflicts does not guarantee that cognitive extractivism will be avoided. On the contrary, the real risk which such extractivist approaches pose to postcolonial academic learning in theology must always lead to deepened self-criticism, which includes the willingness to accept criticism of one's own position. The solution strategies that Mark Lewis Taylor proposes for the postcolonial dilemma of representation in theology (see above, 4.4) can be helpful on this path.

---

106. See Ashcroft et al., *Post-Colonial Studies*, 15–17. The concept of *appropriation* is understood here as the critical and resistant taking up of cultural elements of the colonizing culture by the colonized.

5.7. Beyond the Frontier: Conclusion

The dialogue with and learning from non-Western alternatives that characterize postcolonial theologies serve to liberate theology and Christianity in general from their coloniality and to overcome the legacy of colonialism altogether. This dialogue is not aimed at promoting or creating alternatives in order to achieve a cultural diversity that would be desirable for its own sake. Rather, the goal is to disrupt power relations that are expressed in and maintained through cultural and interreligious devaluation and exclusion. The proposition is not only to resist these power relations but also to show the possibility and the existence of real alternatives to coloniality. When such alternatives are embraced and asserted, it can help end injustice, reverse oppression, and overcome exclusion.

Alternatives may have existed for centuries or be newly created in the course of decolonization. There is no fundamental difference in that. In both cases, the colonial and postcolonial encounter and the decolonizing dynamic trigger processes of hybridization that accelerate cultural transformation and intercultural exchange. Alternatives in the sense of this chapter are not static identities that could assert themselves alongside a colonial or postcolonial identity that is presented as just as static, but are in dynamic negotiations with the prevailing worldviews, even through resistance and conscious distinction. Indigenous or precolonial cultures always have continued to transform over the centuries of colonialism, especially through contact, conflict, and resistance to it.

Like queer theologies (see above, 5.5), postcolonial theologies also make use of the practices of trespassing, transgression, and violation of boundaries. They feel free to use alternatives to the practices that are common and considered right in Europe, the West, or in the various colonial and ecclesiastical centers of the present, both in terms of method and content as well as with regard to the subjects and places of theology. The goal is not theological anarchy, but the liberation of theology[107] aiming at an improvement of its task of serving people's experiences, needs, and liberating practices.

Postcolonial theologies are often consciously based on indigenous, Afro-American, popular, syncretistic, and other knowledge that has been devalued by the power structures of Western colonization. In this way, they also draw attention to the fact that there have always been other,

---

107. The notion of a *liberation of theology* is principally based on Juan Luis Segundo, who understood liberation theology as a fundamental process of restructuring or *liberation* of theology as a whole: Segundo, *Liberation of Theology*.

alternative knowledge systems and knowledge practices beyond the frontiers of Western and colonial knowledge.

This practice of crossing frontiers and criticizing colonial knowledge through epistemic alternatives is very well theorized by Walter Mignolo's concept of *border thinking* and taken up by many authors.

The appeal to Mignolo gives rise to a not unimportant side note: at first glance, it seems to be a contradiction given that Mignolo was mentioned in the last section as an example of the neocolonial appropriation of alternative thinking but is now treated as an advocate for attention to alternatives. In a more detailed analysis, however, this case provides an example of how, in postcolonial thinking, a self-critical distinction can be made between the theoretical contributions of an author and his concrete practice. A valuable element of theory proposed by an author (especially one as widely recognized as Mignolo) remains helpful and is not invalidated by contrary practice. Rather, it can even serve as an element of criticism of just such a neocolonial practice—even if by the same author. The contradiction here is therefore between a certain theory and a certain practice and does not have to be generalized and personalized to the person of Mignolo.

Walter Mignolo's border thinking is interested in the (epistemic) regions beyond the frontiers of knowledge drawn by colonial culture. These frontiers do not exist within knowledge itself but are imposed on knowledge by colonial interests. Beyond these borderlines, a "different space" opens up, an alternative space: "the space of decolonial thinking,"[108] a space in which one can think and conceive differently than in the space of the Western way of thinking. For those who can free themselves from the commitment to Western thinking, new possibilities of knowledge and practice open up:

> Now, once you delink, where do you go? You have to go to the reservoir of ways of life and modes of thinking that have been disqualified by a Christian theology that has proliferated since the Renaissance in the form of secular philosophy and sciences. For, you cannot find your way out in the reservoir of modernity (Greece, Rome, the Renaissance, the Enlightenment). If you go there, you remain chained to the illusion that there is no other way of thinking, acting and living.[109]

For Mignolo, the "reservoir of modernity" possesses this universalistic tendency to deny, devalue, and despise alternatives to oneself.

---

108. Mignolo, "Pensamiento decolonial," 33.

109. Mignolo, *Habitar la frontera*, 177; on *detachment* or *delinking*, see above, 4.7.

At the same time, however, modernity, according to Mignolo, lacks the self-critical attitude that would allow for real change on the scale needed for an escape from coloniality. Rather, the self-centeredness of Eurocentric modernity means that one's own way of thinking is accepted as the only possible basis for self-criticism and for development. Parallels to the well-known dictum of the American feminist Audre Lorde, "The master's tools will never dismantle the master's house,"[110] are striking.

Border thinking makes it possible to seize alternative tools. Mignolo cites two historical examples in which it becomes clear how alternative thinking from across the frontier may engage Western thinking critically via processes of hybridization and can thus fundamentally question it from within: Ottobah Cugoano, a former British slave born in Ghana, and the Peruvian indigenous chronicler Felipe Huamán Poma de Ayala each embraced Christianity and used colonial languages and idioms, but expressed their own values and beliefs within that thinking and were thus able to criticize the European colonizers from the outside, so to speak.[111]

Similarly, Dietmar Müßig's analysis of the *Virgin in the Silver Mountain*,[112] which has been presented above in section 4.6, can be seen as a practice of border thinking: the hybrid image from colonial times shows, on the surface, a depiction of the Virgin Mary, but at the same time refers to traditional Andean religiosity, whose public display and practice had been devalued by colonialism. In the form of this apparently Christian or Catholic painting, however, spiritual worship of these Andean religious elements becomes possible.

These historical examples indicate that these alternatives exist outside of Western thought, and that they have been used to criticize colonialism since the beginning of the colonial era. This critical border thinking also takes on different hybrid forms in the present, but under the current social conditions it often no longer acts as covertly and in camouflaged form as was necessary, for reasons of self-protection, in colonial times. Rather, the epistemological alternatives to coloniality are presented and discussed much more openly today.

For Mignolo, the deconstructive and constructive practices of postcolonial thinking culminate in this border thinking and complement each other. He writes:

110. Lorde, *Sister Outsider*, 110.

111. Mignolo, *Habitar la frontera*, 373–74; see Mignolo, "Pensamiento decolonial," 28–29.

112. Müßig, *Jungfrau im Silberberg*.

> This is neither more nor less than the central question of being
> and thinking on the border, in the exteriority of racism and impe-
> rial epistemic patriarchy in which the rules of good knowledge,
> of good living, of racial and sexual hierarchies, of heterosexual
> normativity and white superiority were made. For those who are
> not willing to inhabit the imperial house and are committed to
> re-existing (and not just resisting, as the Afro-Colombian artist
> and thinker Adolfo Albán . . . reminded us), border epistemology
> is *one* option, which is also the decolonial option.[113]

The examples presented in this chapter from alternative readings
of the Bible, from indigenous, Afro-American, and subaltern theologies, as well as from ecofeminist and queer theologies, make this clear:
Postcolonial theologies criticize discourse practices and power relations in traditional theology in order to free it from the coloniality in
which it has been trapped over the centuries by colonial Eurocentrism.
They resist coloniality and the current power relations that rely on it to
end the bondage and inequality that prevail in postcolonial contexts.
To do this, they resort to alternatives, because these are the ones that
have the ability to overcome coloniality from the outside, and because
their use gives back to the people, who live according to the epistemic
premises of these alternatives, the right to further develop their own
cultural, religious, and political identity.

These alternatives from beyond the colonial frontiers of knowledge
are capable of fundamentally questioning the coloniality of knowledge
in theology, as well as pointing out ways of overcoming it. However, the
colonial exclusion, devaluation, and demonization of these alternatives,
especially through colonial theology and mission, still represent an
obstacle that is difficult to overcome, especially for theology itself. Honest perception and open discussion of the alternatives which surface in
theological border thinking always require a self-critical willingness to
correction and conversion.

Openness to border thinking and the epistemic alternatives that
have resisted colonialism for centuries provides postcolonial theologies
with the necessary space for negotiation and transformative action. Such
border spaces or *third spaces* of postcolonial theological negotiation create
innovative, experimental, and dynamic foundations for a theology that
can contribute to the liberation from the captivity of coloniality.

---

113. Mignolo, *Habitar la frontera*, 374 (emphasis in the original).

6.

Offense or Stimulus for Western Theologies?

CAN WESTERN THEOLOGIES BECOME postcolonial theologies? Can theologians in Europe (and the West) learn something from the postcolonial theologies of the world? Can we let ourselves be inspired to change, maybe even to repent? In what way is this already happening? What challenges arise from postcolonial theologies for the production of Western theologies? As the last step in this introduction to postcolonial theologies, the important question of this chapter is: which learning and reflection processes can be initiated by postcolonial theologies in the West?[1]

It is important to consider not only how this is possible but also what obstacles stand in the way of these processes in the West itself. In German-speaking academia, for instance, it is not a matter of course to let oneself be stimulated or prompted by a theological current that deals critically with fundamental theological, methodical, and epistemological prerequisites.

Judith Gruber narrates various experiences from everyday academic life to show in an exemplary way how in Germany and Austria intercultural, feminist, liberation theological, and also postcolonial theologies are considered by the dominant discourse "provincial," "not representative,"

---

1. This book was written for an academic context in the West, especially in Germany. The importance of a discussion of potential learning processes in the West stems from this context.

and "marginal,"[2] and thus can easily be ignored. She reports anecdotally about the supposedly well-intentioned advice that for her next project she "should not choose a marginal topic again, such as intercultural theology, but should now really turn to a core topic of theology."[3]

Such experiences can easily be repeated when someone attempts to include liberating, feminist, or intercultural theologies in theological journals, editorials, curricula, or scholarly résumés. Especially when such theologies appear with a critical claim to traditional Western forms of discourse, as is the case with postcolonial theologies, such criticism is often brushed aside with reference to an apparent marginality of contextual theologies compared to the assumed universality of Western theology.

Gruber, on the other hand, points out "that a tendency to ignore power relations in theological knowledge production represents in itself a powerful moment in German-language discourse."[4] Sciences are obviously very reluctant to address power relations in these self-same sciences. According to Gruber, a central impetus that emanates from postcolonial theologies is precisely to uncover and critically question these power relations—concerning the marginalization not only of non-Western theological designs but also of them.

With reference to Gayatri Spivak, Gruber explains that it is a question of criticizing the form of power in the production of theological knowledge as a whole and not of presenting one particular theological method as wrong and another as right. Rather, the fact and the structures of these power relations should be uncovered and made transparent, instead of being kept secret and thus made untouchable. On the other hand, postcolonial theologies would not allow these power constellations to disappear or replace them, but would deal with them constructively and conceptually and thus introduce themselves into a power relationship within this exercise of power.[5]

In this respect, postcolonial theologies represent a central and fundamental impetus for the production and teaching of theology in Europe and should not become a matter among others or an intellectual pastime alongside supposedly academic theology. Rather, they challenge it at a fundamental level, criticize its epistemological foundations, and

---

2. Gruber, "Wider die Entinnerung," 24; see 23–25.
3. Gruber, "Wider die Entinnerung," 23.
4. Gruber, "Wider die Entinnerung," 24.
5. Gruber, "Wider die Entinnerung," 26.

ask about the power relations in academia and the society on which it is based.

Postcolonial theologies take a perspective from the outside on Western epistemology and intellectual history. This is a critical look that comes from the experience of being devalued and exploited. With this critical view from the outside, postcolonial theologies do not want to raise the moral index finger toward Western theologies, but rather recognize, analyze, and resist their own dependencies on the coloniality of theology. They are not concerned with correcting European or Western theologies, but with liberating themselves from them. It is crucial for their reception in Europe that this attitude should be perceived, understood, and accepted.

Postcolonial theologies look at Europe from the outside, even when they use European traditions of knowledge and even when—as in some cases—they are developed and taught in European universities. With the help of border thinking (see above, 5.7) they distance themselves from European traditions and face them (self-)critically, even if they enter into a discourse with them. However, they do not evade the postcolonial dilemma described by Dipesh Chakrabarty, according to which Western traditions of thought are "as indispensable as they are insufficient" for postcolonialism.[6]

At the same time, it is not possible to counter the critical postcolonial view of the West with the argument that the West is sufficiently self-critical or that individual elements of postcolonial criticism have already been voiced in Western academia. Postcolonial theologies construct *alternatives* to the theological tradition which they have exposed as an ally of colonialism. That is why they are not primarily concerned with Western theologies being able to learn something or to transform, but with the freedom to work out theological alternatives in resistance to them. In my opinion, if we in Europe want to learn from this, this can only happen with an attitude of conversion and self-criticism. Otherwise, European theologies remain at risk of their traditional arrogance. In a similar vein, the German theologian and social ethicist Michelle Becka argues

> that the findings of postcolonial studies make it possible to
> question something or set something in motion—or could
> set it in motion if these inquiries were allowed. . . . The
> first requirement would be to acknowledge the findings of

6. Cited by Kerner, *Postkoloniale Theorien*, 76. See above, 1.2.

postcolonial theories and studies and take them seriously. The second requirement would be to reconsider our own positions, terms, and concepts of ethics.[7]

In addition to these two requirements, further fundamental questions are presented in this chapter. However, this, too, is not done conclusively and with any claim to completeness. Rather, this chapter serves like the others as an introduction to the critical inquiries made by postcolonial theologies to Western theologies. Within certain theological disciplines and individual topics, as well as from different postcolonial perspectives, present in this book, more detailed, more precise, and more concrete critical examinations can be made.

European and Western theologies must not be understood as a unified, homogeneous structure, even if they are sometimes mentioned collectively in this chapter. The criticism of *the* European theology by postcolonial theologians often addresses an undifferentiated and essentialist caricature of the diverse panorama of European theologies. One or another Western theological current or "school"[8] may be more or less affected by postcolonial critique. Nevertheless, it is important to deal with these criticisms thoroughly and in a joint dialogue in order to attain a postcolonial conversion of theology as a whole. As has already become apparent several times in this book, it will also be evident on the following pages that in some cases this is already being seriously discussed in Western academia.

Within postcolonial theologies, as has been shown in the last chapters, there exist different focal points, due to concrete contextual challenges and individual problems of colonial theologies, which complement and enrich each other. Thus they reflect the necessary breadth and complexity of postcolonial critical strategies. From these varied focal points can result quite different challenges for Western theologies. The following overview serves to take an initial look at the panorama of necessary and possible learning and dialogue strategies in Europe.[9]

7. Becka, "Welcher (V)Erkenntnisgewinn?," 138.

8. For a critique of "schools" in the European theological tradition see Estermann, *Südwind*, 169.

9. The structuring of this panorama into the following four points differs in detail from the division of chapters in this book and also from the structure of this chapter. These differences serve to counteract the impression that postcolonial theologies can be described in clear systematics. There are different focal points in each case, but they are often related to one another and complement one another. They can be systematized in different ways. A uniform system would cover up this inner dynamic and interweaving

- **Postcolonial theologies analyze and critique the different dimensions of coloniality.** This critique takes place along various axes of discursive, cultural, social, economic, and political power relations, and encourages Western theologies to face their own colonial history and to take a critical look at ongoing power relations and claims to power in theological and ecclesiastical practice.

- **Postcolonial theologies describe a "decolonial turn"[10] toward the direction of the perspectives of those negatively affected by colonialism.** This turning point affects theology as a whole, from its epistemological assumptions to its topics of discussion and the way they are discussed, to a shift with regard to the subjects and places of theology. The decolonial turn therefore challenges Western theologies, too, to take a position.

- **Postcolonial theologies resist coloniality in society and theology.** This resistance can also take the form of contradiction or resistance to traditional theologies and church structures. Western theologies are called upon to deal constructively with this resistance.

- **Postcolonial theologies take up non-Western theological and epistemic alternatives in order to construct theology in a hybridizing dialogue with them in such a way that it is able to overcome colonialism.** For Western theologies, this creates the impetus to be inspired and criticized by non-Western knowledge and border thinking.

From a European or Western perspective, these impulses can lead to similar and, in detail, complementary theological strategies that are necessary to learn from the challenges posed by postcolonial theologies and to work toward manifold global ways of postcolonial thinking and theology.

It is crucial for theologians in Europe to recognize that we stand—not as persons but as reflective subjects in a particular theological and epistemological tradition—on the side of those responsible for colonialism and coloniality. The theologies that shape us, or at least shaped us in our theological studies, are directly connected to the theology that also legitimized colonialism and, in some cases, made it possible in the first place. The postcolonial critiques of theology and the resistance against

and rob postcolonial thinking of its creativity and *indiscipline*.

10. See the title of the book by Castro-Gómez and Grosfoguel, *Giro decolonial*.

colonial theologies must be translated into self-criticism by European and Western theologians and will again meet with resistance and contradiction within the West itself.

In the same way, the challenge to learn from non-Western alternatives will be met with resistance in Europe and the West. But the task is not to replace European and Western theologies. Rather, in my view, postcolonial theologies challenge us to listen to one another, to learn together, to take mutual criticism seriously, and to open up *third spaces* from which theologies can grow, which overcome the various forms of coloniality on all continents, i.e., also in Europe.

6.1. Facing Our Own Colonial Past

Europe is the continent from which most of the colonialism of the last five centuries emanated.[11] In most cases, colonial expansion projects that originated on this continent considered Christian were also linked to missionary efforts or were in some other way legitimized theologically. As we have seen, in many respects European theology drew from ideologies that also promoted colonialism, such as in the areas of exegesis, theology of religions, and missiology. No one who deals with postcolonial theologies in Europe can avoid a self-critical examination of their own colonial history.

Postcolonial Studies and theologies hold up a mirror to European-influenced theologies that do not always show what one would like to see in the mirror. Rather, these mirrors reveal historical dark sides that have consequences up to the present. To withdraw from this mirror, to cover it up or simply not to look at it, is neither scientifically honest nor practicable, since postcolonialism already plays a much larger role globally than its reception in theology would suggest. It is therefore necessary to deal with these historical dark sides and to develop the willingness to draw appropriate conclusions from this encounter.

It must be taken into account that the dependency and influence between colonialism and theology in the past was twofold, mutual: On

---

11. Of course it is also possible to speak of colonial expansion efforts in the case of the USA, Russia, China, Japan, and other great powers in past and present. Their policies of expansion and colonization are sometimes also explicitly examined in postcolonial studies and theologies. In none of these cases, however, did such colonial projects as in Europe lead to global empires with effects that lasted for centuries, as in the case of Spain, Portugal, England, and France.

the one hand, the development of the humanities, which promoted colonialism and were promoted by it, also influenced theology. European
claims to superiority also shaped its theology and led, for example, to the
fact that Bible scholars in Europe felt justified to (supposedly) improve the
canonical Bible text through rearrangements and corrections (see above,
2.4). Such erroneous developments in theology—which also led to hidden
racism, universal claims, and centralism—can be broken up and corrected
through an attentive study of postcolonial theologies.

On the other hand, colonial theology also provided arguments
and beliefs that justified colonialism and established cultural domination. The conviction that mission could be practiced through conquest
and cultural assimilation destroyed numerous indigenous cultures,
religions, and peoples, and in some cases even explicitly placed itself at
the service of colonial subjugation (see above, 3.3). The patriarchy that
prevailed in Europe was exported to the colonized countries as an apparently Christian way of life and still influences gender relations in numerous cultures around the world, including the Christian theologies
of Europe. Similarly, postcolonial theologies reveal how many different
theological beliefs that belong to the traditional European canon have
favored relations of domination and exploitation in the past and still act
in this way even in the present, through constellations of coloniality for
example in the image of God and the human-nature relationship (see
above, 3.1, 3.2, and 5.4).

The criticism of the colonial practice of Christian missions from Europe also affects the church practice up to the present, insofar as mission
is often still directed centrally from Europe (or North America). As early
as the late 1980s, in the context of preparing for the commemoration of
the five hundred years of the conquest of America in 1992, the Brazilian
bishop Pedro Casaldáliga brought up a connection between decolonization and *de-evangelization*:

> To "de-evangelize" would mean to decolonize evangelization.
> . . . For us in Latin America, de-evangelizing what has been
> badly evangelized can only mean setting out for full social,
> political, economic, cultural, holistic liberation; it can only
> mean evangelizing the historical processes of our peoples in
> a liberating way.[12]

12. Casaldáliga, *Auf der Suche*, 13–14.

The provocative talk of *de-evangelization* does not mean turning away from the practice of evangelization, which is the central task of the church for Casaldáliga, but a turning point, a conversion in evangelization, combined with the correction of the incorrect forms that accumulated—and in some cases also strengthened—over the five hundred years of wrong or faulty evangelization.

Of course, *de-evangelization* also affects the protagonists of this first, faulty or "bad" (as Casaldáliga writes) evangelization, and that is the church in Europe: In this sense, it too must "de-evangelize," i.e., uncover those practices and theologies and criticize what has led to colonialist evangelization, turn away from them, and convert itself in this sense. Listening to the criticisms of postcolonial theologies can be an important element in this endeavor.

In addition to the already mentioned biblical studies, theology of religions, and missiology, there are many other areas in which postcolonial criticism could lead to a conversion of European theology and church practice. Everyday racism in society and the church is a pressing problem, which is often expressed in the exclusion of and/or condescension toward people from the continents of the South (and Asia), but also, for example, in a sometimes still paternalistic attitude in development aid and church partnerships. Even priests and theologians who come to Europe from southern countries are often affected by this racism, which moreover sometimes fatally overlaps with clericalism, especially in Catholic contexts.

Lack of critical self-awareness of a global responsibility that has grown out of colonialism can also be observed (in Germany) in the role assigned to ecclesial communities that do not use German as their first language. They are often tolerated in a friendly manner, but rarely recognized as part of the universal church or even as congregations with equal rights in their own German local church.

In addition, many other individual examples can be given in which postcolonial thinking could lead to a conversion: availability of non-Western literature in theological libraries, invitation of postcolonial scholars, attention to artefacts stolen during the colonial period in mission museums and archives (and their return), critical review of the honors bestowed on past (and present) missionaries and scholars, etc.

While looking at these specific and important consequences in everyday practice, the need for fundamental corrections in theological epistemology concerning questions of universalism, essentialism, and Eurocentrism must not be forgotten. The following section deals with this.

6.2. European Theologies as Contextual Theologies

Many European theologians will find it difficult to accept that European theologies are contextual theologies (see above, 2.4). The idea that European intellectual history has contributed to a universal clarification of what it means to be human and that philosophy and theology in Europe can be used to say something generally valid about the relationship between God, humans, and the world is all too deeply rooted. At the same time, it conceals the fact that this universalist claim of European thinking has favored and legitimized colonialism's policy of expansion and subjugation.

Following Dipesh Chakrabarty,[13] therefore, a *provincialization* not only of Europe but also of European theology in particular is more than necessary. In this context, provinciality does not mean anything derogatory or negative, but the recognition of the contextuality of European theologies, their internal plurality, and, positively, the achievements of European theologies in dialogue with the respective concrete contextual challenges in dealing with the *signs of the times* of these contexts. Josef Estermann nevertheless recognizes that this renewed self-understanding of European theologies as contextual demands "an epistemological act of humility in the sense that the unspoken or explicitly defended 'universality' of one's own Western-European tradition is put up for discussion."[14]

As early as 1980, Elmar Klinger described the profound importance of the question whether European theology can recognize itself as European in view of the confrontation with Latin American theology of liberation:

> To call our theology a European one reveals . . . a critical stance. This criticism refers to it as a theology . . . . It concerns the horizon in which it stands and takes place. For the horizon of the interpretation of contemporary European theology is the being of humans in general, their existence, while the horizon of interpretation of contemporary Latin American theology is humans' practical being, their existence, insofar as through it

13. See Chakrabarty, *Provincializing Europe.*
14. Estermann, *Südwind,* 158.

they shape the world in which they live. This difference possesses ontological character.[15]

In Klinger's eyes, the claim of European theology to be able to speak for "the being of humans in general" makes it incapable of speaking for specific challenges of being human—be it in Europe or in the world. However, the specific, culturally mediated relationship of theology to its context, to the "world in which they live," and the will to shape it, is linked to the reference to "humans' practical being" in Latin American theology. Only a contextual theology can contribute to shaping the world.

In addition to the claim of universalism, European theology still needs to critically assess the conviction that the concepts of European theology and philosophy can adequately and accurately describe facts of the world and of theology everywhere and in general. For this reason, postcolonial theologies have criticized tendencies toward essentialism in European theology up to the present. For example, Ivone Gebara writes: "We must . . . give up the idea of the Eurocentrism of knowledge and the various imperialist dominances over the truths maintained by the Western world."[16]

This is because truths, especially the "so-called eternal truths"[17] repeatedly criticized by Gebara, are a means of domination. They can justify and secure the rule of men over women, of colonial powers over the colonized, of people over nature. However, such "eternal truths" are still a constant, especially in Western, and not least in Catholic, theology. Gebara correlates them with essentialism:

> One of the most important features of patriarchal epistemology at work in Christian theology is its essentialist character. . . . We are always seeking the essentially constitutive core of each thing, or the way God intended each being to be.[18]

She opposes this essentialist understanding of knowledge and truth with a decidedly contextual one, in which she explicitly includes traditional European theology: "The act of knowledge is contextual; it is conditioned by gender, space, and time."[19] The act of knowledge that leads to a theology which sees itself as universal and valid everywhere has

15. Klinger, "Theologie im Horizont," 48.
16. Gebara, *Intuiciones Ecofeministas*, 42; see 35–89.
17. Gebara, *Intuiciones Ecofeministas*, 60.
18. Gebara, *Intuiciones Ecofeministas*, 51.
19. Gebara, *Intuiciones Ecofeministas*, 47.

this characteristic, and—if it is not disclosed—produces exclusive power relationships that are legitimized theologically.

The alternative to this is a fundamentally dynamic pluralism of truths that does justice to the changing character of contexts and subjects. Gebara writes: "A different path than that of classical Greek philosophy and Thomistic philosophy is possible, even if we may then swim in the sea of uncertainties and doctrinal discussions."[20]

This alternative does not mean constructing or postulating alternative absolute truths, but abandoning the essentialist absoluteness of truth and theological reasoning, in favor of a fundamentally discursive, dynamic, and contextual plurality. If such truths contradict each other, this is no proof of the falsehood of one of them, but a challenge to a more in-depth debate that does not lose sight of the power asymmetries between the different subjects of this debate.[21]

Marcella Althaus-Reid describes another important aspect of the problem of a theology that does not want to recognize its contextual dependency and raises universal claims. She points out that the academic theology presented as universal—without explicitly naming European or Western theology—is incomplete and one-sided because it does not respect, silences, or excludes certain subjects from the discussion:

> Taking otherness on board means also facing the hermeneutical and ecclesiastical challenges of a subject who, up to now, has been forced to remain silent. A subject so defined is unrepresented and unrepresentable in a system that practices symbolic and *a priori* exclusion. Thus, we are facing not only a thematic change, but a radical critique of existing theological methods that are incomplete because they cut out the living potential of the other from our midst.[22]

While Althaus-Reid specifically has queer subjects in mind, which she provocatively describes here as "unrepresentable," she shows that European theology has repeatedly ignored *other* subjects as *unrepresentable*. Above all, subjects whose humanity was not fully recognized (women, indigenous people, Africans . . .) were considered unrepresentable in theology in the past. To this day, however, this still often applies to persons who do not meet a certain Western standard of

---

20. Gebara, *Intuiciones Ecofeministas*, 69. Estermann, *Südwind*, 160, speaks in this context in a similar way of the need to "dehellenize theology."

21. See Silber, *Pluralität*, 78–97.

22. Althaus-Reid, "Queer-Theorie," 88.

education, who work in "unrepresentable" jobs, or who have a cultural background other than that of Central Europe or North America. Numerous discussions in academic committees, editorial offices, and educational institutions, which have to deal with the assumed "unrepresentability" of certain people, so that they are not invited as authors or lecturers, testify to the broad validity of Althaus-Reid's verdict up to the present day. However, this Eurocentric, patriarchal, white, or heteronormative arrogance leads, according to Althaus-Reid's criticism, to an incomplete and thus flawed theology.

Other examples of the effects of essentialism in European theology can be found in the changing description of religions (see above, 2.5), in the essentializing interpretation of the various national, ethnic, cultural, and political groups in the Bible (see, e.g., 2.1), and last but not least in the pictorial representations of biblical scenes as well as of universal church relationships. How are women, how are people in or from Africa, Asia, and Latin America portrayed? In what roles do they appear relative to white, European people, especially men? In 2020, in the German media, it was very widely discussed whether a king figure with blackened skin should be present at nativity scenes or in traditional groups of star singers.[23] This debate brought some of these problems to the consciousness of the congregations and the general church public in German-speaking countries for the first time. This debate also made it very clear how rocky the road to a postcolonial or decolonizing turn in church and theology can be, especially when it comes to very practical questions.

6.3. Uncovering Positions of Power

The analysis of power issues is central to the development of postcolonial theologies. However, it tends to be neglected in European theologies, especially when it comes to the self-critical examination of one's own positions of power.[24] Challenges from postcolonial theologies that refer to the normative power of interpretation of European theologies and church

23. Star singers are small groups, mainly of children, who—following a German tradition—dress on January 6 as the biblical three kings and visit the houses of the parish or village. They pray for the blessing of the houses and families, collect money for poor children, and sometimes sing Christmas carols. There is an ongoing polemic if one of the kings may paint their face black.

24. See, for example, the interdisciplinary discussion of the question of power in Prüller-Jagenteufel et al., *Macht und Machtkritik*.

structures are therefore often ignored, rejected, or played down. Without acknowledging one's own power, both in the form of past colonial power and in current ecclesiastical, academic, and economic power structures, it is difficult or even impossible to take up critical suggestions from postcolonial theologies and work with them constructively.

On the one hand, the problem consists in the coloniality of power in European theological spaces, i.e., in structures, discourses, and other power relations that remain active since the colonial era and still claim validity. On the other hand, the coloniality of power has already been transformed in such a way, in Europe, too, through the checkered history of colonialism, state independence, and neocolonialism, that it is often no longer easy to recognize.

Finally, ecclesiastical and theological transformations, especially in the twentieth century, have altered power relations, so that their coloniality is often concealed and covered up today. Criticisms from outside, which are put forward (e.g.) by postcolonial theologies, can help to self-critically examine and transform these structures. The financial dependence of former colonies on Western states and churches, which is reflected in development aid and missionary projects, and the European (Roman) centralism that prevails in the Catholic Church in particular, have also created new power structures that are often directly linked to colonialism, even if this is not immediately apparent from the external form.

In the field of theology, a dominance of European and North American theological concepts and approaches can be observed worldwide, which often does not promote the development of contextual, local theologies on other continents, but rather prevents them. Last but not least, scholarships for doctoral students and other young theological professionals from postcolonial countries in Germany (or in other Western countries) lead to a deepening and renewal of these power relations, if they are associated with an overvaluation of European theological or philosophical traditions and thus—often implicitly—with a devaluation of non-European ways of thinking. Fortunately, there have been some signs of reevaluation of this problem in recent decades.

In the context of development cooperation, the German theologian Claudia Jahnel criticizes "naivety with regard to the dynamics of power and the distribution of power."[25] In my opinion, this can also be applied

25. Jahnel, "'Religion kann Brücken bauen,'" 316.

to theological dependencies: Jahnel complains that power relations are not sufficiently addressed or are even obscured, and that their importance with regard to the effectiveness of individual measures is underestimated. Above all, those who have a strategic advantage in power relationships often have the least interest in uncovering and clarifying these relationships. Postcolonial criticism must therefore encourage Western, European theologians to recognize and acknowledge their own positions of power. In this way it may become possible to transform relationships and institutional structures of power and liberate them from coloniality.

Jahnel emphasizes—again in the area of development cooperation, but this also applies to other power constellations—the need for increased attention to

> the agency of those affected, their ability and authority in shaping their own ideas for the future. If these ideas and cultural concepts contradict Western ideas about development and quality of life (as well as Western economic interests), the issue of development becomes an issue of power.[26]

Resistance on the part of those affected, the assertion of their own interests and ideas, and criticism of the power of colonialism can therefore provoke resistance from those who are privileged in the global balance of power. The difficulties encountered in the reception of postcolonial criticism in European theologies can be explained, at least in part, by such processes of undesired exposure of power relations.

Similarly, the South African-Swiss theologian David N. Field observes critically,

> that the churches and the theology of the socio-economic centers continue to control Christianity worldwide. The reason for this lies precisely in the fact that they are freed from the struggle for survival that characterizes the lives of the exploited and forgotten. However, if God's intervention rearranges the centers and the margins, we must realize that those of us who are part of the elite are at a grave theological disadvantage.[27]

With the term *elite* he expressly refers to the elites of the formerly colonized countries, which still benefit from the unequal distribution of power and money. These socioeconomic inequalities and injustices are in a complex reciprocal relationship with the relationships of political,

26. Jahnel, "'Future,'" 187.
27. Field, "Über das (Wieder-)Zentrieren," 245.

ecclesiastical, and also theological power. At the same time, they find themselves in open conflict with the theological conviction that the peripheries are favored through "the intervention of God" in the incarnation. Field therefore understands theology as a whole as a "pilgrimage to the margins,"[28] to which the theologies of the centers are also called. For Field, "the pilgrimage begins where we accept our complicity with the powers that forget, oppress, and exclude, and where we accept our responsibility for it."[29]

The uncovering and critical acceptance of positions of power thus includes the critique of one's own "complicity" with the socioeconomic and political relationships of injustice and exploitation, which, like other structures of colonial power, are covered up and played down, especially in the countries of Europe historically most responsible for the rise of colonialism. Theology and the churches as a whole must also acknowledge their "share in a common complicity,"[30] as Field writes, and work together with those affected to ensure that the coloniality of international economic, political, and church relations can be overcome.

This is also a theological task. It promotes a transformation of the doctrines about God, about the church, about Jesus, about salvation, and about the (global) communion in the Holy Spirit, which does justice to the critiques made in postcolonial theologies of these (and other) central statements of Christianity. In this transformation, the real power relations in the world must become signs of the times, through which these traditional doctrines can be recontextualized. At the same time, turning to these *signs of the times* allows alternative theological considerations based on the experience of formerly colonized churches to come into their own. A Western theology transformed and converted in such a way can undertake the "pilgrimage" (Field) of becoming itself a postcolonial theology. Global power issues such as peace, ecology, migration, racism, the world economy, multilateralism, etc. can then lead to a theological exposure to, recognition of, and confrontation with their own positions of power. Doing this, Western theologies could demonstrate their relevance and effectiveness in a completely new way.

---

28. Field, "Über das (Wieder-)Zentrieren," 246.

29. Field, "Über das (Wieder-)Zentrieren," 246.

30. Field, "Über das (Wieder-)Zentrieren," 246.

6.4. Admitting Alternatives and Resistance

In the fifth chapter, it was made clear that the concern of postcolonial theologies is to develop alternatives to traditional theological thinking, which not only deal critically with the colonial inheritance of theology but also develop constructive strategies to overcome colonialism, or at least to transform it. These alternatives concern not only the forms of expression of theology but also its content and methods, as well as the epistemology underpinning it.

Precolonial, indigenous ways of thinking are an important starting point in these alternative designs, as are syncretistic and popular forms of expression of the religions and cultures of those who suffer primarily from colonialism and coloniality. The aim is not—as explained in more detail above—a resurgence of old cults and religions, but in the first place, processes of negotiation and hybridization through which these non-Western traditions, which have also changed and developed over the centuries of colonialism (and in contact with it), can be brought into a new creative dialogue with the challenges of the present and with current critical theories (such as feminism, ecology, religious pluralism, etc.).

Postcolonial theologies also challenge Western theologies in Europe and elsewhere to engage with these theological and epistemological alternatives. It is not enough to value them as contextual theologies while minimizing or ignoring their importance outside those contexts. They pose a fundamental challenge to the question of the contextuality of theology as a whole: Are there contextual and non-contextual theologies? Can European theology claim to be not just European in the sense of a contextual theology, but *theology* in a general, universal sense? Is there a universal theology, and do contextual theologies derive from it? Or do we need to understand that the contextuality of contextual theologies challenges European theology to examine its own relationships to the European context, to recognize the plurality of these European contexts and thus also the plurality of European theologies, and, in a certain sense, to recognize its own provinciality?[31]

In addition to this turning away from European universalism and its claims to hegemony—which have changed since the colonial era but are still influential in many respects, especially in theology—postcolonial theological alternatives from the South also challenge Western theologies in terms of content and methods. These should *learn* from alternative

31. In the sense of Chakrabarty, *Provincializing*; see above, 2.4 and 6.2.

theological approaches and also be *willing* to learn more. Here, the "act of humility" brought into play by Josef Estermann[32] is necessary in order to achieve openness and a willingness to learn after centuries of colonial exclusion of or disdain for indigenous worldviews and spiritualities. This openness does not demand a complete abandonment of one's own tradition and positions but the will to expose them to postcolonial criticism and examine them in the light of alternative concepts.

Western theologies should open up much more than in the past to an attitude of global community, kinship, and solidarity. This includes not to devalue theological ideas and practices from other continents as an echo or imitation of one's own, but rather recognizing them for their independence and intrinsic value, even and especially when they deviate from European theological standpoints or even contradict them. This idea of a global theological community, in which not everyone always represents the same point of view, but all views are appreciated and respected and can contribute to the common learning process of global Christianity, corresponds to a community-oriented ecclesiology and can serve as a model for global processes of theological dialogue.

In the process of negotiation, dialogue, and hybridization, it may also be necessary for Western theologians to correct their own theological ideas, to see them in a new light or from new perspectives, to transform them collectively or to supplement them creatively. Postcolonial processes and strategies such as mimicry, hybridization, syncretism, alienation, ambivalence, and many others can help theologies in the West to enter into a creative and constructive dialogue with postcolonial theological alternatives.

A danger in this process that should not be underestimated is that of appropriation. The balance of power in the postcolonial age does not allow a real dialogue among equals to take place in theology. Taking up theological alternatives from the South can therefore very quickly be misunderstood as cultural appropriation, or actually be it.[33] This risk requires a constant attitude of self-criticism and an honest openness to actual criticism from the South from Western theologies that want to engage in learning from postcolonialism.

After centuries of colonial exploitation and heteronomy, many people in the Global South are not very confident that these European

---

32. Estermann, *Südwind*, 158.

33. See above, 5.6.

attitudes could have changed and not only resist theological hegemony but also express distrust in a willingness to engage in dialogue and unusual openness.

This resistance may seem irrational to us, but it has to do with subject assertion, self-esteem, and dignity that have been challenged or impeded by colonialism and coloniality for centuries.[34] It reflects the violence that emanated from Europe through colonialism and is still having a profound effect today. Such resistance cannot simply be explained away or dissolved, least of all by European actors, who would thereby place themselves in the tradition of other resistance breakers from Europe in history.

In this respect, postcolonial resistance must be taken up self-critically by theologians in the West and translated into a transformation of their own theological standpoints. The resistance against European theologies has a prophetic character. It cannot simply be devalued as backwardness, closed-mindedness, and hostility to progress. On the contrary, representatives of Western theologies who are willing to engage in dialogue must ask themselves whether the resistance they encounter, which can look very differently in each case, should rather be taken as a serious impetus for self-criticism and one's own conversion. Even the refusal or breaking off of a dialogue and other conflictive expressions of resistance may have this prophetic character, or develop it.

Postcolonial resistance to Western theologies can help bring about a change of perspective and theological conversion in Western theology itself, if theologians are willing to take up the critical challenges posed by postcolonial theologies and use them as a spur to the recontextualization of theology in a postcolonial world. On the other hand, such an acceptance of postcolonial positions and alternatives by critical Western theologians, moreover, will also lead to resistance and objection in Western academia and theology. It is not easy to draw the attention of a hegemonic theology to its own hegemony.

Postcolonial theological alternatives will not only transform and develop themselves in this sort of tense and conflict-laden negotiation process but will also contribute to a necessary new evangelization of European theologies. The willingness to allow theological alternatives could promote a fundamentally renewed theological reflection on the fundamental contextuality, plurality, and historicity of theology as a whole and

34. See above, 4.7.

accelerate the farewell to theological concepts of a truth that develops linearly or even is eternally valid. Through such an epistemological transformation process, European theologies would be increasingly able to accept alternatives from the Global South and willingly learn from them.

6.5 Partisan and (Therefore) Relevant

Closely related to the topic of the contextuality of theology is the question of its partisanship. If one extends Fernando Segovia's distinction between "position" and "interest"[35] from reading the Bible to theology as a whole, it becomes clear that the position of a theologian in a specific context will correspond to a specific interest, which shapes their theological reflection in this context.

Politically committed theologies such as liberation theology have always pointed out that, in principle, every theology is guided by such a partisan interest, even those theologies that see themselves as neutral and do not reflect about and explicate their own interests.[36] The refusal to analyze one's own position and interests only leads to a concealment and negation of these interests, which can become all the more powerful as a result (see above, 3.7). Western theologies need to accept the challenge of postcolonial criticism not only to face the contextuality of their own arguments but also to confront their hidden or open interests and to include these in their own discourse in a self-critical manner.

Beyond these fundamental considerations, postcolonial theologies very often make it clear that they speak from the perspective and in the interests of certain subaltern groups, whereby the problem of representation, which has already been discussed several times, must be considered (see above, 4.4). As the examples in previous chapters have illustrated, the subaltern can include groups and people affected by racism, sexism, economic exploitation, and other aftermaths of colonialism, as well as multiple overlapping axes of oppression. The partisanship of postcolonial theologies for these people therefore bears a great resemblance to the option for the poor rediscovered in liberation theology,[37] especially in its more developed, intersectionally profiled version, which has been documented since the 1990s.

35. See Segovia, "Grenzüberschreitendes Interpretieren," 88; see above, 4.1.

36. See Kern, *Theologie der Befreiung*, 15; Segundo, *Liberation of Theology*, 69–96.

37. See Silber, *Pluralität*, 18–21; 30–39; 43–57; 69–74.

From a postcolonial theological perspective, Mark L. Taylor shows that such partisanship and a pronounced interest in the (self-)liberation of the subaltern is necessary in order to escape an arbitrariness of viewpoints and interests. As already quoted, he calls this partisanship of theology "a liberating *a priori.*"[38] Much like the option for the poor in liberation theology, this explicit interest in human liberation predates theological analysis and argument; it is already there a priori. Juan Luis Segundo calls the option for the poor a *hermeneutic key* and ascribes spiritual qualities to it. The partisanship of theology is explained as a consequence of the partisanship of God, who also takes sides with the poor, the subaltern, and the oppressed. It does not *arise from* theological reflection, but *lays the foundations for* it.[39]

The British theologian Chris Shannahan can stand as an example for a consistent implementation of the methods of postcolonial and liberation theology in the cultural and social contexts of Europe. Using these theoretical instruments of the Global South, he researches the social situation of two global European cities (London and Birmingham) and draws attention to cultural differences and plurality, intercultural relationships and questions of power, dynamics and liquidity of urban structures, global economic interdependencies and the public and individual meaning of religions. An important consequence of his study is that it requires the option for the poor as a prerequisite: to be liberating, such a theological study must be rooted in "the divine bias to the oppressed" and at the same time in the "recognition of the complexity of urban oppression and its diminution of the oppressor as well as the oppressed."[40]

The partisanship and perspectivity of postcolonial theologies give rise to their political and public relevance. These theologies start from specific contexts and analyze theological power relations and discursive hegemonies with the aim of changing them. Shannahan takes the concept of the *organic intellectual* from Gustavo Gutiérrez (and Gutiérrez, in turn, from Antonio Gramsci) and applies it to theologians who are part of a social movement and struggle with others to transform unjust structures.[41] This participation in the social movements and their strug-

38. Taylor, "Subalternität und Fürsprache," 283; see above, 4.4.

39. See Silber, *Pluralität*, 18–21; *Befreiung der Kulturen*, 112–28.

40. Shannahan, *Voices from the Borderland*, 227. The "diminution" refers to the obfuscation and belittlement of oppressive structures and the multiple relationships between the oppressor and the oppressed.

41. Shannahan, *Voices from the Borderland*, 12.

gles explicitly reveals the partisanship of theology. At the same time, this commitment can help ensure that the values discussed in theology can also be practiced in public.

This explicit recourse to theology's need of relevance distinguishes postcolonial theology from many intercultural theologies. Without intending to generalize this difference, intercultural theologies often are more interested in mutual understanding and comprehension of one another, but often do not consider questions of power or even methodologically exclude them. While intercultural theologies often work more descriptively and hermeneutically, postcolonial theologies focus on the transformative character of their discourses. Coloniality and its many different faces of oppression, exploitation, and exclusion should be changed, if possible overcome, in order to come as close as possible to the basic equality of all people and the justice and solidarity that is to be striven for between them.

Andreas Nehring and Simon Wiesgickl therefore speak of the "interventionist character"[42] of postcolonial theologies: they intend to change something, to intervene in social, cultural, and thus also religious structures, and to transform them:

> Postcolonial theologies, according to their claim, do not deal with their subjects for their own sake, but to critically question cultural, social, political and economic conditions, and thus also religious relationships, to break them open and to trigger controversies that help to change structures.[43]

For Namsoon Kang, this also has liberating consequences within theology and the churches:

> Postcolonial and feminist theology works *both within* and *beyond* the religious heritage—scripture, tradition, doctrine, creed, etc.—to preserve the liberating legacy while deconstructing, dissolving, and debunking the legacies that generate, perpetuate, justify, and sanctify imperial power over everyday life visibly and invisibly, internally and externally, personally and institutionally.[44]

---

42. Nehring and Tielesch, "Theologie und Postkolonialismus," 23. They adopt this term from Andreas Hepp and Carsten Winter, *Cultural Studies Kontroverse*.

43. Nehring and Tielesch, "Theologie und Postkolonialismus," 24.

44. Kang, "Jenseits," 188.

However, their relevance is not limited to the churches. In collaboration with other social and political movements, be they postcolonial, feminist, anti-racist, or others, the transformative or interventionist relevance of postcolonial theologies aims at overcoming coloniality in society in general. The relevance of postcolonial theologies arises from their partisanship. Their contextual localization and political positioning enable these theologies to play a relevant role in the transformation of coloniality.

In Europe, this relevance must also explicitly focus on the transformation of one's own context, because European cultures are also shaped by colonialism. However, this coloniality cannot simply be determined in parallel or as a mirror image of the coloniality of the former subjugated states. Rather, extremely complex and interlinked relationships between the cultural imprints of the various participants in the complex system of colonialism must be considered. The investigation of the colonial character of the culture of Europe as the continent from which the colonialism of the past centuries largely originated, therefore, represents an important challenge that postcolonialism in general addresses to European scholarship.

In this way, the coloniality of European theologies can also be criticized and transformed. After centuries of colonialism and the lack of a sufficient theological examination of it, this coloniality reduces the relevance of theology. This applies to both Western and colonial contexts. In order to be relevant and effective, it is necessary for Western theologies to self-critically reflect on and disclose their own partisanship. In individual cases, an explicit and clear repositioning toward the option for the poor may be necessary. It would be a spiritual basis for a relevant new evangelization of theology.

6.6. Liberating Uncertainties: Conclusion

Postcolonial theologies can be unsettling. This is definitely their aim. The certainty, clarity, and unambiguity which is often striven for in Western theologies is perceived in the formerly colonized states and their churches as rigidity, petrification, and continued hegemony. An uncertainty in this hegemony can lead to liberation. But any liberation that would establish a new structure of power, a new clarity and security, would run the risk of being oppressive, exclusive, and exploitative again.

For this reason, the strategy of insecurity in postcolonial theologies has at least in part a fundamental character. This character is only *partial* because uncertainty, ambiguity, and insecurity are not declared to be the norm or the goal either: uncertainty serves as a means of liberation, to resolve rigidities or to break them open, to question rule and resist it, to trespass boundaries and thereby transform them into contact zones.

It is therefore not a problem for postcolonial theologies if they appear contradictory or inconsistent, but rather even a mark of quality. But they are not concerned with simply dissolving all certainties and consistencies. Rather, the goal is to gain a deeper sensitivity for othering and petrifying discourse practices, to analyze hidden and taboo structures of domination, to counteract these processes when they curtail people's life opportunities and to show alternatives that can lead to liberated relationships beyond the limits of colonial thought and action.

Postcolonialism, in this sense, is more of a method than a matter, more of a toolbox than a material. Postcolonial theologies do not claim to be recognized as another theological subject in Western academia, but intend to fundamentally unsettle theological methods and thus to challenge and transform them as a whole.

One of the fundamental criticisms leveled at European theologies by postcolonial theologies is the exclusivity of hegemonic theological discourses. Any fundamental criticism of this hegemony runs the risk of being labeled as ideological or as unscientific. For Judith Gruber, postcolonial theologies have the power to hold up a mirror to the theologies of Europe (of the *center* in her terminology) and to unsettle them, because they "are those counter-narratives that break up the dominant power structure of silence, with which the center de-members its powerfulness and obscures its provinciality."[45]

Resistance to this *de-membrance* involves the active memory of colonialism and its interrelationships with theology, mission, and church. To this end, it is important to analyze and criticize the relationship between today's theology and that of the colonial era. It also includes an unclouded view of one's own contextual and historical limitations: Europe's cultural hegemony over most of the world was (and is) the consequence of military and economic dominance and cannot be justified by the alleged superiority of European intellectual history and its supposed

---

45. Gruber, "Wider die Entinnerung," 28. For her, the concept of "de-membering" ("Entinnerung") denotes the refusal to allow remembrance (here specifically of colonialism) and the eradication and prohibition of memory.

universal validity. Rather, European thinking must rediscover a positive, appreciative awareness of its own provinciality.

The unsettling of Western theologies by postcolonialism also affects the global academic and world church power structures that are valid in the present. Due to the growing ecclesiastical and theological independence of the formerly colonized peoples, which can be observed in the worldwide ecumenical movement in the decades since the Second World War,[46] European and North American dominance is being increasingly called into question and is maintained, in the present, first of all by economic dependencies. Ecclesiastical and theological networks, which are increasingly being formed worldwide and which in some cases at most include North Atlantic actors as equals, transform these power structures in many different ways.

Judith Gruber therefore sums up:

> A postcolonial change of perspective exposes theology to a massive epistemological uncertainty. It brings to light a fundamental ambivalence that runs through the Christian tradition: it is never simply given or completed, but a *discourse in which hegemonic and subversive narratives struggle for interpretive sovereignty under asymmetric conditions of power.*[47]

This unsettling ambivalence may paralyze, but it can also lead to a fundamental liberation of theology. The departure from the hegemonic claim to sole representation and from the exclusive unambiguity of theology also sets it free to begin developing a diverse, dynamic, lively, and relevant theology again and again, and together with others. A European theology that is aware of its own colonial and hegemonic significance can be integrated into the mutual learning community of the plural and contradictory theological processes of the world.

In this community, perspectives can change, alternatives and resistance can be taken up and addressed, discourse practices and power structures can be put to the test. This chance of a genuine world church theology as a negotiation, as a dynamic and contradictory process, as mutual insecurity and as fruitful lack of discipline can free theology to political and pastoral, cultural and social relevance. In this liberation lies the promise of vitality, which is combined with the postcolonial insecurity.

46. See Pittl, "Anspruch und Wirklichkeit."
47. Gruber, "Wider die Entinnerung," 36 (emphasis in the original).

Inconsistency and resistance, indiscipline and the apparent lack of seriousness of postcolonial theologies open up a new experience of *joy* in theology. Postcolonial theologies often develop in a playful, lively, passionate, joyful way: they work with unfamiliar narratives, images, and metaphors, arrive at unexpected (intermediate) results, and question the familiar in surprising ways. They experiment with language games, methods, and dialogue partners, and the experiments do not always succeed, so that wrong turns, snaking courses, and processes of conversion are also part of the productive experiences of theology. Theology is not anymore produced for eternity, but *ad experimentum*, provisionally, until the next idea through which a new question can be opened. This sometimes makes it difficult to follow the course of a postcolonial theological debate. However, an overview shows that the diversity, complexity, and ambiguity of the different postcolonial theological discourses worldwide create a picture of a colorful, lively, and very relevant theology, which also contains numerous stimuli and starting points for theologies in the West.

"Offense or stimulus for Western theologies?" is the title of this chapter: Do Western theologies take offense at postcolonial theologies, or do they accept stimuli from them? Do we allow the liberating uncertainty that comes from postcolonial and decolonial movements, studies, and theories, or do we feel insecure and react with resistance? It will not be possible to give a uniform and conclusive answer here. In any case, I am convinced that postcolonial theologies offer an opportunity for conversion for theologians in the West. They can give stimuli if we don't take offense at them, but allow ourselves to be prodded—the passive form is also important here: part of the necessary conversion process is to accept that Westerners are not the protagonists in this process. The unsettling by postcolonial theologies and the promise of provincialization of Europe it represents can free us for new, postcolonial ways of doing theology.

Epilogue: Farewell to the Colonial Goods Store

IN THE *HESSENPARK*, AN open-air museum in the German Taunus mountains near Frankfurt, there is also a colonial goods store.[1] In addition to many other historical relics and furnishings that can evoke vivid memories in visitors over fifty, it contains also racist and colonialist depictions on packaging and advertising materials. It is good when objects like these have a place in a museum where they can remind visitors that colonialism has led to a distorted and degrading representation and treatment of humans, countries, and peoples. However, they should no longer have a place in stores and supermarkets where we actually still shop.

The same applies to "colonial goods" in theology. Critical studies of postcolonialism can guide us to identify these colonial relics, label them appropriately, and, if possible, discard them. They bring to our attention some colonial goods still in stock in mainstream European theology, some of which have been identified, analyzed, and critiqued in this introduction. Beyond this introduction, numerous other remnants of colonialism are described in postcolonial theologies, and others may still be uncovered in the future.

1. In Germany, a colonial goods store originally sold primarily goods imported from the colonies. Later on, the term was generalized to retailers of nonperishable goods. The concept ceased to be in practical use in the second half of the twentieth century.

199

Even if there are no longer any colonial goods stores today, colonial goods such as coffee and tea, bananas, and cocoa still enrich our menu. Global fair-trade networks have been trying for decades to even out the global economic power imbalance to the point where these products no longer contribute to the level of exploitation of the people who grow them as has happened in the past, even if fair global trade relations still are a very long way off.

Transferred to theology, this means that a kind of "fair trade" is also needed here, fair theological and church relations, solidarity, and the recognition of theological reflection of the Global South. As discussed in the last chapter, the idea of conscious or fair consumption is not enough. Rather, there must be a reversal of our theological habits of consumption and production. The metaphor of fair-trade chocolate can be misleading here.

Local and municipal self-sufficiency in theology also deserves strengthening and consideration. Europe is an area of many different contexts, in which very different theologies have to be produced for local use. Regional preferences and tastes, as well as local traditions and needs, must take precedence over global standardization. Theological home cultivation, horticulture, and subsistence farming should also be encouraged and appreciated.

In any case, the supermarket selling the same branded theological goods around the world does not represent the alternative to the (theological) colonial goods stores that postcolonial theologies advocate. Rather, it is much more exciting and fun for the traveler to taste regional products at each local market and to be inspired by them. Some of these can also be linked and exchanged via international networks, thereby stimulating imitation, mixing, and hybridization.

Colonial subjugation and exploitation, however, need to be restricted to the museum. We may be permitted to cultivate nostalgic memories there. But the museum is also a place of critical and transformative memory, an impetus for conversion. The colonial goods store therefore does not have to be demolished and destroyed. Rather, it can become a memorial, a place of remembrance, a memorial that does not let the past fall into oblivion, but instead promotes the renewal processes of the present as a dangerous, constructive, liberating memory.

Theological coloniality belongs in the museum just as much as the colonial goods store. It should no longer determine theological, pastoral, and ecclesiastical practice. Critical inventory and labeling are necessary and unavoidable here. Postcolonial theologies provide us with numerous methods and tools to do this. We should accept this challenge.

Appendix

Short Biographies

A FEW OF THE most important authors of postcolonial theologies are presented here. The selection is primarily aimed to illustrate the diversity and breadth of this global, dynamic current. It cannot be complete, nor does it claim to contain only the "most important" representatives. With the references to the selected literature (see also the literature overviews in the first chapter and the bibliography) and the websites indicated for most of the authors, the research can be easily continued.

Marcella Althaus-Reid

Marcella María Althaus-Reid (1952–2009) was born in Rosario, Argentina, and studied Protestant theology in Buenos Aires. She worked in slums in Scotland and did her doctorate at the University of St. Andrews there on the influence of Paul Ricoeur on liberation theology. She was professor of contextual theology at the University of Edinburgh. Her book *Indecent Theology* (2000) made her world-famous as a representative of a feminist-queer liberation theology. In her work, which is primarily oriented toward theological methodology and hermeneutics, she combined attention to contextuality, gender issues, sexuality, and poverty with questions of decolonization of theology.

Important Publications

- *Indecent Theology. Theological Perversions in Sex, Gender and Politics.* London: Routledge, 2000.
- *The Queer God.* London: Routledge, 2003.
- *From Feminist Theology to Indecent Theology: Readings on Poverty, Sexual Identity and God.* London: SCM, 2004.
- (With Lisa Isherwood, eds.) *The Sexual Theologian: Essays on Sex, God and Politics.* London: T. & T. Clark, 2004.
- (With Ivan Petrella and Luiz Carlos Susin, eds.) *Another Possible World (Reclaiming Liberation Theology).* London: SCM, 2007.

Musa Dube

Musa Wenkosi Dube (born 1964 in Botswana) is professor of New Testament at the Candler School of Theology (USA). She formerly worked as professor at the University of Botswana. She studied in Great Britain and the USA, among other places, and worked in various institutions such as the World Council of Churches in Geneva and at the University of Bamberg.

Dube is best known for her contributions to both postcolonial and feminist exegesis through her dissertation on postcolonial feminist interpretations of the Bible (*Postcolonial Feminist Interpretation of the Bible*, 2000). In addition, through her work with people infected with HIV and AIDS, she has made important contributions to expanding reception-oriented biblical hermeneutics. In 2017 she received the Gutenberg Teaching Award from the University of Mainz (Germany).

https://candler.emory.edu/faculty/profiles/dube-musa.html

Important Publications

- *Postcolonial Feminist Interpretation of the Bible.* Saint Louis: Chalice, 2000.
- *The HIV and AIDS Bible: Some Selected Essays.* Scranton, PA: University of Scranton Press, 2008.

- (With Johanna Stiebert, eds.) *The Bible, Centers and Margins: Dialogues between Postcolonial African and UK Biblical Scholars*. London: T. & T. Clark, 2018.

- (With R. S. Wafula, eds.) *Postcoloniality, Translation and the Bible in Africa*. Eugene, OR: Pickwick, 2017.

Jione Havea

Jione Havea is a Tonga native and Methodist pastor. After studying and doing his doctorate at Southern Methodist University in Dallas (USA), he taught Old Testament/Hebrew Bible at Charles Sturt University in Parramatta (Australia) and has been working as a researcher in religious studies at Trinity Methodist Theological College (Aotearoa New Zealand) since 2016.

Havea's postcolonial research interests relate to cross-cultural issues, with a focus on oral and Pacific traditions, biblical and other written records, and power relations in (post)colonial contexts such as land appropriation, resistance, and religion. Together with other scholars, Havea has edited numerous anthologies on postcolonial and biblical theology.

https://researchoutput.csu.edu.au/en/persons/jhaveacsueduau

Important Publications

- (With Mark Brett, eds.) *Colonial Contexts and Postcolonial Theologies: Storyweaving in the Asia-Pacific*. Postcolonialism and Religions. New York: Palgrave Macmillan, 2014.

- (ed.) *Postcolonial Voices from Downunder: Indigenous Matters, Confronting Readings*. Eugene, OR: Pickwick, 2017.

- (ed.) *People and Land: Decolonizing Theologies*. Theology in the Age of Empire 3. Lanham, MD: Lexington, 2019.

- (ed.) *Religion and Power (Theology in the Age of Empire)*. Minneapolis: Fortress, 2020.

Namsoon Kang

Namsoon Kang studied theology in South Korea and the USA, where she also received her doctorate in theology. She has taught in South Korea and Cambridge (UK), and since 2006 has been a professor of theology and religion at Brite Divinity School in Texas (USA).

Feminism, Postcolonial Studies, world religions, and postmodernism intersect in Kang's theological work. In her research on cosmopolitan theology, she includes transdisciplinary questions of law, justice, and hospitality. She is also involved in international ecumenical organizations and is in demand as a speaker around the world.

https://www.brite.edu/staff/namsoon-kang/

Important Publications

- (with Des van der Water, Isabel Phiri, Roderick Hewitt, and Sarojini Nadar, eds.) *Postcolonial Mission: Power and Partnership in World Christianity.* Cambridge: Sopher, 2011.

- *Cosmopolitan Theology: Reconstituting Neighbor-Love, Hospitality, and Solidarity in an Uneven World.* St. Louis: Chalice, 2013.

- *Diasporic Feminist Theology: Asia and Theopolitical Imagination.* Minneapolis: Fortress, 2014.

- *Cosmopolitanism and Religion: In Search of Perpetual Peace in the 21st Century.* Seoul: New Wave Plus, 2015.

Kwok Pui-lan

Kwok Pui-lan (born 1952 in Hong Kong) has been a professor of Christian theology and spirituality in Cambridge and Atlanta (both USA). She has also been president of the American Academy of Religion.

Since the publication of her seminal book, *Postcolonial Imagination and Feminist Theology,* in 2005, she has made significant contributions to the advancement of postcolonial theologies. Her focus lies in the areas of biblical studies, theology of religions, mission and feminism, and the various relationships between these topics.

http://kwokpuilan.blogspot.com/

Important Publications

- *Postcolonial Imagination and Feminist Theology.* Louisville: West-minster John Knox, 2005.

- (with Laura Donaldson, eds.) *Postcolonialism, Feminism, and Religious Discourse.* New York: Routledge, 2002.

- (with Cecilia González-Andrieu and Dwight N. Hopkins, eds.) *Teaching Global Theologies: Power and Practice.* Waco, TX: Baylor University Press, 2015.

Michael Nausner

Michael Nausner (born 1965 in Vienna) is a Methodist scholar at the Research and Analysis Unit of the Church of Sweden. Until 2017 he taught systematic theology at the Reutlingen Theological University. After studying in Germany, Sweden, and the USA, he received his doctorate in the USA in 2005.

Nausner combines intercultural and postcolonial issues, and directs his attention in particular to the problems of borders and contact zones. Most recently, he has also dealt with questions of religious identity, migration, and participation.

https://www.svenskakyrkan.se/forskning/michael-nausner

Important Publications

- (with Catherine Keller and Mayra Rivera, eds.) *Postcolonial Theologies: Divinity and Empire.* St. Louis: Chalice, 2004.

- "Reimagining Boundaries in Europe: Migrant Utopias and Theological Eschatology." In *Christianities in Migration: The Global Perspective*, edited by Elaine Padilla and Peter Phan. New York: Palgrave Macmillan, 2016.

- "Imagining Participation from a Boundary Perspective: Postcolonial Theology as Migratory Theology." In *Migration und Integration—wissenschaftliche Perspektiven aus Österreich*, edited by Julia Dahlvik, Christoph Reinprecht, and Wiebke Sievers. Göttingen: Vandenhoeck & Ruprecht, 2013.

Nicolás Panotto

Nicolás Esteban Panotto (*1982) is a Baptist theologian from Argentina. He directs the international theological institute GEMRIP (Group for Multidisciplinary Studies in Religion and Public Effectiveness), which he founded. He studied theology, sociology, and anthropology, earned his doctorate in social sciences, and teaches at universities in Chile and Argentina.

In addition to a broad reception of post- and decolonial theories in theology, the public and the public effectiveness of political theology are important to him. Another issue is the importance of religion in and for a secular (laicist) state.

https://unap.academia.edu/NicolasPanotto

Important Publications

- *Teología y espacio público.* Buenos Aires: GEMRIP, 2015.
- (ed.) *Pope Francis in Postcolonial Reality: Complexities, Ambiguities and Paradoxes.* s.l.: Borderless, 2015.
- (ed.) *Indecent Theologians: Marcella Althaus-Reid and the Next Generation of Postcolonial Activists.* s.l.: Borderless, 2016.
- *Descolonizar o saber teologico na América Latina. Religião, educação e teologia em chaves pós-coloniais.* São Paulo: Recriar, 2019.
- (With Luis Martínez Andrade, eds.) *Decolonizing Liberation Theologies: Past, Present, and Future.* New York: Palgrave Macmillan, 2023.

Joerg Rieger

Joerg Rieger, born in Germany in 1963, studied theology at the Reutlingen Theological College and in Durham (USA), where he also received his PhD. He was ordained in the United Methodist Church. He was a professor of constructive theology at Southern Methodist University in Dallas and has been teaching at Vanderbilt University in Nashville, also in the USA, since 2016.

Rieger represents a profound and comprehensive critique of power in religion, politics, and business, which also includes postcolonial issues.

https://www.joergrieger.com/

Important Publications

- *Christ and Empire: From Paul to Postcolonial Times.* Minneapolis: Fortress, 2007.

- (With Néstor Míguez and Jung Mo Sung, eds.) *Beyond the Spirit of Empire: Theology and Politics in a New Key.* Reclaiming Liberation Theology. London: SCM, 2009.

- (With Kwok Pui-lan, eds.) *Occupy Religion: Theology of the Multitude.* Theology in the Modern World. Lanham, MD: Rowman and Littlefield, 2012.

- *Jesus vs. Caesar: For People Tired of Serving the Wrong God.* Nashville: Abingdon, 2018.

Mayra Rivera

Mayra Rivera Rivera (spelled with both one and two surnames) was born in Puerto Rico in 1968 and describes herself as someone who always walks on border paths.[1] Raised in a postcolonial situation, she is (as a Puerto Rican) a US citizen without national voting rights, of African, Native American, and Spanish ancestry; Latina; and Protestant. The complexities, perplexities, and subtleties that postcolonialism deals with are—due to this entangled biography—best known to her.

She studied theology and religious studies in the USA. As a professor of religion and Latinx studies at Harvard University (USA), she combines theology, literature, feminism, and Postcolonial Studies into a critical theological examination of differences and relationships, classifications, and the overcoming of borders. One of her focal points is postcolonial issues in the Caribbean.

https://hds.harvard.edu/people/mayra-rivera-rivera

Important Publications

- *The Touch of Transcendence: A Postcolonial Theology of God.* Louisville: Westminster John Knox, 2007.

---

1. See Rivera, "God at the Crossroads," 187.

- (With Catherine Keller and Michael Nausner, eds.) *Postcolonial Theologies: Divinity and Empire*. St. Louis: Chalice, 2004.

- (With Stephen D. Moore, eds.) *Planetary Loves: Spivak, Postcoloniality, and Theology*. Transdisciplinary Theological Colloquia. New York: Fordham, 2010.

Fernando F. Segovia

The US-American Bible scholar Fernando Segovia, born in Cuba in 1948, has been teaching the New Testament and early Christianity at Vanderbilt University (Nashville, USA) since 1984. Segovia was one of the first to use postcolonial methods to transform the interpretation of the Bible out of this perspective. His focus is on Latin American and Caribbean contexts, as well as the diaspora and minority situation of Latinxs in the USA. He has also published research on Johannine writings.

https://www.vanderbilt.edu/gdr/people/bio/fernando-segovia

Important Publications

- *Decolonizing Biblical Studies: A View from the Margins*. Maryknoll, NY: Orbis, 2000.

- (ed.) *Interpreting beyond Borders*. The Bible and Postcolonialism 3. Sheffield: Sheffield University Press, 2000.

- (With Stephen D. Moore, eds.) *Postcolonial Biblical Criticism: Interdisciplinary Interventions*. London: T. & T. Clark, 2005.

- (With R. S. Sugirtharajah, eds.) *A Postcolonial Commentary on the New Testament Writings*. London: T. & T. Clark, 2007.

Rasiah S. Sugirtharajah

Rasiah S. Sugirtharajah, mostly abbreviated R. S. Sugirtharajah, was born in Sri Lanka, studied theology in India, and received his doctorate in Birmingham (UK), where he taught as a biblical scholar until his retirement. He is a pastor of the Methodist Church. Sugirtharajah can be described as one of the pioneers in the application of postcolonial methodology in biblical studies and theology in general, and published

several important anthologies on postcolonial theology early on. Another important element of his theological work is to give attention to
marginalized voices in theology and biblical interpretation.

https://www.birmingham.ac.uk/staff/profiles/tr/sugirtharajah-rs.aspx

Important Publications

- *Asian Biblical Hermeneutics and Postcolonialism: Contesting the Interpretations.* Maryknoll, NY: Orbis, 1998.

- *Postcolonial Criticism and Biblical Interpretation.* Oxford: Oxford
  University Press, 2002.

- *Postcolonial Reconfigurations: An Alternative Way of Reading the
  Bible and Doing Theology.* London: SCM, 2003.

- *The Bible and the Third World: Precolonial, Colonial and Postcolonial
  Encounters.* Cambridge: Cambridge University Press, 2001.

- *The Bible and Empire: Postcolonial Explorations.* Cambridge: Cambridge University Press, 2005.

- *Voices from the Margin: Interpreting the Bible in the Third World.*
  Revised and expanded 3rd ed. Maryknoll, NY: Orbis, 2006.

- *Still at the Margins: Biblical Scholarship Fifteen Years after the Voices
  from the Margin.* London: Bloomsbury, 2008.

Glossary

Appropriation Cultural appropriation.

Border thinking, especially in the case of Walter Mignolo, describes a thinking that does not subject itself to the prevailing borders or frontiers, especially those caused by coloniality and/or modernity, but goes beyond them. 5.7

Coloniality denotes the cultural, social, economic, and other legacies of colonialism, not least in terms of mentality and epistemology. The term goes back to Aníbal Quijano and is now used in many contexts. 1.2; 3.8

Contact zone can be a space or a place, but not necessarily. This term also and primarily refers to opportunities for contact between neighboring cultures that may be in a relationship of dominance or dependency, and their mutual exchange, which may be influenced by power structures. 4.6

Cultural appropriation or **appropriation** is the adoption of cultural patterns, values, forms of expression by a dominating culture without the consent of those living in the dominated culture, often with the aim of economic or power gains. 5.6

Epistemic violence refers to the deep connections between modes of cognition and knowledge on the one hand and the violent consequences that this knowledge entails or can entail on the other. The term also draws attention to the fact that structural violence can already be exercised through the mode of knowledge and through knowledge itself. 1.2

Epistemology is the study of knowing. In the scholarly field, it also refers to the teaching of formation of scholarly knowledge. **Episteme** and **epistemic** refer to the ways and the act of knowing itself; **epistemological** is related to the teaching and learning about it.

Essentialization, essentialism refer to the rigid attribution of certain characteristics based on an external characteristic such as skin color or gender. 2.2

Eurocentrism is the notion of a centrality or primacy of Europe, European history, or attitudes in different areas of knowledge and power. The idea of a special relationship of all phenomena and events in the world to Europe and the indispensability of European ideas is also called eurocentrist. 2.4

Hegemony is understood, following Antonio Gramsci, as a subtle form of rule in which a seemingly self-evident general interest is constructed through cultural means, which is accepted unquestioningly by the entire population, although it only reflects the interests of the rulers. 2.9

Hybridity: unlike in biology, hybrid does not designate a new identity that arises through fusion or crossing, but (according to Homi Bhabha) a social or cultural formation that is caused by the transformation of power relations between different subjects. 4.6

Identity can be misunderstood in an essentialist way as a definite, rigid, immutable structure of properties rather than a social construction in relationships. It is in this rigid, ideological sense that one also critically uses the adjective **identitarian**.

Interrelationality refers to the mutual relation of things, people, concepts, etc. to each other. It stands in contrast to dualistic, exclusive, and/or hierarchical ideas. 5.2

Intersectionality is the theory (and the fact) of the intersection, overlap, and mutual influence of different axes of social oppression such as sexism, racism, poverty, etc., and the analysis of these relationships. 2.8

Mimicry, following Homi Bhabha, refers to imitation in a colonial relationship of dependency, which is also accompanied by alienation.

Modernity/Coloniality is the name of an important Latin American working group that has promoted decolonial and Postcolonial Studies in Latin America since around the turn of the millennium. With this name, the scientists also refer to the close mutual dependency of both concepts. 1.2

Nativism, nativist denotes a desired return to an original cultural reality and/or identity understood in an essentialist way, that supposedly existed before the beginning of colonization. This project was primarily advocated in the independence processes of some African states, but today it is often viewed critically from a postcolonial point of view.

Negotiation is a term used by Homi Bhabha to draw attention to mutual power relations in dialogue and to characterize the dependence of identity ideas on changing attributions by others. 4.6

Othering describes the socially constructed attribution of identity features to people in a group who display certain (sometimes only claimed) differences from the defining subject. By being othered, these people become "others"; differences are emphasized more than similarities or relationships. 2.1

Provincialization refers to a book title by Dipesh Chakrabarty, who uses the concept to denominate the strategy of describing Europe as a culturally diverse and globally only regional phenomenon. This is intended to counteract Eurocentrism. 2.4; 6.2

Representation of subaltern voices in academic discourse is in principle viewed (self-)critically in Postcolonial Studies, because non-subalterns take the floor for others and thereby transform or even falsify the intentions of subaltern persons. 4.4; 5.6

Subaltern, following Antonio Gramsci, refers to persons who are subjected and excluded and/or exploited in different ways. Significant to Gramsci is the notion that the subalterns are unorganized and unaware of their status and opportunities. In Postcolonial Studies, the term is often used very broadly to denote many types of hierarchical (colonial) relationships at the same time. 4.4

Third space, a term that goes back to Homi Bhabha, describes the relationships between identities that are thought of as binary or opposite and is closely related to his concept of hybridity and the idea of contact zones. 4.6

Bibliography

Ackermann, Cordula. "Die Identität 'der Armen' in der Befreiungstheologie unter postkolonialer Kritik." In *Identitäre Versuchungen. Identitätsverhandlungen zwischen Emanzipation und Herrschaft*. CONCORDIA Monographien 73, edited by Judith Gruber et al., 104–14. Aachen: Verlag Mainz, 2019.

Akper, Godwin I. "The Role of the 'Ordinary Reader' in Gerald O. West's Hermeneutics." *Scriptura* 88 (2005) 1–13.

Althaus-Reid, Marcella María. "Gnade und Anderssein. Eine postkoloniale Reflexion über Ideologie und Lehrsysteme." *Concilium* 36 (2000) 426–33.

———. *The Queer God*. London: Routledge, 2003.

———. "Queer I Stand: Lifting the Skirts of God." In *The Sexual Theologian: Essays on Sex, God and Politics*, edited by Marcella Althaus-Reid and Lisa Isherwood, 99–109. London: T. & T. Clark, 2004.

———. "Queer-Theorie und Befreiungstheologie. Der Durchbruch des sexuellen Subjekts in der Theologie." *Concilium* 44 (2008) 83–97.

———. "Schlimmes Sterben. Kreuzigungen im Volk und nicht beherrschbare Auferstehungen in Lateinamerika." *Concilium* 42 (2006) 523–32.

Althaus-Reid, Marcella María, and Lisa Isherwood. "Introduction: Queering Theology. Thinking Theology and Queer Theory." In *The Sexual Theologian: Essays on Sex, God and Politics*, edited by Marcella Althaus-Reid and Lisa Isherwood, 1–15. London: T. & T. Clark, 2004.

Ashcroft, Bill. "Threshold Theology." In *Colonial Contexts and Postcolonial Theologies: Storyweaving in the Asia-Pacific*, edited by Mark Brett and Jione Havea, 3–20. Postcolonialism and Religions. New York: Palgrave Macmillan, 2014.

Ashcroft, Bill, et al. *Post-Colonial Studies: The Key Concepts*. 2nd ed. London: Routledge, 2007.

Avendaño, Lukas. "Brief eines Indios, der sich nicht festgelegt hat." *Concilium* 55 (2019) 524–28.

Babka, Anna. "Gayatri C. Spivak." In *Handbuch Postkolonialismus und Literatur*, edited by Dirk Göttsche et al., 21–26. Stuttgart: J. B. Metzler, 2017.

Bascopé C., Víctor. *Espiritualidad originaria en el Pacha Andino. Aproximaciones teológicas*. Cochabamba: Verbo Divino, 2006.

Baumann, Martin. "*Götter, Gurus, Geist und Seele. Hindu-Traditionen in der Schweiz.*" In *Eine Schweiz—viele Religionen. Risiken und Chancen des Zusammenlebens*, edited by Martin Baumann and Jörg Stolz, 223–37. Bielefeld: Transcript, 2007.

Bechhaus-Gerst, Marianne, and Joachim Zeller, eds. *Deutschland postkolonial? Die Gegenwart imperialer Vergangenheit*. Berlin: Metropol, 2018.

Becka, Michelle. "Welcher (V)Erkenntnisgewinn? Postkolonialismus und Christliche Sozialethik." *Jahrbuch für Christliche Sozialwissenschaften* 61 (2020) 137–60.

Bencke, Romi Márcia. "Die Irruption des Sakralen, das während der Kolonisation verschüttet wurde. Herausforderungen für das christliche Zeugnis in pluralistischen Gesellschaften am Beispiel Brasiliens." In *Christliches Zeugnis in einer multireligiösen Welt. Eine Einladung zum Dialog*, edited by Klaus Krämer and Klaus Vellguth, 167–77. Theologie der Einen Welt 16. Freiburg: Herder, 2020.

Berner, Ulrich. *Religionswissenschaft (historisch orientiert)*. Göttingen: Vandenhoeck & Ruprecht, 2020.

Bessis, Sophie. *Occidente y los Otros. Historia de una supremacía*. Madrid: Alianza, 2002.

Bhabha, Homi K. *Die Verortung der Kultur*. Tübingen: Stauffenburg, 2000.

Bosch, David J. *Transforming Mission. Paradigm Shifts in Theology of Mission*. American Society of Missiology 16. Maryknoll, NY: Orbis, 1991.

Brett, Mark, and Jione Havea, eds. *Colonial Contexts and Postcolonial Theologies: Storyweaving in the Asia-Pacific*. Postcolonialism and Religions. New York: Palgrave Macmillan, 2014.

Brunner, Claudia. *Epistemische Gewalt. Wissen und Herrschaft in der kolonialen Moderne*. Edition Politik 94. Bielefeld: Transcript, 2020.

Budden, Chris. *Following Jesus in Invaded Space: Doing Theology on Aboriginal Land*. Princeton Theological Monograph Series 116. Eugene, OR: Pickwick, 2009.

Caero Bustillos, Bernardeth Carmen. "'Für Christen ist es ein Vorrecht und eine Freude, Rechenschaft über die Hoffnung abzulegen.' Die ökumenische Arbeit der christlichen Teología India." In *Christliches Zeugnis in einer multireligiösen Welt. Eine Einladung zum Dialog*, edited by Klaus Krämer and Klaus Vellguth, 213–25. Theologie der Einen Welt 16. Freiburg: Herder, 2020.

Caldeira, Cleusa. "Hermenêutica Negra Feminista: um ensaio de interpretação de Cântico dos Cânticos 1.5–6." *Estudos Feministas* 21.3 (2013) 1189–210.

———. "Theo-Quilombismus: Afro-brasilianische Formen spirituellen Widerstandes." *Concilium* 56 (2020) 53–62.

Casaldáliga, Pedro. *Auf der Suche nach dem Reich Gottes. Eine Anthologie*. Wien/Klagenfurt: Hermagoras, 1989.

Castillo Morga, Alejandro. *Sabiduría indígena y ética social cristiana: Los Acuerdos de San Andrés como una forma de contribución ética de los pueblos indígenas a la construcción de la Justicia y la Paz*. México D. F.: CENAMI, 2017.

Castro-Gómez, Santiago, and Ramón Grosfoguel, eds. *El giro decolonial. Reflexiones para una diversidad epistémica más allá del capitalismo global*. Bogotá: Siglo del Hombre, 2007.

Castro Varela, María do Mar, and Nikita Dhawan. *Postkoloniale Theorie. Eine kritische Einführung, 3. Auflage*. Bielefeld: Transcript, 2020.

Chakrabarty, Dipesh. *Provincializing Europe: Postcolonial Thought and Historical Difference*. Princeton: University of Princeton Press, 2000.

Chipana Quispe, Sofía. "Relationale Wissensbestände und Spiritualitäten in Abya Yala." *Concilium* 56 (2020) 43–52.

Chitando, Ezra. "The Bible as a Resource for Development in Africa: Ten Considerations for Liberating Readings." In *Religion and Development in Africa*, edited by Ezra Chitando et al., 399–415. Bible in Africa Studies 25. Bamberg: University of Bamberg Press, 2020.

Clark, Elizabeth A. "Postcolonial Theory and the Study of Christian History: Introduction." *Church History* 78 (2009) 847–48.

Conrad, Sebastian, and Shalini Randeria. "Einleitung. Geteilte Geschichten—Europa in einer postkolonialen Welt." In *Jenseits des Eurozentrismus: Postkoloniale Perspektiven in den Geschichts—und Kulturwissenschaften*, edited by Sebastian Conrad and Shalini Randeria, 9–49. Frankfurt: Campus, 2002.

———, eds. *Jenseits des Eurozentrismus: Postkoloniale Perspektiven in den Geschichts—und Kulturwissenschaften*. Frankfurt: Campus, 2002.

Contreras Colín, Juan Manuel. "Kritik am europäischen Kolonialismus am Ursprung der eurozentrischen Moderne. Perspektiven der amerindischen Völker." In *Theologie und Postkolonialismus. Ansätze—Herausforderungen—Perspektiven*, edited by Sebastian Pittl, 156–67. Weltkirche und Mission 10. Regensburg: Pustet, 2018.

Cooper-White, Pamela. "The Rape of Tamar, the Crime of Amnon: 2 Samuel 13:1–22." In *Tamar Campaign: Contextual Bible Study Manual on Gender-Based Violence*, edited by Fred Nyabera and Taryn Montgomery, 26–28. Nairobi: FECCLAHA, 2007.

Culbertson, Philip, and Tavita Maliko. "'Ein G-String-Tanga ist nicht samoanisch.' Erkundungen zu einer grenzüberschreitenden pazifischen Theologie des Dritten Geschlechts." *Concilium* 44 (2008) 51–61.

Daniel, Anna. *Die Grenzen des Religionsbegriffs. Eine postkoloniale Konfrontation des religionssoziologischen Diskurses*. Bielefeld: Transcript, 2016.

de Jong-Kumru, Wietske. *Postcolonial Feminist Theology: Enacting Cultural, Religious, Gender and Sexual Differences in Theological Reflection*. ContactZone: Explorations in Intercultural Theology 16. Zürich/Berlin: Lit, 2013.

De La Torre, Miguel A. "Identity Cross Dressing while Teaching in a Global Context." In *Teaching Global Theologies: Power and Praxis*, edited by Kwok Pui-lan et al., 75–89. Waco: Baylor University Press, 2015.

Donaldson, Laura E. "Native Women's Double Cross: Christology from the Contact Zone." *Feminist Theology* 10.29 (2002) 96–117.

———. "The Sign of Orpah: Reading Ruth through Native Eyes." In *Ruth and Esther*, edited by Athalya Brenner, 130–44. A Feminist Companion to the Bible, 2nd series, vol. 3 Sheffield: Sheffield Academic, 1999.

Dube, Musa W. "'Liberating the Word'—One African Feminist Reading of Matthew 23." In *Religion and Development in Africa*, edited by Ezra Chitando et al., 417–42. Bible in Africa Studies 25. Bamberg: University of Bamberg Press, 2020.

———. *Postcolonial Feminist Interpretation of the Bible*. St. Louis: Chalice, 2000.

———. "Postkolonialität, Feministische Räume und Religion." In *Postkoloniale Theologien. Bibelhermeneutische und kulturwissenschaftliche Beiträge*, edited by Andreas Nehring and Simon Tielesch, 91–111. ReligionsKulturen 11. Stuttgart: Kohlhammer, 2013.

———. "'Rhodes Must Fall.' Postcolonial Perspectives on Christian Mission." In *Theologie und Postkolonialismus. Ansätze—Herausforderungen—Perspektiven*, edited by Sebastian Pittl, 83–100. Weltkirche und Mission 10. Regensburg: Pustet, 2018.

————. "'To push the boundaries.' Die Grenzen des Wissens weiten. Interview durch Bernhard Offenberger." *Bibel und Kirche* 67.3 (2012) 160–63.

Duggan, Joseph. "Erkenntnistheoretische Diskrepanz. Zur Entkolonialisierung des postkolonialen theologischen 'Kanons.'" *Concilium* 49 (2013) 135–42.

Dussel, Enrique. *Desintegración de la cristiandad colonial y liberación. Perspectiva latinoamericana.* Salamanca: Sígueme, 1978.

Dyrness, William A. "Listening for Fresh Voices in the History of the Church." In *Teaching Global Theologies. Power and Praxis,* edited by Kwok Pui-lan et al., 29–43. Waco: Baylor University Press, 2015.

Estermann, Josef. *Apu Taytayku. Religion und Theologie im andinen Kontext Lateinamerikas.* Theologie interkulturell 23. Ostfildern: Matthias Grünewald, 2012.

————. *Südwind. Kontextuelle nicht-abendländische Theologien im globalen Süden.* Forum Religionspädagogik interkulturell 31. Zürich/Berlin: Lit, 2017.

Fanon, Frantz. *Black Skin, White Masks.* Translated by Charles Lam Markmann. London: Pluto, 1986.

Febel, Gisela, and Paulo de Medeiros. "Romanistik." In *Handbuch Postkolonialismus und Literatur,* edited by Dirk Göttsche et al., 64–74. Stuttgart: J. B. Metzler, 2017.

Federici, Silvia. *Calibán y la bruja. Mujeres, cuerpo y acumulación originaria.* Historia 9. Madrid: TdS, 2010.

Field, David N. "Über das (Wieder-)Zentrieren der Ränder. Eine Euro-Afrikanische Perspektive auf die Option für die Armen." In *Postkoloniale Theologien. Bibelhermeneutische und kulturwissenschaftliche Beiträge,* edited by Andreas Nehring and Simon Tielesch, 225–50. ReligionsKulturen 11. Stuttgart: Kohlhammer, 2013.

Fung, Jojo M. "A Postcolonial-Mission-Territorial Hermeneutics for a Liberative Shamanic Pneumatology." *Voices* 36.2–3 (2013) 97–121.

Gebara, Ivone. *Intuiciones Ecofeministas.* Madrid: Trotta, 2000.

————. "Ökofeminismus." In *Wörterbuch der Feministischen Theologie,* edited by Elisabeth Gössmann et al., 422–24. Gütersloh: Gütersloher, 2002.

Geck, Philip, and Anton Rühling. "Vorläufer des Holocaust? Die Debatte um die (Dis-)Kontinuität von deutschem Kolonialismus und Nationalsozialismus." *Informationszentrum 3. Welt* 308 (2008) 40–43.

Gonçalves, Alfredo J. "La crisis y la vuelta a las fuentes." *Alternativas: Revista de análisis y reflexión teológica* 16.37 (2009) 81–100.

González-Andrieu, Cecilia. "The Good of Education: Accessibility, Economy, Class, and Power." In *Teaching Global Theologies: Power and Praxis,* edited by Kwok Pui-lan et al., 57–73. Waco: Baylor University Press, 2015.

González Casanova, Pablo. *Sociología de la explotación.* México: Siglo XXI, 1971.

Göttsche, Dirk, et al., eds. *Handbuch Postkolonialismus und Literatur.* Stuttgart: J. B. Metzler, 2017.

Gramsci, Antonio. *Gefängnishefte.* Edited by Klaus Bochmann and Wolfgang Fritz Haug. Vol. 4. Hamburg: Argument, 1992.

Graneß, Anke, et al. *Feministische Theorie aus Afrika, Asien und Lateinamerika.* Gender Studies 5137. Wien: Facultas, 2019.

Graul, Stefanie. "Das dritte Geschlecht der Binnizá zwischen Globalisierung und Ethnizität. Hybride Identitäten?" *Forum der Psychoanalyse* 33 (2017) 57–75.

Grau, Marion. "Göttlicher Handel. Eine postkoloniale Christologie für die Zeiten des neoliberalen Empires." In *Postkoloniale Theologien. Bibelhermeneutische und kulturwissenschaftliche Beiträge*, edited by Andreas Nehring and Simon Tielesch, 300–22. ReligionsKulturen 11. Stuttgart: Kohlhammer, 2013.

Grosfoguel, Ramón. "Del extractivismo económico al extractivismo epistémico y ontológico." *Revista Internacional de Comunicación y Desarrollo* 4 (2016) 33–45.

Gruber, Judith. "Wider die Entinnerung. Zur postkolonialen Kritik hegemonialer Wissenspolitiken in der Theologie." In *Postkoloniale Theologien II: Perspektiven aus dem deutschsprachigen Raum*, edited by Andreas Nehring and Simon Wiesgickl, 23–37. Stuttgart: Kohlhammer, 2018.

Gründer, Horst. *Geschichte der deutschen Kolonien*. Paderborn: Schöningh, 2018.

Gutiérrez, Gustavo. *Theologie der Befreiung*. Systematische Beiträge 11. Mainz: Grünewald, 1976.

Hardt, Michael, and Antonio Negri. *Empire. Die neue Weltordnung*. Frankfurt: Campus, 2003.

———. "Empire—zwanzig Jahre später." *Luxemburg*, May 2020. https://www.zeitschrift-luxemburg.de/empire-zwanzig-jahre-spaeter/.

Havea, Jione. "The Politics of Climate Change: A Talanoa from Oceania." *International Journal of Public Theology* 4 (2010) 345–55.

———. "Stirring Naomi: Another Gleaning at the Edges of Ruth 1." In *Reading Ruth in Asia*, edited by Jione Havea and Peter H. W. Lau, 111–24. International Voices in Biblical Studies. Atlanta: SBL, 2015.

Healy, Susan. "Settler Christianity and the Taking of Māori Land." In *Listening to the People of the Land: Christianity, Colonisation and the Path to Redemption*, edited by Susan Healy, 73–95. Auckland: Pax Christi Aotearoa New Zealand, 2019.

Heimbach-Steins, Marianne, et al., eds. "Vorwort." *Jahrbuch für Christliche Sozialwissenschaften* 61 (2020) 9–17.

Hidalgo, Jacqueline M. "Im Kampf mit Herrschaftsmentalitäten." In *Feministische Bibelwissenschaft im 20. Jahrhundert*, edited by Elisabeth Schüssler Fiorenza and Renate Jost, 205–19. Die Bibel und die Frauen 9.1. Stuttgart: Kohlhammer, 2015.

Hölzl, Richard. "Rassismus, Ethnogenese und Kultur. Afrikaner im Blickwinkel der deutschen katholischen Mission im 19. und frühen 20. Jahrhundert." *WerkstattGeschichte* 59 (2012) 7–34.

———. "Wenn die Trommeln schweigen. Koloniale (Nicht-)Repräsentationen im Missionsmuseum." *Jahrbuch für Christliche Sozialwissenschaften* 61 (2020) 33–47.

Jahnel, Claudia. "'The Future Is Not Ours to See.' Postkoloniale Perspektiven auf den religious turn in der (deutschen) Entwicklungszusammenarbeit." In *Theologie und Postkolonialismus. Ansätze—Herausforderungen—Perspektiven*, edited by Sebastian Pittl, 168–90. Weltkirche und Mission 10. Regensburg: Pustet, 2018.

———. "'Religion kann Brücken bauen für Entwicklung.' Postkoloniale Perspektiven auf den religious turn in der (deutschen) Entwicklungszusammenarbeit." In *Postkoloniale Theologien II: Perspektiven aus dem deutschsprachigen Raum*, edited by Andreas Nehring and Simon Wiesgickl, 302–20. Stuttgart: Kohlhammer, 2018.

Jarosch, Sabine. "Koloniale Wunden. Eine Herausforderung für Theologie und Kirche in Deutschland." In *Reformation und die Eine Welt. Das Magazin zum Themenjahr 2016*. Hannover 2015, 46–47.

Jensen, Sune Qvotrup. "Othering, Identity Formation and Agency." *Qualitative Studies* 2.2 (2011) 63–78.

Joh, Wonhee Anne. "Trauer und der Anspruch auf Trauer. Der postkoloniale Spuk des Kreuzes." *Concilium* 49 (2013) 161–70.

Kang, Namsoon. "Jenseits von Ethno-/Geozentrismus, Androzentrismus, Heterozentrismus. Theologie aus einer Perspektive der Überschneidung von Postkolonialismus und Feminismus." *Concilium* 49 (2013) 181–90.

———. "Wer oder was ist asiatisch? Eine postkoloniale theologische Lektüre über Orientalismus und Neo-Orientalismus." In *Postkoloniale Theologien. Bibelhermeneutische und kulturwissenschaftliche Beiträge*, edited by Andreas Nehring and Simon Tielesch, 203–20. ReligionsKulturen 11. Stuttgart: Kohlhammer, 2013.

Kastner, Jens. *Dekolonialistische Theorie aus Lateinamerika. Einführung und Kritik.* Münster: Unrast, 2022.

Kaunda, Chammah J. "Towards an African Ecogender Theology: A Decolonial Theological Perspective." *Stellenbosch Theological Journal* 2 (2016) 177–202.

Keller, Catherine, et al. "Introduction." In *Postcolonial Theologies. Divinity and Empire*, edited by Catherine Keller et al., 1–19. St. Louis: Chalice, 2004.

Kern, Bruno. *Theologie der Befreiung.* Tübingen: Narr Francke Attempto, 2013.

Kerner, Ina. *Postkoloniale Theorien. Zur Einführung.* Hamburg: Junius, 2012.

Kim, Uriah Y. "Die Politik des Othering in Nordamerika und im Buch der Richter." *Concilium* 49 (2013) 152–61.

King, Richard. *Orientalism and Religion: Postcolonial Theory, India and the "Mystic East."* London: Routledge, 1999.

———. "Philosophy of Religion as Border Control: Globalization and the Decolonization of the 'Love of Wisdom.'" In *Postcolonial Philosophy of Religion*, edited by Purushottama Bilimoria and Andrew B. Irvine, 35–53. Berlin: Springer, 2009.

Klinger, Elmar. "Theologie im Horizont der Politik. Die Herausforderung Europas durch die lateinamerikanische Theologie." In *Herausforderung. Die Dritte Welt und die Christen Europas*, edited by Fernando Castillo et al., 47–63. Regensburg: Pustet, 1980.

Knauss, Stefanie, and Carlos Mendoza-Álvarez. "Queer-Theorien und -Theologien. Eine Einführung." *Concilium* 55 (2019) 493–96.

Konz, Britta, et al., eds. *Postkolonialismus, Theologie und die Konstruktion des Anderen [Postcolonialism, Theology and the Construction of the Other]. Erkundungen in einem Grenzgebiet [Exploring Borderlands].* Studies in Theology and Religion 26. Leiden: Brill, 2020.

Kwok Pui-lan. *Postcolonial Imagination and Feminist Theology.* Louisville: Westminster John Knox, 2005.

———. "Teaching Theology from a Global Perspective." In *Teaching Global Theologies: Power and Praxis*, edited by Kwok Pui-lan et al., 11–27. Waco, TX: Baylor University Press, 2015.

———. "Die Verbindungen herstellen. Postkolonialismus–Studien und feministische Bibelinterpretation." In *Postkoloniale Theologien. Bibelhermeneutische und kulturwissenschaftliche Beiträge*, edited by Andreas Nehring and Simon Tielesch, 323–46. ReligionsKulturen 11. Stuttgart: Kohlhammer, 2013.

———. "What Has Love to Do with It? Planetarity, Feminism, and Theology." In *Planetary Loves: Spivak, Postcoloniality, and Theology*, edited by Stephen D. Moore and Mayra Rivera, 31–45. New York: Fordham, 2011.

Lai Pan-chiu. "Teaching Global Theology with Local Resources: A Chinese Theologian's Strategies." In *Teaching Global Theologies: Power and Praxis*, edited by Kwok Pui-lan et al., 91–104. Waco, TX: Baylor University Press, 2015.

Lander, Edgardo. "Ciencias sociales: saberes coloniales y eurocéntrico." In *La colonialidad del saber. Eurocentrismo y ciencias sociales. Perspectivas Latinoamericanas*, edited by Edgardo Lander, 4–23. Buenos Aires: CLACSO, 2000.

——, ed. *La colonialidad del saber. Eurocentrismo y ciencias sociales. Perspectivas Latinoamericanas*. Buenos Aires: CLACSO, 2000.

Laporta, Héctor. "Decolonizing Virgin Mary." *Voices* 37.1 (2014) 103–13.

La Puente Tapia, Juan Carlos. "Widerstand, messianische Kraft der göttlichen Anarchie." *Concilium* 56 (2020) 72–80.

Lee, Archie C. C. "Returning to China: Biblical Interpretation in Postcolonial Hong Kong." In *Voices from the Margin: Interpreting the Bible in the Third World*, edited by R. S. Sugirtharajah, 281–96. Maryknoll, NY: Orbis, 2006.

Lehr, Fabian. "Zum europäischen Rassismus. Drei Thesen gegen den Import US–Amerikanischer Rassismusdiskurse." 2020. https://www.designing-history.world/theorie/europaeischer-rassismus-amerikanische-rassismusdiskurse/.

Londoño, Juan Esteban. "Hermenéuticas postcoloniales." *Alternativas: Revista de análisis y reflexión teológica* 22.49 (2016) 147–64.

López Hernández, Eleazar. *Teología India. Antología*. Evangelio y Culturas 3. Cochabamba: Verbo Divino, 2000.

Lorde, Audre. *Sister Outsider: Essays and Speeches*. Berkeley: Crossing, 2007.

Lugones, María. "Colonialidad y género." In *Tejiendo de otro modo: Feminismo, epistemología y apuestas descoloniales en Abya Yala*, edited by Yuderkys Espinosa Miñoso et al., 57–73. Popayán: Editorial Universidad del Cauca, 2014.

Mabanza Bambu, Boniface. *Das Leben bejahen. Elemente einer Theologie des Lebens aus kongolesischer Perspektive*. Theologie Interkulturell 24. Ostfildern: Grünewald, 2014.

Maldonado-Torres, Nelson. "Sobre la colonialidad del ser. Contribuciones al desarrollo de un concepto." In *El giro decolonial. Reflexiones para una diversidad epistémica más allá del capitalismo global*, edited by Santiago Castro-Gómez and Ramón Grosfoguel, 127–67. Bogotá: Siglo del Hombre, 2007.

Mananzan, Mary John. "Frauen und Religion." In *Theologie des Kampfes. Christliche Nachfolgepraxis in den Philippinen*, edited by Mary Rosario Battung et al., 113–23. Münster: Liberación, 1989.

Mbembe, Achille. *Kritik der schwarzen Vernunft*. Bonn: bpb, 2016.

Mellor, Mary. *Feminismo y ecología*. Mexico: Siglo XXI, 2000.

Mena López, Maricel. "Raíces afro-asiáticas y la descolonización de la Biblia. Desafíos para la educación teológica latinoamericana." In *Re-encantos y Re-encuentros. Caminos y desafíos actuales de las Teologías de la Liberación*, edited by Daylíns Rufín Pardo and Carlos Luis Marrero, 74–84. Havana: Centro Oscar Arnulfo Romero, 2017.

Mena López, Maricel, et al. "Bíblia e descolonização. Leituras desde uma hermenêutica bíblica negra e feminista de libertação." *Mandrágora* 24.2 (2018) 115–44.

Mendoza-Álvarez, Carlos. "Die Entstehung von Rationalität aus dem Widerstand gegen die systemische Gewalt." *Concilium* 53 (2017) 51–59.

Merchant, Carolyn. *Der Tod der Natur. Ökologie, Frauen und neuzeitliche Naturwissenschaft*. Beck'sche Reihe 01084. München: Beck, 1994.

Metz, Johann Baptist. *Zum Begriff der neuen Politischen Theologie. 1967–1997.* Mainz: Grünewald, 1997.

Mies, Maria, and Vandana Shiva. *Ökofeminismus: Die Befreiung der Frauen, der Natur und unterdrückter Völker.* Neu-Ulm: AG SPAK, 2016.

Mignolo, Walter D. *Epistemischer Ungehorsam. Rhetorik der Moderne, Logik der Kolonialität und Grammatik der Dekolonialität.* Wien/Berlin: Turia and Kant, 2012.

———. *Habitar la frontera. Sentir y pensar la descolonialidad. Antología, 1999–2014.* Interrogar la actualidad 36. Barcelona: CIDOB, 2015.

———. "El pensamiento decolonial: desprendimiento y apertura. Un manifiesto." In *El giro decolonial. Reflexiones para una diversidad epistémica más allá del capitalismo global,* edited by Santiago Castro-Gómez and Ramón Grosfoguel, 25–46. Bogotá: Siglo del Hombre, 2007.

Mohanty, Chandra Talpade. "Under Western Eyes: Feminist Scholarship and Colonial Discourses." *Boundary 2* 12.3 (1984) 333–58.

Monroy, Juan Bosco. "Babel: ¿castigo o propuesta? Lectura popular Latinoamericana de la Biblia y pensamiento postcolonial." *Voices* 37.1 (2014) 139–50.

Moore, Stephen D., and Fernando F. Segovia, eds. *Postcolonial Biblical Criticism: Interdisciplinary Intersections.* London: T. & T. Clark, 2005.

Mosala, Itumeleng J. "The Implications of the Text of Esther for African Women's Struggle for Liberation in South Africa." In *The Postcolonial Biblical Reader,* edited by R. S. Sugirtharajah, 134–41. Oxford: Blackwell, 2006.

Müßig, Dietmar. *Die Jungfrau im Silberberg. Ein kolonialzeitliches Marienbild aus Potosí als Zeugnis andiner Theologie.* Weltkirche und Mission 13. Regensburg: Pustet, 2020.

Musskopf, André S. "So queer, wie es nur werden kann." *Concilium* 55 (2019) 497–504.

Nanko-Fernández, Carmen M. "From Pájaro to Paraclete: Retrieving the Spirit of God in Company of Mary." In *Building Bridges, Doing Justice: Constructing a Latino/a Ecumenical Theology,* edited by Orlando O. Espín, 13–28. Maryknoll, NY: Orbis, 2009.

Nausner, Michael. "Heimat als Grenzland. Territorien christlicher Subjektivität." In *Postkoloniale Theologien. Bibelhermeneutische und kulturwissenschaftliche Beiträge,* edited by Andreas Nehring and Simon Tielesch, 187–202. ReligionsKulturen 11. Stuttgart: Kohlhammer, 2013.

———. "Koloniales Erbe und Theologie. Postkoloniale Theorie als Ressource für deutschsprachige Theologie." *Salzburger Theologische Zeitschrift* 17 (2013) 65–83.

———. "Die langen Schatten der Nofretete. Postkoloniale Theorie und Theologie in Deutschland." *Concilium* 49 (2013) 200–209.

———. "Zur Rezeption Postkolonialer Theorie in der deutschsprachigen Theologie. Ein Literaturüberblick." *Jahrbuch für Christliche Sozialwissenschaften* 61 (2020) 183–209.

Nehring, Andreas. "Verwundbarkeit auf Abwegen. Migration, Flucht und der Verlust von Handlungsraum." In *Postkoloniale Theologien II: Perspektiven aus dem deutschsprachigen Raum,* edited by Andreas Nehring and Simon Wiesgickl, 134–54. Stuttgart: Kohlhammer, 2018.

Nehring, Andreas, and Simon Tielesch, eds. *Postkoloniale Theologien. Bibelhermeneutische und kulturwissenschaftliche Beiträge.* ReligionsKulturen 11. Stuttgart: Kohlhammer, 2013.

———. "Theologie und Postkolonialismus. Zur Einführung." In *Postkoloniale Theologien. Bibelhermeneutische und kulturwissenschaftliche Beiträge*, edited by Andreas Nehring and Simon Tielesch, 9–45. ReligionsKulturen 11. Stuttgart: Kohlhammer, 2013.

Nehring, Andreas, and Simon Wiesgickl, eds. *Postkoloniale Theologien II: Perspektiven aus dem deutschsprachigen Raum*. Stuttgart: Kohlhammer, 2018.

Oduyoye, Mercy Amba. *Beads and Strands: Reflections of an African Woman on Christianity in Africa*. Maryknoll, NY: Orbis, 2004.

Pannenberg, Wolfhart. "Notwendigkeit und Grenze der Inkulturation des Evangeliums." In *Christentum in Lateinamerika. 500 Jahre seit der Entdeckung Amerikas*, edited by Geiko Müller-Fahrenholz, 140–54. Regensburg: Pustet, 1992.

Panotto, Nicolás. "Descolonizar lo divino. Aportes para una teología poscolonial del campo religioso latinoamericano." In *Materialidades (pos)coloniales y de la (de) colonialidad latinoamericana*, edited by Laura Catelli and María Elena Lucero, 143–55. Rosario: UNR, 2014.

———. *Descolonizar o saber teológico na América Latina. Religião, educação e teologia em chaves pós-coloniais*. São Paulo: Recriar, 2019.

Pilario, Daniel Franklin. "Mapping Postcolonial Theory: Appropriations in Contemporary Theology." *Hapág: A Journal of Interdisciplinary Theological Research* 3 (2006) 9–51.

Pittl, Sebastian. "Anspruch und Wirklichkeit. Zu einer postkolonialen Theologie und Kirche." *Stimmen der Zeit* 145 (2020) 903–14.

———. "Schmittsche Gespenster. Identität, Diskurs und Entscheidung." In *Identitäre Versuchungen. Identitätsverhandlungen zwischen Emanzipation und Herrschaft*, edited by Judith Gruber et al., 172–81. CONCORDIA Monographien 73. Aachen: Mainz, 2018.

———, ed. *Theologie und Postkolonialismus. Ansätze—Herausforderungen—Perspektiven*. Weltkirche und Mission 10. Regensburg: Pustet, 2018.

Porto-Gonçalves, Carlos Walter. *Amazonía: encrucijada civilizatoria. Tensiones territoriales en curso*. La Paz: IPDRS / CIDES, 2018.

Pratt, Mary Louise. *Imperial Eyes: Travel Writing and Transculturation*. London: Routledge, 1992.

Prüller-Jagenteufel, Gunter, et al., eds. *Macht und Machtkritik. Beiträge aus feministisch-theologischer und befreiungstheologischer Perspektive. Dokumentation des 4. internationalen Workshops "Kontextuelle befreiende Theologien."* CONCORDIA Monographien 70. Aachen: Mainz, 2018.

Purtschert, Patricia, et al., eds. *Postkoloniale Schweiz. Formen und Folgen eines Kolonialismus ohne Kolonien*. Bielefeld: Transcript, 2012.

Quijano, Aníbal. "Colonialidad del poder, eurocentrismo y América Latina." In *La colonialidad del saber: eurocentrismo y ciencias sociales. Perspectivas Latinoamericanas*, edited by Edgardo Lander, 201–46. Buenos Aires: CLACSO, 2000.

———. "Colonialidad del poder y clasificación social." In *El giro decolonial. Reflexiones para una diversidad epistémica más allá del capitalismo global*, edited by Santiago Castro-Gómez and Ramón Grosfoguel, 93–126. Bogotá: Siglo del Hombre, 2007.

———. "Colonialidad y modernidad/racionalidad." *Perú indígena* 13.29 (1992) 11–20.

———. *Kolonialität der Macht, Eurozentrismus und Lateinamerika*. Wien/Berlin: Turia and Kant, 2016.

Quintero, Pablo. "Macht und Kolonialität der Macht in Lateinamerika." In *Kolonialität der Macht. De/Koloniale Konflikte: zwischen Theorie und Praxis*, edited by Pablo Quintero and Sebastian Garbe, 53–70. Münster: Unrast, 2013.

Quintero, Pablo, and Sebastian Garbe. "Einleitung." In *Kolonialität der Macht. De/Koloniale Konflikte: zwischen Theorie und Praxis*, edited by Pablo Quintero and Sebastian Garbe, 7–15. Münster: Unrast, 2013.

———, eds. *Kolonialität der Macht. De/Koloniale Konflikte: zwischen Theorie und Praxis*. Münster: Unrast, 2013.

Rettenbacher, Sigrid. *Außerhalb der Ekklesiologie keine Religionstheologie. Eine postkoloniale Theologie der Religionen*. Beiträge zu einer Theologie der Religionen 15. Zürich: TVZ, 2019.

Reuter, Julia. *Ordnungen des Anderen. Zum Problem des Eigenen in der Soziologie des Fremden*. Bielefeld: Transcript, 2002.

Reuter, Julia, and Alexandra Karentzos, eds. *Schlüsselwerke der Postcolonial Studies*. Wiesbaden: Springer VS, 2012.

Rieger, Jörg [Joerg]. *Christus und das Imperium. Von Paulus bis zum Postkolonialismus*. Theologie: Forschung und Wissenschaft 26. Zürich/Berlin: Lit, 2009.

———. "Theology and Mission between Neocolonialism and Postcolonialism." *Mission Studies* 21.2 (2004) 201–27.

Rivera Cusicanqui, Silvia. *Sociología de la imagen. Miradas ch'ixi desde la historia andina*. Buenos Aires: Tinta Limón, 2015.

———. *Un mundo ch'ixi es posible. Ensayos desde un presente en crisis*. Buenos Aires: Tinta Limón, 2018.

Rivera, Mayra. "Fleisch der Welt. Leiblichkeit in Beziehung." *Concilium* 49 (2013) 171–80.

———. "God at the Crossroads: A Postcolonial Reading of Sophia." In *Postcolonial Theologies: Divinity and Empire*, edited by Catherine Keller, 186–203. St. Louis: Chalice, 2004.

———. "Ränder und die sich verändernde Spatialität von Macht. Einführende Notizen." In *Postkoloniale Theologien. Bibelhermeneutische und kulturwissenschaftliche Beiträge*, edited by Andreas Nehring and Simon Tielesch, 149–64. ReligionsKulturen 11. Stuttgart: Kohlhammer, 2013.

Ruoff, Michael. *Foucault-Lexikon. Entwicklung—Kernbegriffe—Zusammenhänge*. Paderborn: Fink, 2018.

Ruthner, Clemens. *Habsburgs "Dark Continent." Postkoloniale Lektüren zur österreichischen Literatur und Kultur im langen 19. Jahrhundert*. Tübingen: Francke, 2018.

Said, Edward W. *Kultur und Imperialismus. Einbildungskraft und Politik im Zeitalter der Macht*. Frankfurt: Fischer, 1994.

———. *Orientalismus*. Frankfurt: Ullstein, 1981.

Schillebeeckx, Edward. "Vorwort." In *Abschied vom Gott der Europäer. Zur Entwicklung regionaler Theologien*, edited by Robert J. Schreiter, 8–9. Salzburg: Pustet, 1992.

Segato, Rita Laura. *La crítica de la colonialidad en ocho ensayos. Y una antropología por demanda*. Buenos Aires: Prometeo, 2013.

Segovia, Fernando. "Grenzüberschreitendes Interpretieren. Postkolonialismus–Studien und Diaspora–Studien in historisch–kritischer Bibelexegese." In *Postkoloniale Theologien. Bibelhermeneutische und kulturwissenschaftliche Beiträge*, edited by Andreas Nehring and Simon Tielesch, 70–90. ReligionsKulturen 11. Stuttgart: Kohlhammer, 2013.

Segundo, Juan Luis. *Liberation of Theology.* Dublin: Gill and Macmillan, 1977.

Shannahan, Chris. *Voices from the Borderland: Re-Imagining Cross-Cultural Urban Theology in the Twenty-First Century.* London: Equinox, 2010.

Silber, Stefan. "Among Sisters: What Postcolonial Studies Have to Say to Liberation Theology." In *Sozialarbeit des Südens,* Vol. 8: *Indigenous and Local Knowledge in Social Work,* edited by Ute Strabb et al., 83–96. Internationale Sozialarbeit 8. Oldenburg: Paulo Freire, 2020.

———. *Die Befreiung der Kulturen. Der Beitrag Juan Luis Segundos zur Theologie der inkulturierten Evangelisierung.* Würzburger Studien zur Fundamentaltheologie 27. Frankfurt: Peter Lang, 2002.

———. "El eurocentrismo en la teología. Obstáculos para la percepción del pluralismo." In *Teorías críticas y eurocentrismo. Estudio de los componentes teóricos y prácticos de la ideología hegemónica contemporánea,* edited by Juan Manuel Contreras Colín, 289–315. México: La Guillotina, 2019.

———. "Fragmented Identities: Explorations from the Perspectives of Liberation Theologies and Postcolonial Studies." *Louvain Studies* 42.3 (2019) 323–34.

———. *Kirche, die aus sich herausgeht. Auf dem Weg der pastoralen Umkehr.* Würzburg: Echter, 2018.

———. "Laboratorios de culturas. Perspectivas poscoloniales y teológicas al reverso de las ciudades." *Anatéllei—se levanta* 16.32 (2014) 51–63.

———. *Pluralität, Fragmente, Zeichen der Zeit. Aktuelle fundamentaltheologische Herausforderungen aus der Perspektive der lateinamerikanischen Theologie der Befreiung.* Salzburger Theologische Studien 58, interkulturell 19. Innsbruck: Tyrolia, 2017.

———. *Poscolonialismo. Introducción a los estudios y las teologías poscoloniales.* El tiempo que no perece 3. Cochabamba: Itinerarios, 2018.

———. "Synodalität, Befreiung, Widerstand. Neue Perspektiven für die Missionstheologie." *Theologisch-praktische Quartalschrift* 168.3 (2020) 262–70.

Smith, Linda Tuhiwai. *Decolonizing Methodologies: Research and Indigenous Peoples.* London: Zed, 1999.

Sobrino, Jon. *Christologie der Befreiung.* Vol. 1. Mainz: Grünewald, 1998.

Spivak, Gayatri Chakravorty. "Can the Subaltern Speak?" In *Colonial Discourse and Postcolonial Theory,* edited by Laura Chrisman and Patrick Williams, 66–111. New York: Columbia University Press, 1994.

———. *A Critique of Postcolonial Reason: Toward a History of the Vanishing Present.* Cambridge: Harvard University Press, 1999.

———. *The Post-Colonial Critic: Interviews, Strategies, Dialogues.* Edited by Sarah Harasym. London: Routledge, 1990.

Steyerl, Hito, and Encarnación Gutiérrez Rodríguez, eds. *Spricht die Subalterne deutsch? Migration und postkoloniale Kritik.* Münster: Unrast, 2012.

Styers, Randall. "Postcolonial Theory and the Study of Christian History." *Church History* 78.4 (2009) 849–54.

Suess, Paulo. "Prolegomena zur Entkolonialisierung und zum kolonialen Charakter der Theologie innerhalb der Kirche. Aus einer lateinamerikanischen Perspektive." *Concilium* 49 (2013) 190–99.

Sugirtharajah, R. S. *The Bible and the Third World: Precolonial, Colonial and Postcolonial Encounters.* Cambridge: Cambridge University Press, 2004.

———. "Postcolonial Biblical Interpretation." In *Voices from the Margin: Interpreting the Bible in the Third World,* edited by R. S. Sugirtharajah, 64–84. Revised and expanded 3rd ed. Maryknoll, NY: Orbis, 2006.

————, ed. *The Postcolonial Biblical Reader*. Oxford: Blackwell, 2006.

————. "Eine postkoloniale Untersuchung von Kollusion und Konstruktion in biblischer Interpretation." In *Postkoloniale Theologien. Bibelhermeneutische und kulturwissenschaftliche Beiträge*, edited by Andreas Nehring and Simon Tielesch, 123–44. ReligionsKulturen 11. Stuttgart: Kohlhammer, 2013.

————, ed. *Still at the Margins: Biblical Scholarship Fifteen Years after the Voices from the Margin*. London: Bloomsbury, 2008.

————, ed. *Voices from the Margin: Interpreting the Bible in the Third World*. Revised and expanded 3rd ed. Maryknoll, NY: Orbis, 2006.

Synod of Bishops, Special Assembly for the Pan-Amazonian Region. *The Amazon: New Paths for the Church and for an Integral Ecology*. Vatican, October 26, 2019. https://www.vatican.va/roman_curia/synod/documents/rc_synod_doc_20191026_sinodo-amazzonia_en.html.

Tamayo, Juan José. *Theologien des Südens. Dekolonisierung als neues Paradigma*. Theologien der Welt 1. Freiburg: Herder, 2020.

Taylor, Mark Lewis. "Subalternität und Fürsprache als Kairos für die Theologie." In *Postkoloniale Theologien. Bibelhermeneutische und kulturwissenschaftliche Beiträge*, edited by Andreas Nehring and Simon Tielesch, 276–99. ReligionsKulturen 11. Stuttgart: Kohlhammer, 2013.

Tinker, George E. *American Indian Liberation: A Theology of Sovereignty*. Maryknoll, NY: Orbis, 2008.

Titizano, Cecilia. "Mama Pacha: Creator and Sustainer Spirit of God." *Horizontes Decoloniales* 3 (2017) 127–59.

Walsh, Catherine, et al., eds. *Indisciplinar las ciencias sociales. Geopolíticas del conocimiento y colonialidad del poder. Perspectivas desde lo Andino*. Quito: UASB/Abya Yala, 2002.

Warrior, Robert A. "A Native American Perspective: Canaanites, Cowboys, and Indians." In *Voices from the Margin: Interpreting the Bible in the Third World*, edited by R. S. Sugirtharajah, 235–41. Revised and expanded 3rd ed. Maryknoll, NY: Orbis, 2006.

Weiler, Birgit. *Gut leben—Tajimat Pujút. Prophetische Kritik aus Amazonien im Zeitalter der Globalisierung*. Theologie interkulturell 27. Ostfildern: Grünewald, 2017.

West, Gerald O. *The Academy of the Poor: Toward a Dialogical Reading of the Bible*. Sheffield: Sheffield Academic Press, 1999.

————. "Wir werden nicht mehr schweigen! Tamars Geschichte und die Arbeit für Gender-Gerechtigkeit in Afrika." *Bibel und Kirche* 67.3 (2012) 164–70.

West, Gerald O., and Charlene van der Walt. "Eine queere (Eröffnung der) Bibel." *Concilium* 55.5 (2012) 584–93.

West, Gerald O., et al. "Rape in the House of David: The Biblical Story of Tamar as a Resource for Transformation." *Agenda* 61 (2004) 36–41.

Wiesgickl, Simon. *Das Alte Testament als deutsche Kolonie: Die Neuerfindung des Alten Testaments um 1800*. Beiträge zur Wissenschaft vom Alten und Neuen Testament 214. Stuttgart: Kohlhammer, 2018.

————. "Gefangen in uralten Phantasmen. Über das koloniale Erbe der deutschen alttestamtlichen Wissenschaft." In *Postkoloniale Theologien II: Perspektiven aus dem deutschsprachigen Raum*, edited by Andreas Nehring and Simon Wiesgickl, 171–85. Stuttgart: Kohlhammer, 2018.

Wind, Renate. *Christsein im Imperium. Jesusnachfolge als Vision einer anderen Welt.* Gütersloh: Gütersloher, 2016.

Winker, Gabriele, and Nina Degele. *Intersektionalität. Zur Analyse sozialer Ungleichheiten.* Bielefeld: Transcript, 2009.

World Council of Churches. *Together towards Life: Mission and Evangelism in Changing Landscapes.* Busan, 2013. https://www.oikoumene.org/sites/default/files/Document/Together_towards_Life.pdf.

Index

indiscipline, 129–33

insiders, outsiders, power relations and, 84–88

Institute for World Church and Mission (2017), 25

interconnectedness, 146

"Intercultural Theology: Journal for Missiology" (*Zeitschrift für Missionswissenschaft*), 26

intercultural theology, term usage, 27–28

Interkulturelle Theologie (journal), 26

internal colonialism, 17

intersectionality, of coloniality axes, 61–63

Isherwood, Lisa, 89, 161

Jahnel, Claudia, 186–87

Jahrbuch für Christliche Sozialwissenschaften ("Yearbook for Christian Social Sciences"), 26

Jarosch, Sabine, 13–14

Jefferson, Thomas, 106

Jesus
  as a frontier person, 83
  suffering of, 89–91
  titles attributed to, 70–71

Joh, Wonhee Anne, 90–91

Joseph, old Testament figure, 163

Judges, biblical book, 34–35

Jules Ferry Lyceum, 2–3

Jungfrau im Silberberg (Virgin in the silver mountain) (Müßig), 128, 172

Kang, Namsoon, 38–39, 61–63, 92, 194, 204

Kant, Immanuel, 16

Karentzos, Alexandra, 12

Kastner, Jens, 11

Kaunda, Chammah, 158–59

Keller, Catherine, 129

Kerner, Ina, 11

Kim, Uriah Y., 33–35

King, Richard, 52

Klein, Naomi, 166

Klinger, Elmar, 47, 182–83

Knauss, Stefanie, 160

knowledge
  coloniality of, 96
  in theology, 27–31
  understanding of, 183–84

Kwok Pui-lan
  biblical studies, 137
  biography of, 204–5
  Christian missions dialogue, 77
  ecofeminist theologies, 154–55
  on gender relations, 55
  on religious studies, 49, 51–53
  on suffering and sacrifice, 89
  on Western theology, 87
  woman poking out bible verses story, 4–5

La Puente Tapia, Juan Carlos, 120, 132

Lai Pan-chiu, 51, 151

land ownership, 80–84, 108

Lander, Edgardo, 96

Laporta, Hector, 56–57

Las Casas, Bartolome, de, 20, 70, 77

Latinx spirituality, 152–53

lector rebelde (term usage), 108n17

Lee, Archie, 141

Lehr, Fabian, 44

LGBT (lesbian, gay, bisexual, transgender) community, 163, 163n83

liberation of theology, term usage, 170n107

liberation theology, 27–28, 40, 46, 73–74, 87, 115, 140, 192–93

Liew, Tat Siong Benny, 69

The Location of Culture (Bhabha), 126

Londoño, Juan Esteban, 108–9

Lugones, Maria, 95

Mabanza, Boniface, 37n14

Maldonado-Torres, Nelson, 96

Maliko, Tavita, 165

Malinche (interpreter), 107–8

Maluleke, Tinyiko Sam, 84

Mama Pacha (Pachamama), 56

Mananzan, Mary John, 56

marginalized populations, 63, 88–90

Marx, Karl, 16, 117

masterwords, term usage, 40

Maya theology, 142n18

Printed in Great Britain
by Amazon

47735691R00142